The Privatisation of Knowledge

This book deals with the emergence of intellectual monopolies. It explores different ways of producing knowledge, thus showing alternatives to the current dominant paradigm which is based on turning knowledge produced collectively into intangible assets, owned by a few leading corporations. It discusses a paradox: knowledge creation by government-sponsored research infrastructures or by non-profit institutions, including universities, is increasingly appearing in the form of "open science" – ideas and data are widely available in the public domain. However, such knowledge is privatised downstream by new oligopolies. These oligopolies, such as the Tech Giants and the Big Pharma, are protected by legislation on intellectual property rights that restricts further access to knowledge. This process contributes to increasing social inequality.

The book suggests alternative policy options to counteract this process: the design of new players with a public mission and a coalition of governments as patient investors for the long-term benefit not just of the citizens of one jurisdiction but for creating global public goods. Proposals are presented for launching European R&D infrastructures related to three major long-term challenges: health risks, climate change, and Big Data governance. These knowledge-intensive enterprises should offer innovation as a public good, for example, in new biomedical fields underinvested by private firms, disruptive "green" technologies, and digital platforms based on transparent users' ownership of data.

Offering a balanced combination of theories and practical applications including interesting case studies, the book will appeal to students, scholars, and researchers of public economics and governance. It will also find an audience among policymakers, practitioners, and government officials.

Massimo Florio is Professor of Public Economics at the University of Milan, Italy, and co-Chair of the Jean Monnet Centre of Excellence on European research and innovation policy.

Routledge Studies in Public Economics and Finance

The Challenges of Public Procurement Reforms
Edited by Annalisa Castelli, Gustavo Piga, Stéphane Saussier and Tünde Tátrai

Public Financial Management in the European Union
Public Finance and Global Crises
Marta Postuła

Public Goods and the Fourth Industrial Revolution
Inclusive Models of Finance, Distribution and Production
Edited by Maria Płonka

The Privatisation of Knowledge
A New Policy Agenda for Health, Energy, and Data Governance
Massimo Florio

For more information about this series, please visit: https://www.routledge.com/Routledge-Studies-in-Public-Economics-and-Finance/book-series/LICPUBECONFIN

The Privatisation of Knowledge

A New Policy Agenda for Health, Energy, and Data Governance

Massimo Florio

Routledge
Taylor & Francis Group
LONDON AND NEW YORK

First published 2024
by Routledge
4 Park Square, Milton Park, Abingdon, Oxon OX14 4RN

and by Routledge
605 Third Avenue, New York, NY 10158

Routledge is an imprint of the Taylor & Francis Group, an informa business

British Library Cataloguing-in-Publication Data
A catalogue record for this book is available from the British Library

ISBN: 978-1-032-46405-3 (hbk)
ISBN: 978-1-032-46406-0 (pbk)
ISBN: 978-1-003-38153-2 (ebk)

DOI: 10.4324/9781003381532

Typeset in Sabon
by SPi Technologies India Pvt Ltd (Straive)

Contents

List of tables

Preface

This book aims to show a paradox and to propose a new policy. Science, the ultimate source of any economic advance, is increasingly created as a public good. It is both financially supported by taxpayers and intellectually generated by the effort of researchers whose motivation is the intrinsic pleasure of discovery, not their income. However, knowledge is then appropriated as own capital by companies, is effectively privatised and systematically exploited to extract profits for investors. The result is the formation of oligopolies.

Small groups of firms and their investors enjoy huge rents, for example, in the pharmaceutical industry, in the energy sector, and in the digital business. The outcome of this social mechanism is that science, often without knowing it, contributes to inequality. The shareholders of knowledge-intensive companies, such as Pfizer, Tesla, or Meta appropriate rents on an unprecedented global scale. According to Oxfam, a charity, the 10 richest men in the world in 2020 owned collectively more wealth than 3.1 billion people. Their wealth doubled during the pandemic. There are about 2770 billionaires in the world, according to *Forbes*, and most of the top richest people in the list belong to investors in the "tech" industry, the media, telecommunications, health, and other sectors typical of the knowledge economy.

I suggest in this book that the spread of knowledge privatisation is pervasive, has undesirable social effects, and changing this is both urgent and feasible.

My argument starts with a brief historical account of the institutions where knowledge is created: the traditional role of universities and scientific societies, then the R&D departments within companies, and finally the emergence of large-scale public research infrastructures such as CERN for particle physics, or the European Molecular Biology Laboratory (Chapter 1). The issue of social inequality is discussed as correlated to the expropriation of citizens from their data and taxes (Chapter 2). This is not the only source of social inequality, but an increasingly important one given the shift of capital from land and machinery to intangible assets, such as patents, software and know-how.

Three sectors are then examined: health (Chapter 3), energy (Chapter 4), and data (Chapter 5). For each of these broad scientific domains and for some related economic activities, I offer both an analysis of the privatisation of knowledge and how an alternative public model of knowledge creation could counterbalance it.

While each of the three sectors has some specific features, a common pattern is identified and a new policy is proposed. This is based on international public research infrastructures designed as enterprises with long-term missions on health from a global perspective, on the science of climate change, and on data governance.

Any new policy agenda requires identifying a potential actor. I submit that the European Union should be a first mover, with a strategy that would open the newly created public research infrastructures to other countries, following again the example of CERN or the European Space Agency, on a wider scale.

I hope that the book will be of interest not just to my colleagues and students in public economics and other social sciences, but also to scientists, policymakers, and anybody concerned with the curious association in our time between the brilliant advancement of science and the sad reality of global inequality.

Massimo Florio
Milan, 20 June 2022

Acknowledgements

I have been working on the topic of this book for several years. I learnt a lot from research into the social benefits and costs of large particle accelerators such as the Large Hadron Collider (CERN) for basic research, CNAO (Pavia) for medical applications, and synchrotron light sources such as ALBA (Barcelona) for materials science and structural biology. I obtained research funding initially from the European Investment Bank, then from CERN, the University of Milan, and more recently from the Horizon 2020 programme, the Jean Monnet Action of the European Union. Without the sympathy and support at CERN of the Director General, Fabiola Gianotti, as well as physicists Stefano Forte, Tiziano Camporesi, Lucio Rossi, and others, our work would have been impossible. Currently, the collaboration continues in the Future Circular Collider Study, with Michael Benedikt, Johannes Gutleber, and others, together with researchers from CSIL (Centre for Industrial Studies), in particular, Silvia Vignetti, Emanuela Sirtori, Jessica Catalano, and Francesco Giffoni.

This work also led me to observe research infrastructures in fields ranging from cancer adrotherapy to bioinformatics, from molecular genetics to pharmacology, and from energy efficiency to Big Data. In Europe, many of these infrastructures are periodically evaluated by ESFRI, the European Strategy Forum on Research Infrastructures, and the European Commission (especially DG Research and DG Regio), with which my group also collaborated. I have recounted this journey to the places of contemporary science in a recent book (*Investing in Science*, MIT Press, 2019), from which, in a certain sense, I draw here in order to go further and explicitly make proposals that straddle the line between science policy and industrial policy.

I also learnt a lot from research carried out with the Italian Space Agency, particularly on the subject of Earth observation from satellites, with Simonetta Di Ciaccio, Mauro Piermaria, and a team including Paolo Castelnovo, Stefano Clò, Valentina Morretta, Matteo Landoni, Davide Vurchio, Veronica Lupi, and others. I have recently carried out a study with Chiara Pancotti, David Anthony Prochazka, Simona Gamba and other researchers for the European Parliament (STOA) on the possibility of a European biomedical research infrastructure.

I am indebted to Fabrizio Barca for the stimulus to study the relationship between social justice and this way of producing science. The Forum Disuguaglianze e Diversità (Inequality and Diversity Forum) has taken up my proposal of the "Geneva model" for new kinds of public enterprises, a project that is developed here. I would like to thank Giuseppe Laterza very much for convincing me to put my ideas into the form of the Italian edition of this book.

An earlier draft of the book was read by various people, who gave very helpful advice and who are not responsible for what I say here and how I say it. In particular, I would like to thank for their comments on Chapter 3, Letizia Giorgetti (DEMM Department of Economics, Management, Quantitative Methods, University of Milan), Chiara Pancotti (CSIL), and Martina Dal Molin (Gran Sasso Science Institute); Chapter 4, Mario Genco (CSIL) and Veronica Lupi (DEMM); Chapter 5, my colleagues Alfio Ferrara (Department of Informatics) and Stefano Carrazza (Department of Physics) at the University of Milan. I would also like to thank Anna Gialluca, Editorial Director of Laterza, and Kristina Abbotts, Senior Editor of Routledge, for their helpful suggestions on how to improve the structure and style for a non-specialist audience of respectively the Italian and the English language editions. Finally, I thank Martina Gazzo for her patient assistance in preparing the text and Jeremy Kemp for translation work of an earlier version.

Introduction
Science and social justice

The pandemic has forced us to realise that the global market does not offer adequate answers to our most important challenges – the challenges which our lives depend on. When our encounter with SARS-CoV-2 started, there were no ongoing large-scale studies on antiviral drugs and Coronaviruses' vaccines, even if the warning of a possible pandemic had been made almost 20 years previously. It was not deemed worthwhile for the pharmaceutical companies to invest in that area of research. When they eventually did so it was in a hurry and, effectively, in response to governments offering huge research subsidies and advance purchase contracts (i.e., before knowing whether and when effective and safe vaccines would be available). Companies have held on to patents, licences, and technologies despite the public funding they received. They are not allowing vaccines to be produced everywhere in the shortest possible time, and so companies and governments are giving the virus time to mutate, leaving much of the world's population unprotected.

The same is true for climate change: we have known for a long time that we need to find new production and consumption technologies compatible with a radical "green" shift, but companies have other priorities, for example, the use of artificial intelligence for self-driving cars, hybrid combustion systems, electric cars: innovations aimed at supporting the car market rather than the transition to radically innovative transport modes. The companies need to recoup past investments in hydrocarbons and related technologies. The timing of business is not driven by medium to long-term emergencies, but rather by protecting the short-term interests of shareholders and managers.

We note, with resignation, the growing market power over and influence on our lives of a digital oligopoly that exploits everyone's data to accumulate wealth for the few. The knowledge behind these technologies was created by public research in the first place but is now owned by a small group of companies. Much of the data, if managed by organisations with a public mission, could be a vital resource for improving our well-being, from our own health to environmental protection.

We live in a paradoxical situation. Modern science was born – in various ways – as a public good but is now being privatised. This mechanism for privatising knowledge produces social inequality and contributes to an

DOI: 10.4324/9781003381532-1

uneven distribution of income and assets that is undermining the foundations of states and social coexistence.

The scenario could change if there were new players in the field: knowledge-intensive supranational public infrastructures and new types of public enterprises, driven by long-term scientific and technological missions. Europe could be the incubator, learning from the experience of the many excellent research infrastructure projects it already has, such as CERN, the European Space Agency, the European Molecular Biology Laboratory, and several others.

These organisations are manifestations of a way of producing science that has gradually established itself over the past decades and that today defines an original paradigm, different both from the age-old tradition of universities and from big science linked to the military–industrial complex of the great powers, and distinct from the research and development carried out in the world of oligopolistic companies. The new paradigm of science production is inherently based on cosmopolitan scientific communities, it is not tied to national missions but typically to international coalitions of governments, it guarantees universal access to data, eschews secrecy, and seeks to attract the interest of the general public. It justifies the work of researchers not with participation in profit but with the joy of discovery. We need to learn from these experiences and initiate new ones to address the problems that the market is clearly unable to address. Private companies are doing their job: making money for investors. The problem is that we urgently need something else: discovery and innovation in fields in which either no short-term profits can be generated or, symmetrically, in which the creation of oligopoly surpluses would be unacceptable for reasons of both social equity and dynamic efficiency. Subsidising large companies or regulating them does not work. Another way is needed. To understand what is needed, it is necessary to understand the nature of the oligopoly of our times.

Knowledge as an intangible asset

What is so special about the US tech giants Apple, Alphabet (owner of Google), Amazon, Meta (Facebook, Instagram), Microsoft, China's Alibaba, and Tencent that their value to shareholders is greater than the assets[1] of many states?

Rankings based on the value of listed companies fluctuate with the share price. At the top of the ranking – now that a small number of shares have been placed on the market – is Saudi Aramco, the Saudi oil giant. In the past, we would have found ExxonMobil, another oil company, but in 2020, the world's top companies were the seven sisters of information technology. For none of these companies does market value primarily have to do with something tangible. Take, for instance, the balance sheet of Apple, whose market value in the third quarter of 2020 was around 2000 billion USD. To relate this figure to something familiar, such as the GDP of a country, Apple is worth more on the market than the GDP of Italy, Brazil, Canada, Russia, and South Korea. The value has grown about tenfold in ten years, making the fortune of shareholders such as Tim Cook, the company's CEO. What is on the assets side of Apple's balance sheet?[2] On 27 June 2020, against total assets of 317 billion USD, the company reported less than 36 billion USD in assets under real estate, machinery, and equipment: almost 90% of Apple's balance sheet value has nothing to do with computers, industrial plants, or offices.

If the accounting value of these assets is then compared to the market value, it does not even represent two percentage points.

This is no exception. Land, buildings, machines, and deposits no longer: 21st-century capitalism is mainly composed of something else. What does the operator of a search engine or an online sales platform possess that places it at the top of the world? If it were only market power, the question would shift without changing its nature: What determines this market power?

The ingredients of production have been identified by economists for some decades, albeit with models that have many variations and nuances. Essentially, they can be reduced to three groups of factors: fixed assets, labour (including human capital, i.e., acquired skills) and technical knowledge (in the broad sense of the term). The latter determines the combined productivity of the first two groups. The value of a company has to do with how much the market bets on its future profitability, and in turn, this bet depends on productivity. Ultimately, for Apple or Amazon, what the market values is the ability of these firms to sustain their technological leadership over time, which in turn translates into commercial leadership. Therefore, at the heart of these valuations is the perception of market power derived from accumulated knowledge. This is not the case for Saudi Aramco or ExxonMobil, whose value depends on betting on the price of hydrocarbons and the accumulation of rights to exploit reserves, that is, on not believing that the energy transition can take place in the next few decades. The value depends on the past enduring.

The value of Meta Platforms (which operates Facebook, WhatsApp, Instagram, Messenger, and others), on the other hand, depends on the future: it does not lie in the big computers where it stores the data of about three billion users but in the economic potential of the knowledge that Meta possesses thanks to the data it stores and processes every 1000th of a second.

Even for a big pharma company such as Johnson & Johnson (also active in various other sectors in over 60 countries), which is also one of the world's top companies in terms of capitalisation (with annual sales of over 80 billion USD), intangible assets (including patents) are worth more than four times as much as real estate (including factories), respectively, 81 billion versus less than 19 billion USD.[3]

Knowledge is a poorly measured asset in balance sheets, but that does not make it any less decisive in ultimately determining who wins and who loses in the struggle for survival in the marketplace. And so, understanding where knowledge is created and how it is appropriated and translated in a company asset becomes crucial.

Where is knowledge produced?

Let us move further up the chain. The typical places of knowledge production are, on the one hand, universities and research infrastructures dealing with basic science and a significant share of applied science and, on the other hand, companies for further development of innovations. The division of roles is rough, but along this path, oligopolies are created that live from the appropriation of knowledge and its transformation into financial bets. The relations between universities, public research infrastructures, and companies are the starting point of this book. I will argue this thesis: the relations between public (or at least not-for-profit) research and private companies have been configured in such a way as to give rise to a system of privatised knowledge on a global scale, a system which generates social inequalities and which does not help us to face the great challenges of the future.

Gibbons (1999) highlights the decline of the traditional "contract" where universities provide fundamental research while company labs applied research and product development. He points to a new pattern based on four ingredients: co-evolution of science and society, contextualisation of science rather than its ambition for universality, the production of socially robust knowledge within certain boundaries, and the construction of narratives of expertise. This more complex pattern implies in a broad sense a deeper permeability of science and society. Something, in my opinion, most private investors and lawmakers do not fully acknowledge, as the example of legislation and practice shows, where intellectual property is still seen as a reward of individuals. Pagano (2014) writes that "the privatization of knowledge and its direct transformation in the most valuable proprietary asset of the firm" is the "most extreme and most meaningful step" of a more traditional monopolisation of capital process through the ownership of machinery that embody past knowledge, a core idea of Marx.

That knowledge is ultimately the cause of economic progress is – in a sense – a truism. Oil or coal would have no economic value if we did not know how to extract energy from burning fossils. The wheel would be a decorative object if we did not know how to use it to reduce friction when transporting heavy objects.

Wheels, the internal combustion engine, and thousands of other innovative ideas have been incorporated into the symbol of capitalism in the last century: the car, an increasingly concentrated oligopolistic industry. But let us look at a slightly more exotic example – the positron as the antiparticle of the electron.

Hypothesised in a purely theoretical manner by physicist Paul Dirac between 1928 and 1931, it was observed the following year in cosmic rays. Discovering some of its properties has meant knowing how to build machines for positron emission tomography (PET), which allows, for example, certain types of tumours to be seen at an early stage by assessing their location and size, and thus to save lives. In 2018, there were 210 PET scanners in Italy, as well as more than 6000 machines for CT, MRI, and mammography.[4] The accumulated value of these machines in hospitals is several billion euros, and a single service can cost up to 1000 euros (which the patient is often unaware of in a public system). Paul Dirac and other particle physicists have therefore – in some way – given the world the principles on which a technology is based that is incorporated in thousands of machines and millions of tests every year. Science, profits, and lives saved: this is a virtuous narrative.

Innovation and financialisation

It is quite normal that someone "upstream" (in the flow of a river of ideas) discovers something and someone "downstream" appropriates it by applying the new knowledge to innovations of economic value. This has been the case for centuries, and capitalism has proved to be a particularly suitable environment for taking advantage of and stimulating scientific and technological progress. This fact has been an element in the legitimisation of capitalism, an economic system that is in other ways unjust, if only because it is based on unequal property relations, but certainly no more unjust and unequal than ancient Asian production systems, such as Pharaons' Egypt or imperial China. Feudal Europe was not very egalitarian. Marx and Schumpeter in this perspective grasped an element of progress in the dynamic of capitalism compared to other systems, a dynamic based on the exploitation of technological innovation. They went on to draw opposite political conclusions, revolutionary for the former, and conservative for the latter.

Neither of them could have predicted that a structural mutation of capitalism would occur through the combination of two trends. On the one hand, financialisation, a process perfectly captured by Keynes with his definition of casino capitalism with reference to the concrete functioning of stock markets in the 1930s and taken up, for example, by Susan Strange, Hyman Minsky, and, more recently, recalled by Mariana Mazzucato (2018a). The activity that takes place in a casino basically consists of placing bets, and for a bet to make sense, there must be an element of uncertainty. It would make no sense to bet on the fact that the roulette comes out red or black or green (the zero) because this will certainly happen (unless the ball shoots out of the wheel or dematerialises due to an extremely unlikely quantum phenomenon). A lack of knowledge regarding where the ball will fall when the wheel stops spinning is necessary.

Innovation lends itself perfectly to betting. Consider someone patenting a new drug or a new photovoltaic cell or a new algorithm for analysing personal data. Will it work? Will it sell well? Will it allow the patent holder to make a profit? If the holder of the economic rights to the innovation is a listed company, the share price incorporates such bets, along with many other factors relating to predictions about the environment in which the company operates. As in a casino, the winner is whoever has bet on the number that comes up, in this case, the bet is on the profit that will occur in any one moment. Those who place these bets typically do not know much about the innovation they are betting on, they bet on the basis of mental or mathematical models that predict what might happen in future. The roulette wheel spins at the speed of milliseconds for hundreds of millions of bets (equivalent to the number of securities traded and operators). The data tell us something surprising: the profits that can be derived from gaming are far greater than the apparently underlying "industrial" profits that can be derived from innovations. In this context, innovations are in a very precise sense pretexts. Pretexts can also be weather events, political tensions, the personal affairs of individual managers, a pandemic, or whatever is uncertain and "playable".

The Tech Giants' wealth of knowledge presumably did not expand during the months of the Covid-19 lockdown. Alphabet's or Amazon's corporate research and development programmes in February 2020 were presumably not very different from those in January, but the gamblers saw that the knowledge embedded in the share price was now becoming more promising from a profitability perspective. Amazon was worth 970 billion USD in the first quarter of 2020, 1432 billion USD in the second quarter, and has continued to rise. Bezos, founder and CEO of Amazon, owner of 11% of the shares, had a personal wealth of 115 billion USD on 1 January 2020,[5] but on 26 August 2020, he became the richest man on the planet with 205 billion USD. Clearly, this increase is a multiple of the actual increase in Amazon's sales and profits due to the pandemic, reflecting the markets' upward bet. The same is true for the prices of Big Pharma in those weeks since no one could know in advance if, and when, one of them would be able to develop a vaccine or drug against the virus responsible for the pandemic.

The role of government

The second trend not foreseen by Marx and Schumpeter, but the same can be said for Keynes and many other economists of the last century and our contemporaries, is the crucial role of governments in generating a seemingly inexhaustible source of new knowledge, from basic to applied research. The process is entirely or almost entirely at taxpayers' expense. It shifts a large part of the risk of generating knowledge of no economic value onto citizens.

According to UNESCO Science Report (2021), there are around 8.8 million researchers in all fields in the world. This is a formidable legion of brains, many do not work in companies, but rather in universities and other public or non-profit institutions, including hospitals.[6] While more than two-thirds of research and development (R&D) expenditure is financed by businesses, one has to dig into the numbers to get a more realistic picture. Many of the business expenditures accounted for as R&D are much further downstream of the knowledge production process, sometimes bordering on market research, public relations, or even operational activities. Much of this expenditure is supported by explicit or implicit forms of public subsidies for private research. This includes capital transfers in various forms, tax credits, technology-intensive supply contracts (particularly in the military sector), and perhaps the greatest benefit of all: the initial training of corporate human capital through education up to the level of PhDs and often post-docs by 90,000 higher education institutions in the world.[7]

Perhaps, if the correct calculations were made, the public contribution to global R&D expenditure in all its forms could be closer to half, rather than a third. This scale was unthinkable in the time of Marx, but also in the time of Keynes and Schumpeter. Even if, especially in Germany, universities and scientific societies at the end of the 19th century were already strong, the organisation and financing of knowledge production on the present scale is essentially a phenomenon that started initially with the First World War, established itself at the end of the Second World War and (literally) took off with the Cold War: science became big science with the race for nuclear weapons and their launchers, with radar systems, computers, satellites, space missions, and government-sponsored biomedical research. The number of scientists and researchers is growing by leaps and bounds. As their numbers increase, so does the confidence of scientists in the social value of their work. In Europe, in particular, supranational communities are emerging that are able to persuade governments to finance research agendas that are decoupled from the military–industrial apparatus.

A new narrative is emerging. Science no longer has to justify itself (exclusively) by citing military reasons and national strategic missions. It can proudly claim to be an end in itself. The social utility of the production of science is based on the realisation that sooner or later mankind will know what to do with the work of scientists, even if they are dealing with the strangest of topics: elementary particles with an extremely ephemeral life that have not existed in nature for billions of years, gravitational waves and black holes in galaxies light years away, genomes of species that have been extinct for aeons, and much more. The claim that all this could "sooner or later" lead to social utility is a dogma widely shared by scientists. I will argue that this narrative is on the whole realistic, though difficult to prove, if only because a few decades are not enough time to see the ultimate impacts of most of the strange things scientists are studying.

Science and gambling

On the contrary, one does not have to wait decades to observe a phenomenon that is – on the current scale – new: the co-evolution of the production of science as a public good and the creation of oligopolies based on the private appropriation of knowledge. The mechanism is almost invisible and yet powerful. Citizens finance scientific and technological research with taxes (and in other ways that we will discuss), discoveries are continuously made, and new languages, new methods, and new hypotheses are invented. It is an immense knowledge production machine that has its own autonomy, its own rules, and – as we shall see – has given itself its own organisation.

Every year, perhaps more than 7 million articles are produced and published in more than 34,000 scientific journals.[8] For every single publication, there are pre-prints, conferences, hundreds or thousands of online message exchanges between research groups, video calls, and conversations in laboratory cafeterias. This entire flow of ideas and data takes two routes: the main one leads back into the scientific community and results in reputation, careers, recognition, and frustration, as with any other community. The other route takes this knowledge elsewhere, to companies where ideas are sifted through more or less effective filters and selectively incorporated into investment decisions. There is an incessant flow of people and ideas from the world of science to companies (and backwards), perhaps with the mediation of intermediary bodies, such as development agencies, or simply carried inside the head of the young researcher newly recruited from the university community. Companies drink from this flow directly or through the innovations they observe in other companies that have done so. They filter one idea out of 10,000 and create a project.

This is where the casino managers come in, who in turn place their bets: on a new molecule with possible therapeutic properties, on a new way of manufacturing an electronic component, on a material with unique properties. These bets can take various forms, from venture capital to other techniques of casino capitalism. Some bets are successful. Cumulative processes are set in motion, which can spread throughout the economy in a wide and capillary way or concentrate in points of the system. The oligopoly of our times is essentially a local thickening of diffuse knowledge and innovation, around which winning financial bets have been mounted. As in the example of Amazon, there is an initial core of knowledge (in the management of incoming and outgoing online orders), but around this core, a financial mechanism is created that raises barriers that cannot be penetrated by competitors, at least for a sufficiently protracted time. Business profits based on initial innovation, which in turn is downstream of scientific and technological progress, pale in comparison to the financial returns associated with the casino. A bit like quantum physics, if you think you can predict exactly where the ball will land, you have not understood the concept. Nobody knows how to make these predictions. If anyone knew, the game would be dead.

A side effect of this system is that public money ultimately creates opportunities, not only for the emergence of oligopolistic businesses, but also for contributing to the huge inequality between the wealth accumulated by Jeff Bezos and associates and what goes back to the hundreds of thousands of human beings who make the deliveries, manage the warehouses and logistics (800,000 people), and to the consumers themselves. To get an order of magnitude, let us magically distribute an equal share of the stock to all Amazon employees. Since the company was worth around USD 1600 billion in July

2020, each of them would have assets of USD 2 million. In reality, the average wealth of Amazon's employees is about zero (net of mortgages and other debts). The abnormal profit also measures the overpricing on costs paid by consumers, who are also happy to pay because they often have no equally convenient alternatives.

While Amazon is an information technology company, it also owes its fortune to the invention of the Internet, the World Wide Web, and other technologies, as well as to a massive financial gamble by third-party investors. If, for instance, as Amazon has announced, would switch to large-scale delivery by drones, it will be using a technology developed over the past decades for military purposes, notably by the aeronautical engineer Abraham Karem in Israel during the Yom Kippur War and later perfected in the US by Karem himself with his Californian start-up.[9]

The fact that the value created by DARPA (Defense Advanced Research Projects Agency), a public agency, somehow ends up in the assets of Bezos and associates is the result of a round of roulette, it has nothing to do with the contribution of ideas or work of one person. According to Herbert Simon (Nobel Prize in Economics 1978),[10] at most 20% of a person's income is "earned". The rest of the income is the product of the social accumulation of capital, which includes intellectual and human capital, that is, knowledge. In the case of Bezos, this would still attribute 40 billion USD of personal wealth as the specific fruit of his ideas and work, a sum that still seems rather difficult to justify.

The combination of large-scale accumulation of scientific and technical knowledge, private appropriation of incremental knowledge (with or without legal mechanisms such as patents) and the lottery of financial markets are at the basis of an unacceptable distribution of income, wealth, and power. Bezos is also the owner of the *Washington Post*, a monument of liberal information: but nothing would prevent private fortunes from supporting newspapers and social networks of the extreme neo-nationalist right. It just depends on where the roulette ball falls.

Policy failures

In principle, there could be instruments to correct for the accumulation of rents, that is, of income that does not derive from the remuneration of productive factors, but from circumstances such as oligopolistic power, control of scarce resources, or benefits from externalities. However, for various reasons, traditional corrective policies, such as taxation of profits and capital and regulation of markets, have not prevented a, possibly, unprecedented, concentration of power and wealth. Taxation of corporate income and capital gains in general is inversely proportional to the size of the tax base. The larger the fortunes, the easier it is to have an avoidance strategy that leverages the possibility of moving the location of the legal taxpayer to where taxation is lower or almost zero.

The case of Apple in Ireland is significant in this respect. In 2020, the European Court of Justice ruled that the European Commission's assessment that Ireland had in fact granted state aid to Apple in the form of tax breaks was not sufficiently proven. But according to Professor Baistrocchi of the London School of Economics, the Apple–Irish government–European Commission dispute has shown in detail how things stand in the relationship between multinationals and governments. According to his estimate, for example, in 2014, for every million USD of profits, Apple paid 50 USD in taxes in Europe, equivalent to an effective income tax rate of 0.005%.[11]

This is just one example, among hundreds, of the fact that while for small- and medium-sized companies the costs of implementing an international tax avoidance or evasion strategy are prohibitive, for large multinationals it is extremely convenient to seek out countries where it is easier to escape the tax burden. Tech Giants, Big Pharma, and Oil&Gas in this sense, given their size, can successfully implement these strategies. The market regulation policies are even weaker and have been implemented with some determination in hi-tech sectors, such as telecommunications. The best-known case was the forced break-up of the US telephone giant AT&T in 1984. AT&T is also an important case because of the "Schumpeterian" role in scientific and technological research played by its Bell Laboratories (later acquired by Nokia) in the presence of near-monopoly power. The result was less incentive for in-house research, a phenomenon observed in general in many of the large privatised and liberalised companies. In any case, policies as aggressive as those that led to the break-up of AT&T have not been proposed again by the competition authorities of various countries, presumably resigned to the idea that the technological oligopoly is unbeatable and perhaps its elimination is undesirable. The seven regional companies resulting from the break-up of AT&T were called "Baby Bells". Nobody today would propose creating a "Baby Amazon" for every 30 million inhabitants.

Moreover, the economic power that is concentrated in one out of every 1000 taxpayers, partly as a result of the mechanism I have described, makes politics – let us say euphemistically – very susceptible to the influence of these interests. Tax legislation and market regulation for some decades now, especially in the USA, has been shaped with the rhetorical support of economists opposed to tax progressivity, capital taxation, controls on the movement of capital between jurisdictions, and generally redistributive policies, rejected en bloc as being "socialist and inefficient".

The emphasis of economic theory in recent decades on the importance of innovation as a factor in R&D spending within the framework of theories of endogenous growth, from a policy perspective, has taken the form of subsidies to private firms to invest more in R&D. These policies, practised on a very large-scale in the form of direct subsidies or as tax credits and other forms, have probably had the effect of amplifying the phenomenon we are dealing with here, the formation of rents based on the appropriation of knowledge produced using public resources.

Economists also give some credit to the instrument of innovative supply contracts between public bodies and private companies in order to promote applied research. These contracts have reached their peak in the defence sector not only in the USA but also in other countries. There is no doubt that they can stimulate R&D and innovation in supplier companies, but they may not be the most efficient and, above all, the fairest mechanism when they end up reinforcing oligopolistic positions, as is particularly evident in the case of the US military–industrial complex.

A new policy agenda

If one wants both to support the accumulation of intellectual and human capital, that is, of economically productive forms of knowledge, and to pursue the objective of social justice, the recourse to taxes and subsidies or to competition and market regulation policies seems, on the whole, to be contradictory. The policy suggested in this book takes another route.

I propose that international coalitions of governments should launch new public actors that intervene in the very structure of the oligopoly, counterbalancing it on the supply side of knowledge and of the goods and services that embody its value. These actors should be designed as combinations of research infrastructures and knowledge-intensive public enterprises[12] oriented by long-term missions. Research infrastructures in Europe (but also elsewhere) are an important reality of the knowledge production landscape. More than a thousand of them have been identified and some of them are of considerable size in terms of the human and financial resources they mobilise. Public or publicly owned companies are also still well established in Europe and often make a significant contribution to R&D, especially in certain fields. Now that the privatisation frenzy has died down, not least because of the disappointments it has caused in crucial sectors such as energy and telecommunications, it should be recognised that governments today already have instruments for implementing industrial policies that are more direct and effective than market regulation and tax instruments. I am also convinced that some of the more far-sighted private companies might be interested in contributing to these combinations in the form of partnerships on an equitable basis, if only because sooner or later they will pay a price for the exaggerated power they have accumulated.

I propose – in order to illustrate the idea effectively – three missions and, therefore, three strategic subjects: human health, climate change, and data governance. The European dimension of these enterprises could be ideal for guaranteeing their success for a number of reasons: because no European state can do it alone, because there is a solid base of scientific and technical expertise to build on, and because the European Union, with the pandemic, is experiencing a moment of re-foundation, favourable to investment and wide-ranging public missions.

The first proposal is prompted by what we are learning from the pandemic. The relationship between public spending and the pharmaceutical oligopoly shows that there is room for a European player to start up (the verb is not chosen by chance) the research, development, production, and distribution of the drugs and biomedical innovations that Big Pharma will not give us.

The second proposal concerns the science and technology of climate change. This topic is at the top of the list of EU priorities, for example, the European Commission's indications for the allocation of Next Generation EU funds. However, the role of companies controlling the energy markets and of some industries that have invested in past technologies is underestimated. The risk of dispersion or capture of these funds is significant, in the absence of an entity that internalises a long-term scientific and technological mission and acts as owner and manager in the collective interest of a break with the current model.

Finally, I think we could study the feasibility of a European platform capable of opposing the seven sisters (and their cousins) of information technology and affirm an alternative model of public governance of data. While the previous two examples dealt with the oligopoly of Big Pharma and the oligopoly of Oil&Gas and the automotive sector, here we are dealing with the Tech Giants. Can you really challenge them to do something more useful for our future with our data than they are doing to make billions in profit? I try to discuss this.

These proposals might be feasible, not only from a scientific and technological, economic and financial point of view, but they could also enter the political agenda of the contrast between a progressive Europe and a Europe that looks backwards, sometimes excessively so. Now is the right time to talk about it.

Notes

1 An asset is a good that is expected to provide future benefits to its owner (individual, firm, government). Assets can be current (as cash), financial (as shares), fixed (as buildings or equipment), and intangible (as patents or software).
2 Apple Inc., Condensed Consolidated Statements of Operations (Unaudited): https://www.apple.com/newsroom/pdfs/FY20-Q3_Consolidated_Financial_Statements.pdf
3 https://www.wsj.com/market-data/quotes/JNJ/financials/annual/balance-sheet
4 https://ec.europa.eu/eurostat/statistics-explained/index.php?title=Healthcare_resource_statistics_-_technical_resources_and_medical_technology#Use_of_medical_technology
5 https://www.forbes.com/sites/sergeiklebnikov/2020/10/12/jeff-bezos-is-again-worth-more-than-200-billion-as-amazon-stock-soars-ahead-of-prime-day/?sh=39e71e7c5f42
6 According to Eurostat, in the EU, around 45% of R&D personnel is employed by universities and the public sector. https://ec.europa.eu/eurostat/statistics-explained/index.php?title=R%26D_personnel#Researchers
7 HESA, 2022.
8 Fire and Guestrin, 2019.

9 Thanks to a 40 million USD contract with DARPA, which is the same US defence agency behind the Internet. The project then continued with another military supplier, General Atomics, with the Predator project (which in September 2020 was awarded a 7.4 billion USD contract to supply a new type of drone to the US Air Force).

10 Cited by Mariana Mazzucato (2018a).

11 https://tbr.ie/2020/10/06/what-the-eu-court-ruling-on-the-apple-ireland-tax-case-means/

12 A public enterprise can take various forms: state-owned corporations, government-invested companies, or other not-for-profit entities.

1 The places of knowledge

From Big Science to research infrastructure

For centuries, science has been produced in small-scale laboratories, by solitary intellectuals or with a small group of disciples and collaborators. We are familiar with the narratives about Marie Sklodowska Curie and her husband Pierre sifting through uraninite ore in a shed to extract radium, Alexander Fleming focusing the microscope on moulds in his laboratory, and Watson and Crick cutting out strips of cardboard to build the three-dimensional double helix model of DNA. Scientific informal networks, the social capital of science, have been evolving over time. According to Latour (1987) and other sociologists,[1] no scientist is acting as an individual but as part of a complex mechanism of shifting interactions within networks of relationships. However, the way of working of a small-scale laboratory in the 20th century was not radically different from that in the previous centuries: Galileo scanning the moons of Jupiter with his self-made telescope, Newton making drawings and calculations using geometric methods, Galvani sacrificing frogs with his wife to study electricity, Darwin breeding pigeons to observe natural selection. As far as we know, many centuries earlier, Archimedes, Euclid, or Eratosthenes probably worked in a way that was not radically different.

A large part of contemporary science still seems to involve a certain amount of artisanal activity: a principal investigator with a group of younger researchers and a few PhD students in a laboratory. But a different large-scale organisational paradigm has now emerged. When in 2012, Fabiola Gianotti, then spokesperson for CERN's ATLAS experiment, announced (together with her colleague Joseph Incandela of the parallel CMS experiment) the empirical confirmation of the existence of the Higgs boson, she was speaking on behalf of a collective entity.

The ATLAS[2] scientific collaboration does not have per se a principal investigator. The spokesperson is elected in rotation by the members: around 3000 scientists from 181 research institutes in 38 countries across every continent. Hundreds of small groups within the collaboration deal with specific aspects of the research, coordinate in committees, continuously exchange results, and, ultimately, publish them, after mutual review, by signing them collectively. The system is astonishing, not least because very few, perhaps none, of the participants can master all the aspects of research that is so complex that

DOI: 10.4324/9781003381532-2

it requires a "microscope", an object that is 27 km in circumference in a tunnel that lies under two countries at a depth of 100 metres. The Large Hadron Collider (LHC) is a particle accelerator made up of millions of components, requiring billions of calculations to analyse an astonishing amount of data generated in its lifetime. The generation of an immense amount of data is often a crucial aspect of the new model of knowledge production.

Over the past few years, I have closely observed the way things are done at CERN. Together with my research group, we have assessed the potential socio-economic impact of the LHC, followed by its upgraded High-Luminosity version due in 2025, and are currently working on the Future Circular Collider project (a hypothetical 100 km circumference accelerator to succeed the LHC after 2035). Automatically, as participants in the FCC collaboration, we were included as co-authors of the publications. The 250-page article on the Conceptual Design Report of the FCC-hh (one of the possible versions of the accelerator, the one with the highest energy), published in the European Physical Journal, is signed, in strict alphabetical order, by some 1200 authors from 352 universities and research institutes. We are a long way from artisanal production here. This way of producing science is changing the landscape forever.

While particle physics may be considered an extreme case, much of contemporary science is radically influenced by the organisational model of research infrastructures. For the first time, the Human Genome Project (HGP) has mapped some 92% of the three billion bases (the pairs of components of the double helix) of our DNA. From 1990 to 2003, the HGP included at least 20 different institutes and universities in the USA, UK, Germany, Japan, China, and France, with the involvement of at least 250 scientists.[3]

A well-known example, if only because of its use in the media, is the open-access pandemic data dashboard operated by the Center for Systems and Engineering Science at Johns Hopkins University,[4] based on real-time data from hundreds of sources, with tens of thousands of professional users.[5]

This model of broad collaborations, which often combines tangible infrastructures in a physical place (a campus, a laboratory, a research centre) with digital infrastructures that create virtual communities of collective intelligence,[6] no longer has much to do with traditional Little Science. Nor is it the Big Science[7] linked to the military–industrial complex, to quote the title of the successful book by de Solla Price (1963), who was the first to study the transition between two eras of knowledge production. The distinction between different modes and places of contemporary science is useful to understand its dynamics and final social impact.

The knowledge production of our times has global dimensions that were unthinkable a few decades ago, and it has evolved in different forms, linked by cumulative processes. To get some idea of the scale: Web of Science, the Clarivate database of the 22,000 most authoritative scientific journals (plus 250,000 conference abstracts) contains 80 million articles in over 250 disciplines.[8]

Patent databases represent another indicator of the extent of progress in knowledge. In the year 2017 alone, 3,170,000 patent applications were filed, with China ranking first in terms of number of applications.

Global R&D expenditure around 2020 was estimated at 1.7 trillion USD PPP (at purchasing power parity). According to the OECD,[9] the US spent more than 610 billion USD in 2015, China 515 billion, and the EU (without the UK) 311 billion. More than 70% of the expenditure was incurred by businesses (including public enterprises, which are still very important in some countries) and the rest directly by governments and to a small extent by non-profit bodies. The role of governments, however, is also indirect, through support in various forms of business R&D. In fact, almost all basic research, a significant proportion of applied research and a fraction of technology and product development is directly supported by taxpayers. The rest is ultimately financed by consumers through the price of products sold on the market. Considering only OECD countries, government spending on research was about 490 billion USD (current PPP USD) in 2020, meaning that each citizen contributed about 360 USD per year through taxes, and the rest through what they pay to buy the products that benefit from the results, from drugs to smartphones.[10]

Public research plays a crucial role in keeping the knowledge machine going. Gheorghiou et al. (2017), in a survey of the economic justifications and impact of public funding of R&D activities, suggest that public funding of private R&D investment is needed because of five bottlenecks faced by firms: a) scientific, technological, and market risks; b) high investment, high sunk costs, and long time lags before paybacks; c) inability to fully appropriate the R&D returns; d) lack of financing; e) spillovers to other firms. A survey of firms by the European Investment Bank[11] finds other constraints, particularly general uncertainty, lack of staff with the right skills, business regulations. High sunk costs are often needed for market-creating disruptive technologies. These arguments have supported the view that government should offer subsidies in different forms to "first mover" companies, usually without much consideration of the distributive impact of this transfer of resources from taxpayers to investors. Or perhaps with the belief that in turn taxpayers will benefit at a later stage. Business research is only the final stage of this process based on new actors, not yet fully understood and assessed in terms of their socio-economic impact. According to Georghiou et al. (2017), an increase of aggregate R&D investment of 0.2% of GDP would create an increase of 1.1% of GDP. This would be a rate of return of over 500% per Euro spent, not considering social benefits not accounted for GDP (e.g., life expectancy). The empirics of these calculations is however tricky, as the same authors report the traditional result that at firm level the net return would be between 10% and 30%. The externality, id est the gap between private and social returns, would hence be huge. The variability of findings across countries, industries, fields, and time is very large.

Table 1.1 shows a selection of 40 key and emerging technologies for the future. These fields will attract most of the public and private investments.

Table 1.1 Selected key and emerging technologies

Advanced materials	*Biotechnologies*	*Digital*	*Energy + Environment*
Additive manufacturing	Biocatalysis	Artificial intelligence (AI)	Advanced energy storage technologies
Carbon nanotubes	Biochips and biosensors	Big Data analytics	Autonomous vehicles
Functional materials	Bioinformatics	Blockchain	Biofuels
Graphene	Health monitoring technology	Cloud computing	Carbon capture and storage
Nanodevices	Medical and bioimaging	Gaming	Drones
Nanomaterials	Neurotechnologies	Grid computing	Electric vehicles
	Personalised medicine	Internet of Things (IoT)	Fuel cells
	Regenerative medicine	Modelling simulation	Hydrogen energy
	Stem cells	Photonics and light technologies	Micro- and nanosatellites
	Synthetic biology	Quantum computing	Photovoltaics
	Tissue engineering	Robotics	Precision agriculture
			Power microgeneration
			Smart grids
			Wind turbine technologies

Source: Table based on OECD, Science, Technology and Innovation Outlook 2016.

Big Science and the military–industrial complex

The transition from traditional Little Science to Big Science[12] initially took place slowly and gradually during the first half of the last century but experienced a sudden acceleration during the Second World War. The most representative case was the Manhattan Project, whose sole scientific and technological objective was to translate some newly discovered phenomena of nuclear physics (in particular, by Enrico Fermi) into the design and construction of the atomic bomb: this would result in two types of nuclear weapon based on different principles.[13]

It was not the only large-scale science production project with a direct or indirect military purpose: missiles, radar, computers, satellites, nuclear reactors and much more came from a Big Science model characterised by strategic missions determined by national governments and the military–industrial complex of the great powers.

Let us quickly look at some aspects. First of all, it is more than a coincidence of timing that the affirmation of Big Science occurred in the last century at a time when organisational models of the production of goods and services based on high-intensity fixed capital and high technological content were consolidated. This is not only the case of the Fordist factory, where human labour is organised around the operation and timing of machines and plants, but it is perhaps even clearer in the development of network infrastructures: large railway systems, electricity generation, transmission and distribution, and telecommunication networks. In all of these examples, human labour is part of technologically complex organisations, with an architecture that exploits economies of scale (and in some cases economies of variety, when the same infrastructure can efficiently deliver different services) to the utmost. The scientific principles underlying the production of electricity or the transmission of information via electromagnetic waves, to give just two examples, determine technologies that in turn contribute crucially to the organisation of work, though not exclusively: labour costs, organisational knowledge, the rules of market functioning and many other circumstances constitute other factors.

It is therefore no coincidence that we speak of research *infrastructure* (RI), a term used in economics and engineering. But already in Big Science, which is traditionally linked to the military–industrial complex, the intersection with large-scale enterprise organisation models are clearly visible, as well as those stemming from the industrialisation of military equipment. I have mentioned the Manhattan Project as the birth of Big Science in specialised historiography. I will briefly recall some of its dimensions. Firstly, its orientation towards a precise scientific and technological mission: to produce the atomic bomb. It may seem trivial to point this out, but an organisation with a specific mission that conditions its funding and operations is very different for the scientists working in it from the university environment from which they typically come. Universities for centuries have had the generic mission of producing and passing on knowledge, not specific missions. I will return to this aspect later when I discuss the interaction between universities and research infrastructures today.

The scientists and engineers of the Manhattan Project, as well as the administrative workers, labourers, and military personnel, were not employed to produce knowledge in general, but specifically to produce the knowledge needed to exploit the not-yet-fully-understood principles of nuclear fission for military purposes. While military applications of science were already relevant for several laboratories before and during the First World War, and even before, the scale of operations in the case of the Manhattan Project can be grasped by considering the numbers involved: total cost of 1.9 billion USD in the 1940s, equivalent perhaps in 21.7 billion USD at 2019 prices (a small fraction of the costs of the war for the US); 130,000 employees (most workers and technicians), over 30 sites, 90% of the costs of building and operating plants to produce fissile material (uranium and plutonium) experimenting with a variety of chemical and physical methods to obtain the required isotopes. More than 600 companies and 400,000 people were examined by the secret service to maintain strict security protocols in the internal and external organisation.[14] As we know, this project was responsible for the bombing, each with a single device, of the Japanese cities of Hiroshima and Nagasaki (August 1945). In the years that followed, the USA (pursued by the USSR and, on a smaller scale, by others) created an atomic arsenal that peaked in 1986 with an estimated stockpile of 64,452 bombs.[15]

Another example often cited is NASA's Apollo programme,[16] which was also conceived in the strategic context of the Cold War. The US response to the USSR's successes in space (Sputnik in 1957) came with the landing of astronauts Armstrong and Aldrin on the Moon (1969), preceded and followed by a series of other missions that played a very important role in the development of scientific computing tools, innovative materials, electronic systems, transmission of radio signals over very long distances, and much more. Here too, the collaboration between scientists, engineers, government agencies, and private companies developed on the scale of Big Science.

This model of organising the production of knowledge did not disappear with the end of the Cold War, although it became less visible. The Manhattan Project in the United States was inherited by the Department of Energy, which manages – in cooperation with consortia of universities and other bodies – the original sites. Most of them have been converted to non-military research, but not all of them, since the mandate of the Office of Science, heir to the Atomic Commission, and thus to its budget, continues to include management of the nuclear arsenal, research into the effects of radioactive contamination and other related issues. Scientific and technical organisations of this kind are still active in France (given the military–civilian duality of the country's nuclear strategy), Russia, China, and elsewhere.

I summarise below the essential features of the Big Science model and how it is different from the model of large scale in research infrastructures that I discuss in the next section. First, in Big Science scientists are involved in missions decided by a national government as part of a political strategy. It may also be that scientists convince governments to set certain priorities. This has happened many times, as exemplified by the famous letter to Roosevelt in support of the atomic bomb project written in 1939 by Hungarian physicist Leo Szilard and signed by Einstein. The Big Science model is, however, typically top-down. Scientists, even when they enjoy a certain degree of decision-making autonomy, substantially depend on a government-appointed management. This implies that their political and ideological loyalty must be somehow guaranteed or at least monitored. Secondly, and closely related to the first aspect, the organisation cannot be too open to international collaboration, except with "reliable" countries (the UK and Canada in the case of the Manhattan Project) and even then, only up to a certain point. The predominantly national dimension of this type of Big Science obviously contrasts with the markedly cosmopolitan character of the scientific communities in their autonomy.

A third implication is that the scientific and technological agenda is relatively rigid, as the focus on a prevailing mission does not allow for significant digressions, which are often the basis of serendipity, the unexpected encounters that broaden the view of science. A further aspect is the secrecy, or at least the non-applicability of the open science/open data model because it would be too risky to make acquired knowledge available to rivals.[17] Finally, the media are mobilised not so much in the function of informing and engaging the public, but in the co-creation of an apologist narrative. In the case of NASA, this propaganda aspect is particularly developed, for example, by co-funding science fiction films about human exploration and the colonisation of Mars. NASA thus tries to gain public favour for the Mars Exploration Project[18] adopted by the government and the agency, despite the exorbitant cost and risks of bringing astronauts to that planet, compared to the cheaper alternative of using only rovers (as the flawless Perseverance rover that arrived at its destination on 18th February 2021).

The "Geneva model" and its evolution

After the Second World War, in parallel with the Big Science linked to the military–industrial complex of the major powers, an alternative paradigm of science production emerged.

In many ways, the model of CERN in Geneva – which, not surprisingly, was established in a neutral country – overturns the principles of Big Science. The most important aspect is that the mission is primarily dictated bottom-up by the scientific community, with no other objective than to explore possible answers to the questions posed by scientists using a technological platform accessible to different groups. I use the term technology here in a broad sense: a combination of fixed investments and operational activities that efficiently enable the production of new knowledge. In other words, it is knowledge embedded in a technology that in turn produces more knowledge: to paraphrase Sraffa (1960), "production of knowledge by means of knowledge".

It takes a lot of science and technology to build a large radio telescope, such as the Square Kilometre Array (SKA) in South Africa, which will search for signals from objects that are immensely distant from us in space and time. The Human Genome Project was not only about organising hundreds of researchers to analyse the DNA puzzle but also involved the development of new machines and computational methods without which the process would have been unthinkable. A cancer therapy centre with a proton and carbon ion accelerator, such as the National Center of Oncological Hadrontherapy (CNAO in Italian) in Pavia, is both a place of medical research and a complex requiring sophisticated machines, equipment, and electronic systems.

In this context of cutting-edge research, governments receive possible priorities from the scientific community, and take on a funding role, but are not able to enter the decision-making process in the same way and depth as when there are military or national strategy implications (e.g., in the field of energy self-sufficiency). In funding RI, governments give control of these enterprises to scientists. The latter, in turn, having no particular reason to see their research as an expression of specific national policy, pursue an international dimension in the projects and organisations in which they work. The greater the cutting-edge nature of the research, the more the scientific communities are cosmopolitan. A telescope, an oceanographic ship, a biodata bank, regardless of location and funding source, if they do advanced scientific research, they will inevitably tend to host international groups and address the entire world scientific community.

Typically, the major RIs are therefore supported by cooperation from different countries, often giving rise to supranational bodies, with their own statutes and self-governing mechanisms. Supranationality changes the rules of the internal game, governance depends less on the objectives of a national minister or parliament and more on the ability of scientists and management to be convincing about their own agenda.

In contrast to secrecy, the model adopted is that of open science. Data and results are made public relatively quickly. Hierarchies are fluid and agendas are flexible. The recruitment of scientists is not conditioned by political loyalty but by merit, in a race to attract the necessary human resources. A crucial aspect of RI is that it is open to the use of a wide range of researchers from different fields.

A concrete example can clarify this mode of access that is open to a variety of users. In order to examine details of matter at the molecular level, very high-resolution "microscopes" are needed, and this can be achieved with "synchrotron light" instead of ordinary light. This involves generating photons with a very high frequency and therefore very high energy, several orders of magnitude higher than the X-rays used in medical and industrial practice. These photons can be obtained by repeatedly accelerating beams of electrons, forcing them to follow approximately circular orbits by means of magnetic fields and thus causing them to emit "synchrotron light" along the way. These highly energetic photon beams can be extracted from the ring in which the electrons are circulating and sent to experimental stations along the ring.

Such a machine is the European Synchrotron Radiation Facility (ESRF), located near Grenoble in France, run by an autonomous European body, it originally comprised 11 member states, which were later joined by 11 others, including Russia. Before the upgrades, the ESRF currently had 44 beamlines, that is, photon extraction lines, each of which is connected to an experimental station, where samples of materials of many different types (biological, chemical, and even archaeological) can be analysed by a research team that has access for one shift – typically eight hours – after being selected by a call for tenders. The service for researchers from universities and other non-profit organisations is completely free of charge (companies can gain access for a rather modest hourly fee to cover the cost). In recent years, typically over 2000 applications for beamline access are submitted to the ESRF each year, amounting to about 28,000 shifts, and 1000–1500 are selected, amounting to about 13,000 shifts. In 2015, an average of 769 experiments were carried out at the ESRF by teams of four researchers over nine shifts. In total, almost 3000 scientists (external to ESRF staff) from hundreds of universities and third-party organisations used the infrastructure in fields ranging from structural biology to materials science, medicine, chemistry, and cultural heritage. In essence, ESRF is a "microscope" collectively used in turn by thousands of researchers, who produce almost 2000 scientific publications each year using the experimental data. The protocols for access to data by third parties in an open science perspective are regulated by a series of protocols that users must sign in order to gain access.

The RIs also invest in communication with the non-specialist public, thereby playing a cultural as well as a scientific role. The aim is to create a climate of consensus around often esoteric research, which cannot be justified by military rhetoric or national ambitions.

Obviously, communication is never an entirely "pure" narrative, but in the best cases, it is aimed at transmitting sparks of passion from the scientists to the general public. It is therefore less apologist than the narrative of Big Science, even though it may be just as prone to spectacularising the hunt for black holes, the oddities of quantum computing, and the wonders of biodiversity. I will return in the next chapter to the socio-economic implications of this way of producing science.

How widespread is this model globally? How many scientists are involved? How much science is produced today using it? It is impossible to give an exhaustive answer to these questions, not least because the RI concept has changing contours. Even a large scientific library can be considered an RI, whether it is based on a paper archive or digital documents. Thus, the Library of Alexandria (3rd century BC), with 490,000 scrolls available to scholars, may have been the first RI in the world. Not counting libraries, scientific collections in natural history museums and other traditional forms, in Europe alone, according to the European Portal on Research Infrastructures,[19] there may be more than a thousand organisations that fit the RI pattern. A map of them is also available on the website of the European Commission (DG Research) and some basic data in the aforementioned portal. The largest RIs are systematically monitored by the European Strategy Forum for Research Infrastructures, which periodically publishes indications of which ones could – by consensus of the participants and evaluators – be considered priorities for the European Union. According to some estimates, there could be around 300 major RIs of more markedly international interest due to the communities they involve. The size varies widely, from 2500 employees at CERN, to 1700 at the European Molecular Biology Laboratory (EMBL) at six different sites, to 650 at ERSF, to a few dozen at virtual infrastructures such as Elixir (Cambridge, UK) for accessing biodata.[20] But these numbers are not indicative of the actual size of the operation, given the very nature of RIs, what counts are the numbers of scientific communities accessing the services provided.

Some of these communities have structured themselves in the form of stable collaborations, as in the example of ATLAS mentioned above, and hundreds of other networks. The order of magnitude of European RI access in this perspective could exceed 1 million researchers, including doctoral students, post-docs, and various others. The digital libraries managed by the EMBL-European Bioinformatics Institute are accessed yearly by an estimated 450,000 to 500,000 unique primary users.[21] This brings us directly to the next topic: the relationship of RIs with universities.

How university research is changing

The establishment of the RI paradigm as a reference model for the production of science has important implications for universities. For centuries, universities have been the favoured place of the traditional paradigm of the master with his students, merely to mention the most remarkable cases: the medieval universities of Bologna, Padua, Naples, Oxford, Paris, and Salamanca. That model was never exclusive, but coexisted with academies, such as the Lincei in Rome and the Cimento in Florence in the 17th century, the Royal Society of London for the Improvement of Natural Knowledge (1660), the first French Grandes Écoles (18th century), and the dozens of German scientific societies (from the Astronomische Gesellschaft founded in 1800 to the various societies for physics, geology, meteorology, pharmaceuticals, and the current large organisations named, respectively, after Planck, Helmholtz, Leibnitz, and Fraunhofer, which we will discuss later).

For many reasons, the German case is the most relevant in the contemporary perspective, since until the catastrophe of the Second World War, Germany was undoubtedly the scientific locomotive of the world, with by far the largest number of scientific journals, universities, patents, Nobel prizes, and practically every indicator relating to the production of science,[22] before giving way to the USA (partly due to the brain drain from the Third Reich).

Despite the prestige of university institutions in their various national forms, it must be considered that their distinctive feature, in past centuries as well as today, is the combination of both creation and transmission of knowledge: research, teaching, and, to a lesser extent, the so-called "third mission" of knowledge transfer to society. For many reasons, this model of mixed missions has been successful for centuries.

Firstly, in elite universities, teaching a select few students allowed them to be directly involved in the research carried out by the mentor, a feature that could no longer be maintained when we moved to large numbers and inevitably the need to devote much of the teaching to the simple transmission of established knowledge.

Secondly, and this should not be underestimated, directly (through fees) or indirectly (through public grants) the presence of students (and former students, the alumni) ensured private and public funding. The social capital of a university is provided by the network of contacts and the reputation of the professors, which for obvious reasons is multiplied by the relationships with students whose careers often take them to other universities, but also to public administration and business: this was the case for Oxbridge in the British civil service, for the Grandes Écoles in the French high administration, and for the major technical-scientific universities in the management of industry in Germany.

A consequence of this plurality of missions of the university model is often the inefficiency of subject specialisation. Although there are important exceptions, etymology can help here: in Latin, universitas stands for "a set of several things, a totality of things", hence "*universitas studiorum*", that is, a corporation that ran the educational institutions and at the same time corporation of masters and students, hence the more common designation of *universitas magistrorum et scholarium*. From the contemporary perspective, one can see the university as an organisation that emphasises economies of variety and only secondarily economies of scale.

My university, the "Statale" of Milan, with 5000 lecturers and technical, administrative, and library staff and over 60,000 students, offers 77 three-year degree courses, 64 two-year second cycle degrees, 32 doctorates, and over 140 master's degrees and specialisation schools. Teachers and researchers work in 33 departments, with over 50 interdepartmental centres and hundreds of laboratories and groups. Seen up close, this large university is a kaleidoscope, with even the strongest groups rarely reaching a dozen researchers. Indeed, it is a wide and diversified aggregation of Little Science, even in terms of equipment, the most expensive of which is, in any case, smaller than that found in specialised research infrastructures.

If you visit the Massachusetts Institute of Technology (MIT), you can still see a 6 Megawatt research reactor, which was built in 1958 and is still maintained by a small faculty and student community of just over 20 people. Although good teaching and niche research can also be done there, it is essentially one of many small-scale neutron sources (there are a few dozen in the world). The scale of RIs specialising in cutting-edge nuclear research is beyond the reach of any university. Remaining in the field of neutron generation, which can be used for a wide variety of basic and applied research, the European Spallation Source (ESS), under construction in Sweden (with a data centre in Denmark), is an RI involving 13 member states, 40 partners, and about 130 universities and other bodies. As in the case of synchrotron light sources, an accelerator carries high-energy particles (in this case protons), which are fired at a rotating target in order to obtain – as opposed to the massless photons as at ERSF – beams of heavy neutrons. Here too, the beams are extracted from beamlines and sent to experimental stations for the development of new materials, for example, for the pharmaceutical, aerospace, plastics, IT, biotechnology industries, and other possible fields of application. Full operation is planned for 2023, and during the start-up phase of the experiments there will be a community of 2–3000 user scientists (in Europe alone there are an estimated 6000 scientists working on neutron physics applied to this type of research).

It is clear from this example that the future for universities in many fields may not be to invest their financial and human resources mainly in in-house projects, but rather to contribute to international projects, by providing the collaboration of their own research teams, as well as, in some cases, parts of machinery, instruments or software, or even directly a share in the budget. In the case of the European Spallation Source, the in-kind contributions will be 30% of the total construction cost of 1843 billion euros. Clearly, on this scale, a research group at a European university interested in a neutron "microscope" is better off adopting a cooperative approach rather than trying to compete using its own infrastructure.

In the USA, a number of universities have set up specific bodies which, in a consortium (also with companies), have bid for the management of research infrastructures owned by the Department of Energy (DoE), such as the 17 National Laboratories, the heirs of the Manhattan Project, for example, the University of Chicago co-manages Fermilab, the main seat of particle physics in the USA (1750 employees). The University of Chicago participates in a consortium (Fermi Research Alliance) for this purpose. In turn, this alliance is part of the University Research Association (URA), to which 90 mainly American universities (but also Pisa for Italy) belong.

There is, however, a much more pervasive aspect of the impact of RI on universities, even without a formal association between universities and these organisations. Indeed, through various degrees of open science and open data policies, researchers all over the world have the possibility to access the knowledge generated by these organisations. An example might help: with one click of a mouse, a PhD student in genetics from New Zealand or China can access, free of charge and in real time, all the information on the human genome and on many other living and extinct species (more than 42,000 genomes), on more than 70 million protein sequences, and on more than 125,000 macro-molecular structures by connecting to the above-mentioned portal of the EMBL-European Bioinformatics Institute.

Every day, researchers from a 100,000 different computers (individual IPs) do this, and the numbers keep growing. So, the student might work in a small laboratory in a small peripheral university, but through this digital infrastructure, she has access to continuously updated data from a global community: a new form of Big Science without masters and national governments standing guard at the door. The library of Alexandria has risen from the ashes, the scrolls have been replaced by bytes of digital information, and it is physically distributed in many places, wherever there is Internet access.

How R&D is changing within firms

The innovative enterprise is at the heart of the vision of a dynamic capitalism as conceived by classical economists, Marx and Schumpeter and the more recent endogenous growth theory. Albeit with different formulations, the intuition shared by the economists of our time is that something called "capital" (if it could somehow be measured) would have returns that decrease with its quantity given the same amount of labour employed and given the other factors of production. A tailor with a Singer treadle sewing machine (you can find them at auction) produces a shirt in an hour and a half; a tailor with two of these machines, albeit with some acrobatics, perhaps produces a shirt and a half in the same time. But a tailor with ten Singer machines would certainly not know what to do with all that capital. If, however, traditional sewing machines are replaced by something more automated – the foot pedal, for example, is replaced by an electric motor – the relentless diminishing returns can be offset.

The problem for the progressive tailor is to find someone to invent the electric motor, and further upstream, someone to invent the generation, transmission, and distribution of electricity. He is not able to do it, and neither is Singer. For many economists, it has been taken for granted that research and development of new products and processes should essentially take place within companies, though not necessarily within the individual company, of course. So one does not expect tailors to invent the industrial use of electricity to improve the sewing machine, nor Singer to do so, but one hopes that some investor will seize ideas that are in the air and turn them into innovative projects. The theory of endogenous economic growth replaces knowledge that falls from the sky with deliberate research and development. However, it is noted that it may be less than socially optimal because of the inability of the individual innovator to escape the fact that some of the benefits of innovation are appropriated by others: an externality, seen as a market failure, for example in a famous article by Paul Romer (1990), 2018 Nobel Prize winner in economics.

This narrative has been variously used as a justification for public policies to support R&D in businesses: capital subsidies or subsidies to certain types of business expenditure, creation of technology parks on favourable terms, tax credits, legal protection of intellectual property, loans on better than market terms, and other measures.

As important as the issue of market failure in knowledge creation due to externalities may be, this narrative is somewhat incomplete, if not misleading. The scientific and technological progress of the contemporary world not only has the enterprise as its locus, but it increasingly requires the contribution of the other mechanisms we have described in the previous sections: the role of governments in the emergence of Big Science linked to the military–industrial complex, the role of universities and other specialised forms of knowledge production and transmission, and, in recent decades, research infrastructures.

Much has been written about the interaction between the first two modes of interaction, those between military research and universities on the one hand, and universities and business on the other. Here I will argue that the third, more recent, mode connecting business and research infrastructure deserves careful study.

Let us return to the example of synchrotron light sources. There are dozens of them in operation around the world (from various technological generations). They are used for both basic and applied research. How do companies benefit? In the case of ERSF, about 30% of the groups that take turns at using the beamlines have projects with potential industrial applications. A much smaller percentage of the shifts are assigned directly to groups working for company R&D. As mentioned above, access is for free or is paid for at a relatively modest hourly rate, but the mechanism for passing on experimental knowledge to companies mostly follows a different path.

Companies rarely invest in research that requires the science and technology of synchrotron radiation. Mostly they wait patiently for ideas to mature. Scientists who carry out experiments at ERSF sooner or later publish their results. About 1600 articles each year use experimental data from research carried out at Grenoble. These articles are in turn cited by other articles, which are in turn cited by others, in a cumulative process. Approximate calculations indicate that a synchrotron like Grenoble directly generates in its decades-long life, a literature of tens of thousands of papers and contributes to hundreds of thousands of publications citing them. A fraction of these papers will contain ideas that have commercial applications. Their authors may have direct contact with companies, such as pharmaceutical companies, or there may be people within companies who monitor the literature and extract ideas and data from it.[23]

A crude way to measure this impact is to look in patent databases at the citations a patent makes of a scientific article. It turns out that the results of research done in Grenoble, as in dozens of other similar research infrastructures, publicly available in millions of pages of scientific articles, contribute to the patents filed by companies, that is, to the private legal appropriation of the economic benefits of a service freely provided by a public infrastructure to the scientific community.

The more open the science upstream, the higher the likelihood that in the impact cascade it creates downstream, there is – along the way – an opportunity for profit, not necessarily embodied in a patent, since in various sectors ownership of ideas and designs is defended in other ways.

This mechanism, the transformation of knowledge into capital or "assetisation", was already applied to some academic research in the centuries of the industrial revolution, but Little Science was a craft and companies could also be founded by a lucky inventor, sometimes an amateur. Research infrastructures, on the other hand, are large-scale industrial knowledge factories, whose impact is amplified by the digitisation of scientific outputs. With the mediation of scientific communities in universities and other specialised institutions, and with the support of the digitalisation of information and its almost instantaneous transferability, a river of potential innovation opportunities is created. It makes sense for companies to equip themselves to fish on the river with targeted investments, and it makes sense for finance to support these knowledge-intensive investments in order to place its bets on them. The process is taking place before our eyes. It has extraordinary economic and technological results that benefit us, for example, every time we make a purchase with our smartphones, every time we get a Magnetic Resonance Imaging to see how our knees are doing, or every time a photovoltaic panel on the roof of our house gives us a few watt-hours of power. But there is a side effect: science's surprising contribution to social inequality.

Before dealing with this issue in the next chapter, let us take a closer look at some of the mechanisms of the direct social impact of RI. As we shall see, the effect on inequality is an indirect effect and it is useful to analyse the mechanisms separately.

The social impact of research infrastructure

From the perspective of interest, the distinction I made earlier between science for the military–industrial complex and science for the scientific community is crucial. While in the latter case, as I will argue, one can credibly compare social benefits and costs, in the former case this is impossible. A thought experiment can help to understand the problem.

As I mentioned, the Manhattan Project was explicitly proposed by Szilárd and Einstein as a reaction to news coming out of Nazi Germany. It was known that Werner Heisenberg, one of the most brilliant physicists of his time and one of the fathers of quantum mechanics, had been put in charge of a project that could have led Hitler to the atomic bomb. Hitler preferred to give priority to the work of another Wernher, the famous von Braun, who would design the V2 missiles with conventional explosive warheads. The aim was to overcome British resistance after the failure of the Battle of Britain with carpet bombing. But if Heisenberg had had the means and the iron determination (some have imagined that he did not) to give Hitler the atomic bomb, and the two scientists had collaborated, Germany could have been in possession of missiles with nuclear warheads long before the Soviets and the US, who were far from possessing missile systems at the time.[24] Fortunately, this coincidence of circumstances did not occur; Hitler did not gain the capability for ballistic carriers armed with nuclear warheads. But the example shows that it would be unimaginable to discuss the social costs and benefits of developing the science and technology of the atomic bomb and guided missiles without considering the strategic and political implications. The death toll in Hiroshima and Nagasaki, the cost of destroying two entire cities, and the fact that we now know that some scientists within the Manhattan Project had proposed a demonstrative use to induce Japan's surrender, have led many to consider those bombings a crime against humanity. Nor does it help much in the balancing of benefits and costs to resort to the counterfactual history scenario of lives saved if the Pacific war had continued for some time until Japan's inevitable surrender.

If I recall these events of the last century, it is because the current narrative about science, tends to lose sight of the banal, but no less true, consideration that scientific progress is not automatically associated with social justice. It is, therefore, useful to clarify: the following analysis does not apply to Big Science specifically related to military uses, although obviously, any scientific and technological advancement may ex post have both civilian and military uses, as is the case, for instance, with radar and earth observation satellites.

On the other hand, it is possible, though not easy, to assess the socio-economic impact of large-scale RIs, even if it is impossible to predict what mankind might make of the experimental knowledge that the Higgs boson exists, that the collision of supermassive black holes produces gravitational waves, that the genome of the Neanderthal man can be sequenced, and much more. Fortunately, it is enough to assume that this knowledge on average can do no harm and move on.

A social cost–benefit analysis of RI can rely on a number of principles. First, from a cost perspective, RI is often quite similar to other types of infrastructure, such as energy production or telecommunications, and one can rely on all that we have learnt for decades about how to correctly assess social costs across time and, in particular, how these costs can differ from financial costs. Second, it may be useful to break down the benefits of large-scale RI according to the social groups involved.

In the following discussion, I identify three classes of benefits of RI, as a preliminary step to talking about their impact from the perspective of social justice: First, I examine the benefits for scientists and young researchers; then I discuss the direct benefits for companies and then for the users of innovations; finally, I analyse the direct and generic cultural benefits (the "non-use" values).[25] I will leave the issue of the surprising distributional implications of value creation through science to the next chapter.

Science for scientists and the creation of human capital

Scientists are both "producers" and "consumers" of the output of research activity. They contribute to increasing the stock of knowledge at various levels (incremental, true discoveries or "breakthrough" discoveries) both in their own and other scientific domains. Research output is often measured, albeit imperfectly, by considering scientific publications and preprints.[26] The subsequent impact on the scientific community can also be measured by tracking the number of citations through bibliometric analyses.[27] What is the social value of these activities and, therefore, of the contribution that a large collective scientific enterprise makes to them?

For scientists, an RI is a working tool that enables them to efficiently acquire large-scale experimental data and empirical evidence which – after an analysis process – will flow into the most typical knowledge products: publications, conference proceedings, books, and other communication vehicles. This process is not linear. In order to design a radio telescope, a satellite system for studying climate change, or a machine for sequencing the genome, it is necessary to imagine at the outset the research questions to be answered by systematically collecting certain data. The design of the Future Circular Collider (FCC) at CERN, if an accelerator that costs around 25 billion euros is actually built by 2040, is not just an engineering problem. A 100-kilometre-long tunnel at depths of over 100 metres is required, as well as a system of upstream interconnected pre-accelerators including the current LHC itself, at least four extremely sensitive detectors to "read" what happens when various types of particles collide, and a powerful set of filtering, processing, transmission, and data storage systems. For years, the world's scientific community has been engaged in the process of selecting different variants of this project, not without heated controversy. Some would prefer CERN to opt for a competing linear accelerator project, while others argue that it should instead participate in projects in Japan or China and in the meantime experiment with acceleration technologies based on entirely new scientific and technological principles. FCC supporters include those in favour of a machine that initially collides electrons and then, in the same tunnel, is replaced by a machine that collides protons (the two-stage solution currently in the majority), while others suggest skipping the intermediate stage and going straight for the most ambitious project. Each of these variants potentially answers different research questions and has different chances of success, particularly in going beyond the Standard Model of Physics. This model is an admirable theoretical construction that has been experimentally verified with extreme precision but is so incomplete that it does not allow gravity to be included in its framework and many other aspects of our universe to be clarified. The decision-making phase within the scientific community can take many years, more than ten, not to mention the need to convince governments to offer funding.

Therefore, in reality, behind every piece of data collected and every publication that uses it, there is a very complex process that can also lead to dead ends, projects that will never come to light, or that will turn out to be less promising than expected.

The easiest way to put a value on this for scientists is to think of publications, books, and conference proceedings as the manifestation of an investment of time. In this perspective, an RI is a factory of publications, which – whatever their content – have a statistical impact that averages out between the few works that make the history of science and the many that simply turn out to be background noise. The *minimum* social value is the opportunity cost of the time taken to produce the publications.

It is important to emphasise that this is not the value of the knowledge embedded in publications, which is certainly much larger, although often unknown. We now know how to use the photoelectric effect, in particular, that it could be an alternative source of energy to the unsustainable production of energy from fossil fuels. But when Einstein gave his interpretation of what happens,[28] the technological and industrial implications were completely unknown. The social value of the book you are reading should not be too much less than the value of the time I am spending writing it, plus the cost of publishing it for the publisher. If, then, the book will have any impact on European science policy, it is better to be cautious and avoid confusing the concrete editorial product, this book, with the uncertain hope that it will influence the world.

To sum up: using the concept of opportunity cost of time and examining both publications and citations and other scientometric indicators, it is possible to assign a minimum average value to scientific communication, regardless of the knowledge embedded in the publications themselves (a point to be considered separately). As RIs are factories of scientific publications, this is their first impact. From a social point of view, it is a smaller impact than the others I discuss here, because it affects a smaller number of people. For instance, the world community of particle physics represents perhaps 0.0004% of the human population, and the publications it produces, partly thanks to machines such as the Large Hadron Collider, evaluated with the criterion of the social opportunity cost of this community's time, are of much less value than the technological and cultural effects I will discuss later.

There is also a group (only partly overlapping with scientists) for whom RIs are likely to have a very significant impact in terms of human capital creation. Namely, the students and young researchers who spend a period of study and/or work at an RI and benefit from it in terms of learning skills.[29] From this perspective, a very important component of the benefits of RIs concerns precisely their contribution to human capital formation. Although this effect may also concern scientists and technicians in the early and intermediate stages of their careers, the effect is crucial for young people (PhD students, post-docs and others involved in laboratories, data analysis, and other RI activities).

The benefit for human capital can be measured with methods that have been developed in education economics. The idea is this: working – for a period of one's life when one is still in the training phase – in an environment which allows for on-the-job learning is a great advantage in several respects. Firstly, because the practical experience one can gain in one's own university is limited by the fact that – as I said above – university laboratories do not usually have the tools available to RIs, which were created precisely because of the economies of scale and variety that can be achieved in a single specialised organisation, as opposed to the inevitable fragmentation of academic departments. Secondly, because in addition to more advanced tools, the nature of the problems to be solved is generally more challenging and stimulating. Thirdly, and no less importantly, becoming part of large groups of young and experienced researchers in a specific field, even more so if in an international environment, enhances at the same time human capital and what has been defined as social capital: the value for an individual of his/her participation in a network of interpersonal relations based on trust and reciprocity. This also contributes to the reputational benefit of the young researcher, who will be able to boast of this training on his or her curriculum vitae.

Several studies based on interviews with young researchers have confirmed the importance of these three aspects for those who were able, during their university studies or immediately afterwards, to participate in this type of experience within international RIs. One way to empirically estimate the economic value of the effect of human capital accumulation and related social capital is to extend the models used in the economics of education to the context of RIs. In these models one tries to estimate the effects of education on people's future wages, for example, as a difference between those who stop at high school and those who proceed to university, between those who stop at a bachelor's degree and those who are admitted to a master's or a doctorate, and within this progression between those who are educated in the humanities and those who are educated in mathematics, engineering, biology, etc.

The pay premium for those involved in training in an international RI seems to be significant. At CERN, our group has estimated it (using various survey methods) as an average annual effect of around 10% higher pay (compared to those without this experience) over the professional life of a young physicist or computer scientist. In most cases, however, this young person will not go on to university research but will go on to work in industry or finance (where certain computational skills are highly valued). To the extent that salaries even approximately reflect the productivity of people, it is as if RIs create value in the form of human capital "given" to students and young researchers as a positive externality (since they usually pay nothing to be admitted during or immediately after their doctorate). In the case of CERN, year after year, thousands of young people are involved, mostly through the scientific collaborations of the universities they belong to, and over the often multi-decade life of a particular RI, the cumulative effect concerns tens of thousands of people, hundreds of thousands of years of work, and billions of euros in salary premiums.

To a certain extent, this effect presumably occurs in all fields in which the young researcher can add experience in this environment to his/her university curriculum. For example, it can only be beneficial for a marine biologist to have undertaken a sufficiently long period aboard an oceanographic ship or another type of research vessel, such as – in the Italian context – the "Laura Bassi" of the Istituto Nazionale di Oceanografia e di Geografia Sperimentale, acquired in 2019, an 80-metre unit suitable for polar exploration that can accommodate 50 researchers per mission, rotating between various scientific users. There is an illustrious precedent to these missions, the five-year voyage (1831–1836) of the very young Charles Darwin on the ship the HMS Beagle, which provided the material for the theory of evolution that developed over the following decades.

Not everyone can aspire to become Charles Darwin, but the European Molecular Biology Laboratory hosts 240 PhD students each year in the international institutional programme, from 40 countries, plus PhD and Masters students who, despite being based at their universities, participate in research projects at the various EMBL sites. There is no doubt that a PhD at one of the best biology laboratories in the world has an impact on the entire career of these researchers, some of whom come from good but small or peripherical universities that could not have offered them a comparable environment in terms of instruments and stimuli.

Direct impact on businesses

The construction of RIs, even those that appear to be less capital-intensive (such as the Human Genome Project), has required significant technological advances, especially from companies supplying components and systems. These advances include new materials, specialised machines, data extraction, processing and transmission, and much more.

We find here a significant manifestation of the paradox of open science, a public good that generates private profits.[30] Very often, RIs do not patent technological innovations, and collaborate freely with supplier companies to help them overcome the innovative challenges of building non-standardised components. As a result, companies have an extraordinary, often unique opportunity for experimentation and learning and later, sometimes with several years of gestation, they are able to file patents or otherwise generate innovative products and services for customers in different markets. This impact on business profitability is measurable and often represents a significant share of the benefits of RIs. There are further downstream effects that multiply these effects, for instance, in the field of medical imaging technologies or materials from space missions.

Let us look at some of the pathways that serve to transmit such impacts. Suppliers interact with RIs to provide them with technology, goods, and services that are instrumental to the research activity. Technological purchases typically consist of state-of-the-art instruments and/or services that often do not exist on the market and have to operate under extreme conditions. Certain types of space launchers must be able to withstand both very high and very low temperatures, they must withstand impacts with objects that can hit them at high speed (including debris from the disintegration of other space objects), but they must be as light as possible for obvious reasons of launch efficiency. The superconducting magnets of a particle collider must operate at temperatures close to absolute zero, lower than the temperature of interstellar space.

Interactions and knowledge exchange between RIs and (usually private) technology-supplying firms is a source of mutual learning,[31] innovation, and enhancing the success of the supplying firm in the market.[32] Benefits acquired by direct suppliers can be (partially) transferred to their sub-suppliers.[33]

Studies conducted for the European Space Agency, CERN, and other operators of large RIs have concluded that, typically, for every euro spent by these institutions in the procurement of high technology from supplier companies, three euros of net revenues in other markets are generated for these companies, thanks to the knowledge acquired and transferred as an external benefit.

With my collaborators, we have verified this effect as statistically significant on samples of several hundred CERN suppliers and, more recently, we have found this kind of effect on suppliers of the Italian Space Agency (ASI) and the European Space Agency (ESA).[34] We interviewed more than 100 Italian companies in the space sector who stated that, thanks to the supply contracts with the commissioning agency, they have improved their technical know-how (in 90% of cases), the quality of their products and services (76%), their R&D capabilities (71%), their management and organisational skills (62%), their production processes (54%), developed new technologies (63%), new products (55%), and new services (48%). In addition, 75% of companies claim to have increased their turnover, and a significant percentage claim to have increased the number of customers, employees, and markets in which they operate. Examining the balance sheet data and patent information for 272 Italian companies in the space industry (thus without possible distortions deriving from the interviewed sample) in a regression model, controlling for the amount of assets (tangible and intangible), the number of employees, and year/sector fixed effects, we found that the ASI variable (which identifies being awarded a supply contract) has a positive and statistically significant coefficient on the average turnover of the companies. In another multivariate regression model, controlling for the same exogenous variables, we find that the variable ASI has a positive and statistically significant coefficient on the number of patent applications by firms, a result that is confirmed with respect to a control group. These results go in the same direction as what we found for hundreds of CERN supplier firms, both when interviewed and when studying balance sheet and patent data, thus confirming the more fragmented evidence available in other studies. Another important channel through which RIs have a social impact is the benefit for software and database users. These two mechanisms deserve to be discussed separately, not least because they are little known outside the scientific community.

The policy of CERN and various other RIs is to develop the software it needs in an open-source and free form. This means that anyone can access the codes and not only download existing software libraries free of charge, such as those of an advanced statistics programme like ROOT or a simulation programme like GEANT, but can also modify and integrate them, thus creating an ever-growing library built by open communities of computer scientists from all over the world. At present, software is being developed and released into the public domain that is initially adapted to the needs of high-energy physics, but which in many cases proves to be of great use in other application domains, for example, in the interpretation of images obtained from CT scans and other forms of radiology, or even in the industrial field. According to some estimates made by our group, the value thus created and donated by CERN amounts to billions of euros, counting the value of the time saved by users along the entire IT product development chain.[35]

A similar approach can be applied to the value created through the free transfer of data generated at RIs given the policy of open data that is often adopted. Research at the European Bioinformatics Institute (EMBL) has estimated the value of the time saved by researchers around the world who can freely access online databases containing a wealth of information on the genome of different species and other biodata. This value is much greater than the cost to taxpayers of funding the digital infrastructure that makes this data available.

Finally, there is a third channel, which is certainly the most important one: the benefits for businesses and consumers of innovative products downstream of the RI, deriving wholly or partly from upstream scientific and technological contributions. They include new services, products, processes, or applications used in secondary markets and/or in areas other than the initial field of research. I will come back to the public funding of academic research and private enterprises later on, but the point I want to make here is that RIs also generate innovations developed independently and then incorporated into many industrial and manufacturing sectors.

There are several examples that could be cited: the approximately 3000 spin-off products of technologies developed by NASA for space exploration, the use of some 40,000 particle accelerators in medicine and other fields, the use of around 5000 orbiting the Earth satellites for telecommunications, Earth observation and geo-positioning, and drugs resulting directly from biomedical research carried out by public bodies.

Cultural impact and social attitudes towards science

I have mentioned the cultural impact of RIs, directly or indirectly associated with research activity.[36] The Kennedy Space Center (KSC) is the most emblematic example in this sense: it is visited every year by more than one million people, willing to travel, to pay a rather expensive ticket, to spend time having fun with science. CERN welcomes more than 100,000 visitors every year and is currently working on a major project "The Science Gateway", designed by the famous Italian architect Renzo Piano, to upgrade the public reception area. There are many other examples, as even smaller infrastructures organise open days, handle relations with journalists at special events, and maintain websites. Many RIs also regularly organise permanent or temporary exhibitions, guided tours, lectures, dissemination, and awareness-raising events for the public and lay people. Dissemination activities can also be conveyed via social media through webinars, making digital resources available for recreational activities, etc.[37]

In the economics of cultural heritage, rather robust and proven methods have been developed to measure the social value of these activities (such as those based on travel costs to visit a museum and the opportunity cost of time). There are examples in the field of "science tourism" but also in the involvement of citizens in the co-production of science (citizen science), or in the use of websites and other communication tools.

Finally, there remains the unpredictable value for all of us of scientific discoveries generated in RIs. Given that this value is unpredictable ex ante, the crucial arguments in favour of public investment projects in fundamental research cannot be anything but qualitative. However, it may be interesting to examine the willingness of citizens to pay for investment in the production of science. Reflected in this attitude, even in people who work in completely different fields, have never visited a research site, and have never read a scientific publication, we find an expression of the curiosity of scientists which – as such – is the expression of a more general human attitude towards knowledge.

To what extent are citizens willing to bear this cost, for instance, through taxation (since this is ultimately what happens with public RIs)? Empirical survey methods developed in environmental economics to assess public goods, such as the conservation of ecosystems, or in the economics of cultural heritage, can be adapted to the sphere of science.

In this perspective, all citizens have a dual role: on the one hand, taxpayers and on the other hand, beneficiaries of non-use values. RIs produce knowledge, which is often, in fact, a public good.[38] In the case of RI, typically, the production of knowledge is financed by the participating states through public expenditure; thus, in the last instance, taxpayers are the financiers of knowledge production. But why should they be willing to pay? One possible answer is that there might be a public preference for science, for the possibility of making new discoveries and knowledge advances for its own sake[39] without taxpayers directly benefiting from it. Therefore, value emerges which in environmental economics is called "non-use".[40]

Our group's first experiments in this field, looking at the willingness of French and Swiss citizens to pay for future investments in CERN, yielded surprisingly positive results.[41]

In the case of France, more than a thousand respondents were interviewed (2018), with a representative sample of the country's population over the age of 18. An online questionnaire was administered in which, after ascertaining the individual's degree of interest and attitude towards science in general, the degree of knowledge of CERN was measured in comparative terms with other institutions such as UNESCO or the World Health Organization. Then, with a short introductory video and other informational material, a contingent valuation experiment was conducted, in which two alternative scenarios were presented regarding CERN's future investment in a new accelerator: a scenario with a new project and a scenario of maintaining and then phasing out the current research infrastructure. It was then asked whether to sustain a future accelerator the respondent would be willing to increase the taxes he/she pays by a certain annual amount, dividing the sample into subgroups, each with a different virtual tax baseline, in the range of 3–50 euros. If the respondent says he/she is not willing to pay that level of tax, a lower level (different for each subgroup) is proposed, whereas if he/she is willing, a higher level is proposed. In addition, a maximum level of willingness to pay is asked of everyone. In addition, information was collected on gender, age, per capita net income, level of education, and residence. The statistical analysis of the results (with different econometric models) shows three interesting aspects: as expected, the willingness to pay for investments in basic research is positively correlated with income, level of education, attitude towards science and information level regarding CERN; an albeit narrow majority of the respondents was willing to contribute; the average willingness to pay is about 50% higher than the per capita tax implicit in the annual contribution of the French state to CERN.

The study confirmed these results for Switzerland (the other CERN host country with main access to the campus near Geneva). Again, there were more than a thousand respondents, with a representative sample of the population. The structure of the experiment was identical to that in France, except for an adjustment of the reference values of virtual taxes and a further division of the sample into two subgroups of 500 people each. One group was given the information that they already implicitly pay taxes for CERN (6 Swiss francs per year), while this information was not given to the other group. The result was that it makes no difference whether the level of effective taxation is disclosed or not (so there is no "anchoring" effect) and again it was found that the average willingness to pay of Swiss taxpayers is significantly higher than the actual taxation. Moreover, the proportion of those who are unwilling to contribute is lower than that in France.

It would be interesting to repeat these experiments in other countries and in other fields of scientific research that are based on large investments. Despite the occasional belief that fake news and other irrational attitudes create hostility towards science, the data on attitudes measured by a monetary yardstick, which has the advantage of "weighting" the results, seem to say that the majority of citizens are aware that knowledge has a social value, even when it is a public good with no visible concrete benefits.

Summing up

Analysis of the social costs and benefits of RIs suggests that the social return is often positive. The investment could pay for itself in terms of economic welfare, even without wild speculations about the economic impact of systematically mapping planets outside the solar system or detailing every type of virus on our planet.[42]

In some cases that we have studied in depth, the total social benefits of RIs (as far as it is possible to measure them) are greater than their costs, generating a net benefit to society. For example, the LHC accelerator at CERN produces measurable social benefits in the above categories. The benefit–cost ratio (B/C) is 1.2[43] which increases to 1.8 when considering the upgrading of the accelerator with the High-Luminosity LHC project, planned for 2025 with an investment cost of 950 million Swiss francs.[44] In other words, the social benefits will outweigh the costs by between 20% and 80% (with a very high probability, tested with simulation models based on random sampling of tens of thousands of scenarios).

A large synchrotron for medical cancer research, such as the CNAO in Pavia, has an even greater benefit–cost ratio.[45] These and other more qualitative studies produced by other research groups since the 1980s[46] suggest that RIs could therefore generate net social benefits even before the cascading economic effects of scientific progress can be predicted from the perspective of long-term innovation.

These are the impacts that can be measured as aggregate effects. But how are the ultimate social benefits of the production of science distributed to society through large RIs in particular? Does scientific and technological progress ultimately increase or decrease inequality today? This is clearly a different question. We need to move away, hence, from the abstract study of the impact on the "average" citizen, an unrepresentative subject of the human population in an unequal world. This is the subject of the next chapter.

Notes

1 Science and Technology Studies is an interdisciplinary field, mainly in the domain of sociology looking at science and technology in the social and historical context. See Hackett et al., 2007.
2 https://atlas.cern/Discover/Collaboration
3 The list of signatories of the pioneering article in *Nature*. Lander et al., 2001.
4 Dong et al., 2020.
5 An example of our times is the development of virtual laboratory projects on Covid-19 such as the OpenCovid19 Initiative, which aims to develop low-cost open-source tools, including tracking methods and prediction models in response to the pandemic, and purports to have attracted over 4000 volunteers and experts. https://app.jogl.io/program/opencovid19
6 Malone, Bernstein, 2022.
7 The term "Big Science" appeared perhaps for the first time in a famous article in the journal *Science* by the American physicist A.M. Weinberg (1961).
8 Over 100,000 selected books, 171 million records, and 1.9 billion cited references. https://clarivate.com/news/clarivate-launches-new-web-of-science-to-accelerate-the-pace-of-research-and-discovery/, accessed September 2022.
9 OECD (2022), Gross domestic spending on R&D (indicator): https://data.oecd.org/rd/gross-domestic-spending-on-r-d.htm, accessed September 2022.
10 https://data.oecd.org/pop/population.htm; https://stats.oecd.org/Index.aspx?DataSetCode=GBARD_NABS2007
11 EIB Investment Survey: http://www.eib.org/about/economic-research/investment-survey.htm
12 de Solla Price, 1963.
13 Hughes, 2003; Gosling, 1999; Galison, Hevly, 1992.
14 https://en.wikipedia.org/wiki/Manhattan_Project#Manhattan_District
15 Based on Federation of American Scientists 2022: https://ourworldindata.org/
16 Lafleur, 2010; Scott, Jurek, 2014.
17 Weinberg, 1961.
18 https://mars.nasa.gov/
19 https://www.riportal.eu/
20 Martin et al., 2021.
21 Beagrie, 2021.
22 Watson, 2010.

23 Catalano et al., 2021.
24 After Germany's capitulation, the Soviets faithfully copied the V2 and used it for their first space launches. The USA hired former SS major von Braun as a designer for NASA, until the Saturn V triumphed in the Apollo moon mission (to date, the largest launcher used for missions with astronauts on board).
25 For a more detailed analysis, see Florio, 2019.
26 European Commission, 2014; Martin, 1996; Pinski, Narin, 1976.
27 Carrazza et al., 2016; Ferrara, Salini, 2012.
28 There were previous experimental studies by Hertz, Hallwachs, Righi, and others.
29 Camporesi et al., 2017.
30 According to Pagano (2014), "there seems to be an evident paradox in the institutional tendencies of modern capitalism: the knowledge-intensive characteristics of its technologies should favour a democratic economy made up of small firms employing non-rival knowledge; by contrast, however, thanks to knowledge private ownership, big global firms, whose shares are traded on global financial markets, are increasingly predominant in the world economy. [...] Moreover, when knowledge is privatised, the size of the firm matters: each unit of proprietary knowledge can be used an infinite number of times, generating a dramatic form of (firm-level artificially restricted) increasing returns, and allows the exploitation of economies of scope arising from the complementarities with a greater number of other units of knowledge. [...] In the words of Kenneth Arrow: 'Information overlaps from one firm to another, yet the firm has so far seemed sharply defined in terms of legal ownership. I would forecast an increasing tension between legal relations and fundamental economic determinants. Information is the basis of production, production is carried on in discrete legal entities, and yet information is a fugitive resource, with limited property rights'" (Arrow, 1996, p. 651).
31 Autio et al., 2004.
32 Castelnovo et al., 2018; Nordberg et al., 2003; Sorenson, 2018; Edquist et al., 2015; Edquist, Zabala-Iturriagagoitia, 2012; Williamson, 2008; Lundvall, 1985.
33 Florio et al., 2018; Nordberg et al., 2003.
34 Florio et al., 2022.
35 Florio et al., 2016.
36 Martin, 1996.
37 European Commission, 2014.
38 Stiglitz, 1999.
39 Archibugi, Filippetti, 2015.
40 Florio, 2019.
41 Giffoni, Florio, 2023.
42 Social cost–benefit analysis of a RI has nothing to do with financial analysis in terms of returns of investment on similar indicators. See Florio, 2019.
43 Florio et al., 2016.
44 Bastianin et al., 2022.
45 Battistoni et al., 2016.
46 Martin, Irvine, 1983; Irvine, Martin, 1984.

2 Science, inequality, and public policy

A successful programme of the Italian public broadcast in the 1970s was titled "Impossible interviews", with imaginary conversations with the greats of the past. No social scientist was among the 80 or so guests. Let me try to speculate what three of them would say looking around in our times.

Karl Marx would not fail to notice that machinery capital is no longer the prevailing form of accumulation. He would have to admit the need to update his analysis of the exploitation of the proletariat by the industrial bourgeoisie. I imagine he would announce to the interviewer that he is already planning a fourth volume of *Das Kapital* to take this into account.

Karl Polanyi would declare that he is working on an updated edition of *The Great Transformation*. In the new edition, the impoverishment of the English rural population brought about by the enclosure of common lands would only be a historical antecedent to the invisible fences that enclose common property in our times in the prairies of knowledge.

Perhaps the most interesting interview would be with Joseph Schumpeter, by no means the most modest of the three. Asked by the journalist if he didn't think he should revise something in his analysis, I think he would answer that, on the contrary, he had already foreseen everything: in *Capitalism, Socialism, and Democracy* (written at Harvard in 1942), there is the decline of the entrepreneur-innovator replaced by the large managerial enterprise, in which research and development becomes a corporate function and not the creative activity of an individual.

The imaginary Schumpeter would state that looking around he finds confirmation of his pessimistic prediction that monopoly is less and less an essentially temporary phenomenon brought about by innovation adopted by one firm in advance of the others, increasingly taking the form of enduring market power with a smaller role for creative destruction.

I think that these great minds of the past would, when prompted by the interviewer, recognise however that there is no mention in any of their analyses of the crucial role of the state in creating the basis for scientific and technological progress, and hence for contemporary oligopolies. We need a new perspective on capital accumulation in the 21st century.

DOI: 10.4324/9781003381532-3

Governments, through their policies towards universities, research infrastructures, and the support of business R&D, have effectively created a broad ecosystem of knowledge as a public good,[1] but also of a good produced at the outset by public policies. Knowledge thus originates as a good that is in principle available to all but is then transformed along the way, in part still due to some public policies, such as patents, into the creation of "value", an asset, that is, wealth for private investors. This is not an entirely new phenomenon, but what is new is the scale and pervasiveness of the process.

Others have written about it, such as Mariana Mazzucato (2013) in *The Entrepreneurial State*. I analyse here the mechanisms from the perspective of knowledge production and its societal impact.

Firstly, the privatisation of knowledge aggravates the malady that afflicts our societies, inequality, because it shifts part of the share of income produced from labour to capital and simultaneously creates capital concentration. I will show several examples below.

The profits created by the oligopolistic appropriation of knowledge could be curbed in various ways. In this book, I propose a strategy that returns to citizens the benefits of what they themselves have helped to create in the form of knowledge-intensive public enterprises as an evolution of research infrastructures. It is often thought that the containment of profits can be left to taxation and to market regulation. But it must be acknowledged that defining effective taxes and rules to counter the rents of the new oligopolies is not easy, and above all that it fails to structurally change the agenda of the creation and social use of knowledge because it is not only a matter of private appropriation of a public good but also of a consequent socially damaging distortion of priorities in the creation of knowledge.

The channels of privatisation of knowledge

If productive capital is nowadays largely knowledge-based, and intangible in nature, then an important mechanism for generating inequality is to be found in private appropriation and the extraction of returns from knowledge. To take an analogy: for many decades, the most successful capitalist enterprises in terms of market value and profits have been the oil companies, such as Royal Dutch Shell, BP, ExxonMobil, and Chevron, heirs of those seven sisters challenged in the early 1950s by Enrico Mattei, the founder of ENI, the Italian oil company, and by other state-owned enterprises. Those oil&gas companies were to a large extent based on the private appropriation of subsoil resources, resources that were often considered public in national legislation, but then in various ways given in concession to private investors. In that case, the enclosures fenced the subsoil instead of the pastures, privatising the energy sources and the related profits.

It has sometimes been argued that oil concessions were the counterpart of private investment in the exploration, extraction, processing, and transport of hydrocarbons. But we know, of course, that it is not necessary for private capital to invest exclusively in these activities. This is demonstrated by the success of state-owned enterprises such as ENI itself and several other oil companies, including the world's largest company by capitalisation, Saudi Aramco, but also Norway's Statoil (now Equinor), China National Petroleum Corporation, Russia's Rosneft, and several others. Obviously, there are big differences in the way oil revenues are administered by such enterprises in Saudi Arabia and Norway, which have to do with the quality of public institutions in these countries, but the point here is only to acknowledge that it was not and is not essential that oil revenues are privately appropriated by private oligopolists. The allocation of rights to the subsoil is essentially based on political choices, and as such is reversible.

The oil of our times is knowledge, information, and digital content in all forms. The new "seven sisters" are the Tech Giants (Alibaba, Alphabet, Amazon, Apple, Meta, Microsoft, and Tencent), but similar oligopolies are the Big Pharma, aerospace, telecom and media, and defence companies. The enclosures here deal with intangible assets, such as digital information. As such, they are invisible, but by no means non-existent.

Let us look at some of the mechanisms of this appropriation and why, just as in the case of hydrocarbons, land, and industrial capital itself, these mechanisms of appropriation always presuppose institutions and policies that define the process, as Karl Polanyi had seen. I will point out five such mechanisms, apparently very different from each other: intellectual property legislation, the creation of national champions in high-tech public procurement, the appropriation of public investments in human capital, permissive legislation for digital platforms, and the private appropriation of Open Science. The list is not exhaustive, but I hope it is illustrative.

a A first mechanism, certainly the best-known and most controversial one, concerns intellectual property legislation. This legislation establishes a legal monopoly on the economic exploitation of inventions, typically for 20 years. It is a deliberate deviation from free market ideology and policy. The stated aim is to protect the inventor because it is believed that otherwise there would be no adequate incentive to innovate. This is an old-fashioned interpretation of the way research and development, and thus innovation, have operated for several decades. While, on the one hand, it is certainly true that there are researchers who contribute individually with their insights to the accumulation of knowledge, on the other hand, the process is increasingly cumulative and collective.

  A patent application[2] must mention whether there are any previous patents on which the invention is based and also the previous scientific literature directly used. But these citations have a rather limited meaning in the historical era of large-scale knowledge production. The scientific literature on a single topic, for example, a certain pathology, its diagnosis, prognosis, or therapy (pharmacological or otherwise), often consists of hundreds, thousands, or even tens of thousands of articles that can be found in bibliographic databases, such as PUBMED. Families of patents related to a significant innovation may themselves number in the tens of thousands. There are also products that are more difficult to classify, but these too are often easy to find with a web search: preprints, slides of seminar presentations, conference abstracts, and videos. As we shall see later, a researcher or a group can access datasets related to their topic, often freely accessible through large digital databases. No patent can exhaustively cite the antecedents and no one can actually reconstruct exactly how the germination of an idea in the mind of a researcher may have directly or indirectly tapped into this common reservoir of knowledge. The patent thus establishes a legal fence and creates a rent and, in fact, it establishes a private intellectual property relationship over potential innovations that have many mothers and fathers, and certainly many uncles, aunts, and cousins. If these relatives do not claim their share of ownership, it is because it would be too expensive and uncertain to do so. Stories about who first invented something, whether or not it is decided by the courts, may be narratively more or less convincing in the individual case, but they are certainly a weak basis for asserting a "natural" individual property right to ideas. Above all, they are an unconvincing basis for proving the counterfactual that without that legal mechanism, the innovations would not have taken place. The empirical evidence is ambiguous. There are many high-tech sectors where patents – for various reasons – are not considered important or even desirable. Moreover, hundreds of thousands of researchers, in universities and elsewhere, voluntarily forego legal protection for what they discover and invent, preferring to publish their findings and thus give them away before the common pasture is fenced off. Evidently, there are incentives other than patents and associated returns in the creation of knowledge.

b A second mechanism is technology-intensive supplies for the public sector. The positive externality from research infrastructures to firms discussed in the previous chapter can help to create dominant positions in some markets. This is well known in the case of, for instance, the aerospace sector and has been one of the key mechanisms of Big Science in its relationship with the military–industrial complex. This is not only true of the Manhattan Project, but also of countless technologies developed thanks to military orders, or in some cases of strategic interest: these include research on radar, telecommunications, including the Internet, earth observation satellites, missiles, aeronautical technologies, information technology (including Turing's famous machine for decrypting the German WWII Enigma code), and dual-use nuclear power (as in the French nuclear programme). The case history is vast. The scientific and technological knowledge created on commission by the military or specialised public agencies has not only been financed with generous funds, but also by mobilising networks of relations that, especially in the USA, but also in the USSR, France, and Israel – to name but a few examples – have even created personal links between the governing bodies of companies and public decision-making centres. This has led to the creation of monopolistic companies or participants in oligopolies concentrated in certain fields, protected not only and not so much by patents, but rather by decades-long relations with public clients. The world's top ten companies (excluding China and Russia) for defence contracts include the US companies Lockheed Martin, Boeing, Raytheon Technologies, Northrop Grumman, General Dynamics, L3 Harris Technologies, the UK's BAE Systems, the European multinational Airbus, France's Thales, and Italy's Leonardo. Revenues (2020) for each company in this top group (some are diversified into the civil sector) range from 65 billion USD at Lockheed Martin to 15 billion at Leonardo (Italy).

c The creation of human capital at the expense of the public sector in universities and research infrastructures is another channel, which is perhaps not yet widely explored from our perspective of interest. Ultimately, knowledge does not travel so much in documents filed for patents, in articles published in journals, or in reports at scientific conferences, but in people's heads. When a post-doc in particle physics, with his/her skills in data analysis and solving complex computational problems, is hired by an investment fund to work on asset management models, the knowledge embedded in human capital is largely privatised. In most cases, it has been the taxpayers of a country who have financed the path from higher education that has led a young person to a degree in physics, then to a PhD conducted partly in one of the places themselves financed by the taxpayers of various countries, where cutting-edge research is carried out, and again to a period of several years of post-doctoral research. Such collective investment in the creation of human capital takes 10–12 years. Conceived as a path within the creation of scientific knowledge as a public good, it can then lead to the provision of these rare skills in the finance casino, with the benefit of the high salaries offered, the greater certainty of prospects and the fact that in certain fields of scientific research, the supply of brilliant brains is greater than their demand in the public or non-profit sector.

d A fourth mechanism is legislation that actually allows the commercial use of data collected for other purposes by digital platforms. We are so used to taking for granted what Amazon, Google, Facebook, Instagram, and YouTube do with our data that it probably escapes us that whether this appropriation occurs is neither due to the fact that they have superior technology to all their potential competitors, nor to lawmakers' distraction.

The huge prairies of personal and industrial data have been fenced off in a totally artificial way, giving ownership of them to some private companies, but not to others, through contracts that we all sign with a couple of clicks without reading them and without a public authority checking whether citizens are informed about what they are signing (contrary to what should happen in regulated network services, such as energy or telecommunications). I will come back to this issue in the chapter where I make a proposal, but I will make two points here. The algorithms with which search engines or social platforms work, however secret they may be, do not imply scientific and technological knowledge beyond what is within the reach of university departments where advanced research on information technology, including artificial intelligence and in general Big Data processing techniques, is carried out. On the contrary, the seven sisters of the digital economy attract knowledge and human capital and put it at the service of a capital accumulation agenda. If this is happening unhindered, it is also because the legislation that was intended to apply to consumer protection and market regulation in sectors such as mobile telephony was not intended to apply to these platforms. There is nothing inherently technological about this; it is a political choice resulting from reversible circumstances. So, it is no accident that digital platforms do not commit to letting us own our data or to manage it only in the public interest on the basis of a transparent protocol, in fact, the data are exploited for commercial purposes or political communication. It is a political choice that the legislation was so loose, which was made in the belief that it would be expedient to give private investors free rein in these fields. As we shall see, this type of "invisible" choice also concerns Big Pharma and other sectors.

e A counterintuitive mechanism, which I have already mentioned, is related to open science. This is a policy that seeks to extend the principle of open access to research practices, methodologies, and, above all, research results, and is a strategic objective of the European Union in the funding it allocates to research. European Open Science Cloud (EOSC),[3] for example, is an initiative that aims to improve and promote more effective sharing and circulation of scientific knowledge (mostly produced by publicly funded research infrastructures) and related services. Research results, such as data and publications, will be managed and distributed in a way that ensures their discovery, access, interoperability, and reuse by other researchers or economic operators according to the principles summarised in the acronym FAIR: Findable, Accessible, Interoperable and Reusable. This approach, which in itself is driven by the very idea that knowledge should be considered a public good, creates a paradox. On the one hand, the existence of a vast wealth of open science resulting from the research of thousands of universities and public research institutions would represent a great potential for increasing social justice. But on the other hand, this wealth could have the opposite effect: private companies downstream, thanks to the investments in knowledge already made upstream, with their own R&D activities, privately appropriating knowledge. For example, it is certainly a great time and cost saver for pharmaceutical companies to have free online access to the resources of the EMBL – European Bioinformatics Institute (EBI), Hinxton (Cambridge, UK), with its staff of nearly 600 people from over 60 countries. This public research infrastructure, one of the hubs of the European Molecular Biology Laboratory

(EMBL), provides 24/7 free access to its databases, partly through collaboration with similar centres in the USA, Japan, Switzerland, and elsewhere. In addition to the data, EMBL-EBI offers free software to analyse the data as well as online and in-person courses to learn the relevant techniques. In 2019, the EBI website received around 60 million requests for biodata every day, from over 3.2 million IP addresses registered monthly. It is not known how many of these data downloads come from research of direct interest to pharmaceutical companies or biomedical-related industries. A study carried out in 2016[4] on a sample of over 4500 EMBL-EBI data users observed that the academic users participating in the survey accounted for 83% and that of the remainder, more than half were researchers working in companies. It seems obvious to assume that a substantial proportion of the researchers using these biodata will, directly or indirectly, contribute to the development of commercially interesting products and processes. For example, a study carried out for ELIXIR, a network of databases in which EMBL-EBI and 21 member states participate, identified between 2014 and 2017 (just four years), 8000 patents citing bioinformatics databases. Of all these patents on, for example, vaccines, biological markers, and industrial enzymes, about 15% of them draw on these data. The trend can only be increasing, because it is advantageous for companies to draw on open data instead of building their own databases. The above-mentioned study on EMBL-EBI users estimates that there are 1.7 million researchers worldwide in the life sciences and that of these, in 2016, 13%, that is, almost 200,000 researchers, were regular users of the data made available by the institute. This is just one example, albeit on a large scale, among hundreds of online resources, including access to free software, which directly or indirectly offers business R&D an opportunity for the private appropriation of publicly available knowledge.

The new oligopoly and inequality

These mechanisms of knowledge privatisation have wide-ranging and multifaceted consequences in society. In recent years, social inequality, measured in various ways, has increased in developed economies and, particularly in terms of the distribution of wealth and income, has reached almost dizzying heights. According to studies by Credit Suisse,[5] the situation in terms of net wealth (i.e., not counting debts such as mortgages) is such that:

- The top 1% of wealth holders hold 46% of the world's total wealth; and
- The top 12% of adults hold 85% of the world's total wealth; and
- The 55% of the inhabitants of the planet hold only 1% of its total wealth.

There are in 2020 about 68,010 with wealth above USD 100 million, of which 5332 are worth over USD 500 million (see below on the billionaires).

According to Oxfam, half of humanity lives on USD 5.5 a day.[6] While these facts are fairly well known, the ultimate causes of this extreme inequality are debated, and I do not intend to go over this literature here, referring to the excellent discussion by Anthony Atkinson (2015) in his last book.

The aspect I am interested in emphasising is the relationship between knowledge privatisation, oligopoly, and social inequality. A somewhat "photographic" way of introducing this topic is to find out in which sectors those individuals with a net personal wealth of more than a billion USD operate. *Forbes* publishes a list of these people every year, and the 2020 report lists 2095 (as of 18th March).[7] In the top 20, we find several ultra-rich people among the champions of the technology sectors (which represents information technology) and by connection "telecoms" and "media":

1st – Jeff Bezos, Amazon
2nd – Bill Gates, Microsoft
5th – Larry Ellison, software
7th – Mark Zuckerberg, Facebook
11th – Steve Ballmer, Microsoft
12th – Carlos Slim, Telecom
13th – Larry Page, Google
14th – Sergey Brin, Google
16th – Michael Bloomberg, media
17th – Jack Ma, e-commerce
20th – Ma Huateng, Internet media

Thus, more than half of the world's top 20 richest men owe their fortunes not to finance or oil, but to sectors that are more directly related to the technological change brought about by the digital economy. *Forbes* writes:

> The 20 richest people in technology are worth a combined $740 billion. In all, there are 241 technology billionaires on Forbes' 2020 billionaires list, up from 215 last year. Combined, they are worth a whopping $1.4 trillion — 16% of the total net worth for all 2,095 billionaires on the list this year.[8]

The list of the 241 fortunate few includes people whose contribution to innovation is presumably zero, such as the former Mrs. Bezos, whose divorce in 2019 from the better-known Jeff secured her a quarter of Amazon's shares, giving her a personal fortune of 36 billion USD. Or Steve Jobs' widow, Laureen Powell, who inherited 16.4 billion USD from the late Apple co-founder.

Obviously, other sectors are involved in the mechanisms that interest us here: I have already mentioned telecommunications and the media, but the pharmaceutical and other health sectors are also part of the debate on the private appropriation of knowledge, not least because of the increasingly close relations between digital technologies and the biomedical market, a topic I will return to later.

If this information is suggestive, from an analytical point of view it seems tenable that there is a relationship between oligopoly, that is, concentration of market power, and concentration of wealth in terms of distribution of personal wealth. Although these are distinct phenomena, it is nevertheless true that in the final analysis private companies, typically quoted on the stock exchange, are owned by someone, either an individual or a financial investor, so that the effects on personal wealth can be direct (this is the case of founders or top managers paid, for example, with stock options) or indirect, through the participation of individuals in the wealth of legal persons who are the reference shareholders of oligopolistic companies. The ownership of listed companies, although diluted, is not so diluted as to break any link between market power and the personal wealth of the major shareholders.

More generally, technological change and the production of new knowledge interact with the distribution of economic resources and, in particular, with the degree of social inequality in multiple ways. According to Schumpeter (1942), a technological "disruption" (and the creative destruction it brings with it) is linked to the market power enjoyed by the firms that first master the technology or knowledge. According to an optimistic reading, such power is temporary: on the one hand, it is of little concern (since monopolistic innovators are not only threatened by imitators, but they are also subject to potential competition from other innovators); on the other hand, it would be necessary to provide private actors with adequate incentives to invest in research (which a competitive market configuration would not provide).[9]

In a static sense, therefore, the production of new knowledge becomes a precursor of monopolistic (or oligopolistic) power concentrated in the hands of technological leaders to the detriment of other firms. Taking competition as a reference, in relative terms, oligopoly certainly has negative implications in terms of social welfare. However, if it is true that the effects of innovation must be examined in a dynamic sense, it seems that Big Data and the parallel dissemination of information technology have become crucial factors in determining power and success in markets, leading to new organisational forms and the intensification of inequalities. Everything would perhaps be more acceptable if the technological oligopoly were really temporary and if, in the meantime, taxes on income and wealth were redistributive. To put it simply: the private appropriation of knowledge would not be so bad if oligopolistic firms were open to competition and/or the rents they generate (I use the word rents or excess profits and not "profits" deliberately) were taxed. This is not the case.[10]

Corrective policies

From the point of view of equity, in the presence of rents resulting from market dominance, the solution of public economics textbooks is the monopoly income tax. Students are taught that this tax is efficient because the monopolist cannot avoid it by changing its behaviour. The demonstration is simple. All private companies aim to maximise profits, which implies that the optimal quantity to be produced is no greater than the quantity for which the change in total costs (marginal cost) is greater than the change in total revenues (marginal revenue). If by producing 101 units instead of 100 my total profits fall, because that additional unit is a loss, it is better to stop at 100. On the other hand, if by going from 99 units produced to 100 units, my total profits increase, because I still have the possibility of earning something from the additional unit, it is better to produce 100. Therefore, the monopolist produces 100, no more and no less, following the rule that marginal revenue and marginal costs are equal for the chosen production plan. Since each quantity produced corresponds to a price that consumers are willing to pay, the rule simultaneously determines the "fair" price for the monopolist, which is, however, "unfair" to the consumer, since it contains a monopoly rent. If the market were perfectly competitive, the price would be equal to the marginal cost, otherwise, an incoming competitor could enter and take all the customers away from the incumbent.

First textbook solution: tax the profits of the monopoly, as the firm will be taxed while continuing to produce 100 because any other choice would make things even worse. Second textbook solution: prevent the monopoly through pro-competitive policies. Let us quickly see why neither solution works in our context.

The taxation of monopoly excess profits is generally not very effective because companies with market strength have a clear incentive to deploy avoidance or outright evasion strategies. These strategies have costs, for example, it is necessary to pay highly specialised professionals to engage in a game of cops and robbers with tax administrations, possibly within the limits or margins of legality; it is necessary to play on various tables in various countries with artificial tax domiciles; it is necessary to set up transfer pricing systems within multinational groups that increase costs where taxation is highest; to fund economists, journalists, politicians, and think tanks who, with a wealth of "brilliant" arguments, argue that taxing profits and high capital income is bad for the economy, for investment, for employment and thus for the incomes of the poor. Occasionally or systematically, as a last resort, tax officials need to be bribed.

It is, therefore, unsurprising that, according to the above-mentioned Oxfam report, only 4% of the overall tax revenues of governments come from the taxation of wealth of natural and legal persons. Moreover, for the reasons mentioned above, the taxation of capital income in general also has much lower tax rates and tax base than the taxation of labour income.[11]

There is also a more subtle, but no less important, aspect that makes it difficult to tax excess profits that derive specifically from the privatisation of knowledge: the extreme difficulty of separating in the balance sheets of companies the income component derived from public research from that derived from downstream innovations supported by private R&D. Consider the mechanisms mentioned above. Intellectual property legislation is aimed at creating a legal monopoly, even if only temporarily, and it does not seem logical that the excess profits deriving from the exercise of this legal monopoly should be taxed, and the incentive given by one hand is removed by the other hand. Moreover, there is the difficulty of identifying revenues from the company that are specifically related to intellectual property rights.

Similarly, public procurement for innovation policies aims to stimulate the R&D of firms supplying public purchasers by means of contracts which, while not necessarily containing generous conditions in the first instance (although the Pentagon and NASA are not renowned for negotiating down to the last penny on contracts), implicitly expect companies to subsequently capitalise on the knowledge acquired exclusively by working with public research infrastructures, health systems, defence, or transport administrations.

Likewise, the policy of public investment in human capital formation assumes that there is not only an individual but also a collective positive externality (measured empirically as the gap between private and social returns from education) in "donating" these investments to society. It is acknowledged that the education market is imperfect for various reasons and that it is socially desirable for taxpayers to provide free or below-cost advanced education that would not otherwise be offered and demanded in the market. Although not everyone shares this view, particularly in the USA where private universities dominate and where student debt to meet tuition fees is a major factor in household debt, in Europe public education up to PhD level prevails. It seems neither logical nor possible to recover this public investment by taxing companies that employ, for example, PhDs; on the contrary, as I will say in a moment, public policies are going in exactly the opposite direction.

Instead, taxation of digital platforms has been widely discussed in the form of a web tax on online transactions that bypass other types of taxation. But these proposals go more in the direction of standardising indirect taxation than in the direction of specifically taxing the revenues from data appropriation. It is also difficult to imagine taxation of rents from private appropriation of knowledge in the form of open science and open data. Ultimately, although some tax corrections applied to the revenues related to the knowledge economy can be imagined, it does not seem very realistic to correct the impetus it provides to social inequality.

Equally misplaced, I fear, would be the hope for the role of "creative destruction" in high-tech fields, perhaps with the help of market regulation policies. Even if new members join the club and others leave, the economies of scale and variety of the Tech Giants, Big Pharma, and other high-tech sectors seem unbeatable. Players may change, not the game.

Extremely vigorous competition policies in the 1990s broke up (mostly public) monopolies and some oligopolies in network industries, for example, in telephony or electricity, albeit often at the price of socially costly equilibria in the long run, with the formation of new oligopolistic equilibria rather than the establishment of competitive markets (I have tried to demonstrate this in my previous studies on British privatisation and network industry reforms.[12]

However, there is no trace of such aggressive policies in the field of information technology and related businesses, even if regulators occasionally introduce partial remedies. The big question is: where do the economies of scale and variety come from that make it so difficult to challenge Meta, Amazon, or Microsoft? If the question is not one of tangible fixed capital, as in network industries, which automatically leads to a natural monopoly (average costs decreasing with the quantity of product), why don't many Googles emerge (whereas rival search engines have actually exited the market or been relegated to the margins)?

The answer relates to the prohibitive costs for market entrants of overcoming the inertia of users who have been captured by receiving the main service for a free or negligible price. The key aspect of the natural monopoly is not that the fixed capital is tangible, but that the average and marginal costs are continually decreasing and for the services offered by tech companies they are to the extent that the service is offered at zero or near zero price, obtaining revenues in other markets.

If this is the case, creating competing baby Amazons or baby Googles (as was done by creating "Baby Bells" in 1984 out of the break-up of AT&T, the US telephone monopolist) would be extremely costly. In fact, a barrier to entry has been created under the distracted gaze of governments that may perpetuate the oligopoly for even longer than the traditional oil, gas, electricity, and telephone industries, to name only the best-known and most important. For Big Pharma and other high-tech sectors, things look different because of the role of their legal and political protection, whereby aggressive competitive regulation of the market is ruled out at the outset. But even in those cases, the stock of acquired knowledge constitutes the real capital of the firms, which makes their production cost structure such that a competitive market is precluded or difficult to achieve.

Let us summarise. A tension has arisen between public policies that favour, through various mechanisms, the appropriation of knowledge by private enterprises, and the need, shared by many, to combat growing inequality in our societies. Ex-post income redistributive mechanisms are ineffective, since they mainly affect the relative positions of labour income recipients, while at the heart of inequality lies the inequality between labour income and capital income (sometimes disguised as managerial remuneration).

To a large extent, citizens finance the production of knowledge through taxation by means of public expenditure on scientific research, education, and direct and indirect R&D support for companies. In the face of these social costs, the benefits end up being captured to a large extent in the form of capital appreciation of private oligopolistic companies. A regressive redistribution is at work, invisible because it is linked to intangible assets, difficult to estimate, but nevertheless significant.

Mainstream economists, who for decades, between the 1950s and 1980s, interpreted neoclassical growth theory as an argument in favour of policies supporting public and private investment, later, with the theory of endogenous growth, recommended that governments adopt policies to support business research and development, that is, the creation of intangible capital.[13] Contributions such as Romer (1990) focused on the externality arising from knowledge spillovers between companies. This externality was seen as a brake on investment in research and the theory helped to persuade governments to implement generous policies both directly in favour of firms (subsidies and tax expenditures, i.e., tax rebates) and indirectly through universities and other institutions. However, this policy ignored the concomitant effect of monopoly rent formation and the regressive impact on income and wealth distribution.

If one tries to mix policies with very different objectives, one ends up in a quagmire. On the one hand, growth-supporting policies offer firms contributions "in kind" (as in fact are the free services offered by public research infrastructures and universities) and monetary and legal incentives for corporate R&D. If these policies are successful, they create oligopolies and rents for investors that increase inequality. At that point, taxing those rents or trying to break oligopolistic structures becomes practically impossible, given the legal basis that supports them in the first place. For example, if pharmaceutical companies are given unconditional access to public research, to the training of researchers in public infrastructures and universities, to direct funding and tax rebates for their share of R&D expenditures, and finally a 20-year legal monopoly on patented drugs, it becomes impractical at that point to try to weaken their market power and profitability with ex-post corrective policies.

There seems to be no alternative to a world dominated by Tech Giants, Big Pharma, Top Defence, and other oligopolies without the old oligopolies of finance, energy, and large-scale distribution having faded away; on the contrary, they are being transformed in the new context of the knowledge economy (as is the case, for example, with Tesla in the automotive sector, which I will discuss later).

There is however an alternative in the arsenal of economic policy. It is a matter of rediscovering the idea of the public enterprise and hybridising it with that of the research infrastructure: a new type of enterprise as a pole of knowledge creation. This type of organisation could manage as social property the intangible capital resulting from public research in certain fields, creating a portfolio of projects whose returns would feed a fund intended both for reinvestment in that same research and for social programmes to promote equality of access to new knowledge. Before entering this discussion, it is useful to briefly mention the concepts of "knowledge commons" and "collective intelligence". The former refers to arrangements by communities or users to collectively own and manage data.[14] A well-known example is Wikipedia. Open science can be framed in this conceptual tradition. Collective intelligence goes a step further, as it assumes that sharing of information may lead to consensus decision-making.[15] While these concepts are widely explored in the perspective of sociology, computer science, and other literature, the concept of a knowledge-based public enterprise may be a possible way to structure in precise economic terms some of the mechanisms of research infrastructures presented in the previous chapter.

Rethinking public enterprise

Public enterprises (or state-owned enterprises, public corporations, state-invested companies, etc.) in energy, telecommunications, and transport – to mention essential services – arose from strategic considerations, under-investment by private capital, and oligopolistic tendencies arising from the economy of scale of the networks. Historically, public enterprises have been fundamental instruments for breaking the private oligopoly. At times, they were also supported by economists and politicians of liberal persuasion, including Keynes. For more than three decades, however, the subject almost disappeared from academic research and the industrial policy debate. The focus was on privatisation and market liberalisation. For some years now, particularly since the start of the Great Recession in 2008, it has been back on the agenda. In reality, public enterprises, understood as organisations owned or controlled ultimately by the state, have never disappeared in most developed economies, from France to Germany, the Scandinavian countries, and the post-Soviet economies. China's large state-owned enterprises, although suspected of receiving state aid and violating the good rules of international competition, have often proved successful.

The share among the world's top 500 companies of companies with significant state control or ownership has doubled in recent years and is around 20%. The main sectors covered by this type of company are energy, telecommunications, defence, transport, and public utilities, but also social services (although the legal form of hospitals, universities, and others remains mostly that of a public body in Europe).

In briefly reviewing the history of these organisations and their importance in the economy of the 21st century, it is noted that the portfolio of state holdings in enterprises has varied over time, responding to different strategic problems, including military ones. I therefore present the conceptual model of a new type of economic entity that combines some traits of research infrastructures and public enterprises. A number of issues related to the proposal of these new entities are outlined: relevance in contemporary economies, internalisation of public missions, ownership, governance, financing, the relationship between scientific research and technological development objectives and innovative public service objectives.

In the last century (with significant precursors in the 19th century and even before), public enterprise emerged as an instrument of government intervention to respond to various problems, some of which were concomitant, which I will briefly mention here, referring you to the vast literature on the subject.[16]

By public enterprise I mean here, beyond the legal form, an organisation that combines capital, labour and technological knowledge, produces goods or renders services that in principle could also be provided by private organisations, but which has a mission assigned by a government (or a coalition of governments), enjoys wide managerial autonomy, has its own budget, is under the proprietary control of public bodies, not necessarily with a total or majority share of the capital. I will quickly justify this definition from the bottom up.

Legislative, judicial, and governmental activities in the true sense cannot be privatised, so they cannot give rise to organisations with public enterprise characteristics. Railways, telecommunications, electricity, hospitals, universities, credit, and many other services, on the other hand, can be provided by both the public and private sectors. The production of all these services always requires tangible and intangible assets, labour, often highly skilled, and technological knowledge: the ingredients must be coordinated by a management that is in a position to exercise a certain degree of discretion, given the changing circumstances. The reasons why, in some sectors, states have created economic organisations in the form of enterprises under public sector control, instead of relying on the private sector, can be summed up as follows.

Firstly, as the economic historian Robert Millward (2013) points out in particular, the strategic-military reasons cannot be underestimated. Millward mentions the French and German railway networks (which depended directly on the Ministry of War), but also the arsenals of Her Majesty's British fleet. I would like to add the important antecedent of the arsenal of Venice, a complex organisation capable of producing up to three ships a day in the 16th century to maintain control of the maritime power of the Serenissima. The relationship between science, technology, and military–industrial complexes has already been discussed. Here it is sufficient to mention that some of the companies still under state control are among the most advanced in terms of R&D in various fields (from electronics to materials science).

Secondly, states decided to create this type of organisation when in some industries, critically based on high long-term investment in fixed capital, the private sector tended towards a natural monopoly[17] and consequently to market, to monopoly, or to an (often collusive) oligopoly. Excessively high prices, inadequate production and investment, and financial instability were typical of old private oligopolies. Especially in Europe, these problems have led to the creation of public enterprises in sectors such as railways, energy, and telecommunications.

Thirdly, relying exclusively on private provision has been considered by many national and local governments as unsatisfactory in the field of social services such as health and education, essentially because of the pricing policy and the heterogeneity of the supply in terms of quantity and quality by private organisations. This is where the growing view of the welfare state as a cohesive social mechanism to counteract the inequalities inherent in capitalist development comes into play.

Finally, governments have intervened in the credit market and monetary policy with their own instruments, such as central banks, development banks, and publicly owned commercial banks, in order to overcome endemic problems of instability in a sector that periodically gives rise to serious economic crises. Policy choices, such as the direct control of natural resources (subsoil, water, forests, and others) and territorial and social rebalancing, have been added to all these motivations, partly through the locating of public enterprises in lagging behind areas.

Despite the fact that governments have privatised a substantial proportion of public enterprises in various sectors over the last three decades, these types of corporations have shown surprising resilience, often returning to the fore in the form of mixed capital or state-invested enterprises, with renewed organisations, as opposed to the sometimes entrenched ones of the previous phase in which they operated under conditions of legal monopoly.

In general, the quality of governments, for example, in terms of transparency and honesty of politicians, and the quality of the management of public enterprises, for example, in terms of selection of managers and their autonomy, are related. This has implications for efficiency.

In the electricity distribution sector, Borghi et al. (2016) observed that in 16 European countries the total factor productivity of public enterprises is higher than that of private enterprises, but only in countries with high indicators of government quality, otherwise the opposite is true. The same is found in the telecommunications sector,[18] where with a few exceptions (such as Italy, Spain, and the UK) governments have retained state ownership stakes in firms, for example, in Scandinavian countries, Germany, France, and elsewhere.

In terms of R&D investments and patents, state-owned companies often outperform their private counterparts, a fact that can be explained by an attitude that is less bound to the need to show short-term returns to shareholders and financial markets.[19] The correlation between R&D investment and a "patient investor" attitude, with a long-term view, is well known and – although some private organisations may also play this role – public enterprises are good candidates in technology-intensive sectors, if their mission is well defined in this direction.

This last point is the decisive one for the proposals I will make in the next three chapters. Indeed, many economists underestimate incentive mechanisms other than profit maximisation. They are wrong. As Herbert Simon has written[20] the market paradigm is much overrated compared to the paradigm of the organisation as a lens through which to view our societies. Fortunately, in many organisations, it is not contracts with economic objectives that govern the relationships between people. Research infrastructures are a good example of how people can be stimulated to do frontier work in terms of mental and even physical commitment (long shifts in laboratories) without monetary incentives. No large hospital could function, as we have seen in the tragic circumstances of the Covid-19 pandemic, if the relationships between managers, medical, nursing, and technical service staff, including cleaners, functioned solely on the basis of contracts and monetary incentives.

And, this not only concerns emergencies, but the daily life of organisations, even large and complex ones, in which intrinsic motivations to work and collaborate for common objectives prevail, whether they be scientific, health, educational, or in a broader sense shared by a community.

Internalisation of missions

One of the problems that in the last century, and to some extent still today, has weakened the potential role of public enterprises in some fields is an inadequate designation of missions by governments to boards of directors or bodies with analogous management functions (to which I will return later). This is an important point for the proposals I will make and in general for mission-driven innovation policies, as Mariana Mazzucato, in particular, has defined them in a report to the European Commission[21] and in related publications.[22] According to Mazzucato, innovation is not only characterised by its growth rate but also by the direction it takes. In the 21st century, major social, environmental, and economic challenges include climate change, health, demography, and inclusive and sustainable growth. In this perspective, we need mission-oriented, systemic policies that draw on frontier knowledge to achieve defined goals: "big science to meet big problems".

In the context of Mazzucato's discussion of policies, there are five necessary conditions: missions must be bold, and broadly relevant to society; they must set time-bound and measurable goals; research and innovation must be ambitious but realistic; actions must be interdisciplinary, cross-sectoral, and involve various actors; multiple and bottom-up solutions must be sought.

While I agree with this way of framing mission-oriented policies, I tend to think that something is missing. I suggest that the creation of a coalition carrying a public mission requires that there is a key actor in the field who takes on that mission and has the resources to change the game: a game changer rather than a game player. It cannot be the state as such, because it usually does not have the structure and competences to design and execute missions operationally.

From this perspective, the historical experience of public enterprises is relevant from two points of view. Firstly, because their experience shows that they work well when the management of the enterprise receives clear indications from the public body to which it refers as to what is expected (this applies to a federal government as well as to a municipality): to continuously provide drinking water of guaranteed quality to households, to bring electricity to all users with a minimum of interruptions, to bring digital broadband connections even to rural areas, to guarantee reliable emergency medical services in a quantity appropriate to the needs, and so on. However, when the mandate becomes vague or contradictory (protecting health, protecting the environment, securing jobs, and a dividend for the public purse), even well-intentioned management does not know what the priorities should be. It may choose its agenda according to criteria of its own, which may not be meritorious.

However, this is still not enough, the organisation needs to have the right incentives to take the public mission seriously. There are several ways in which this can happen, not necessarily alternatives. Firstly, the organisation's legal statute can be sufficiently clear about this and outline the mission, so that trustees and staff, including researchers, receive a sufficiently informative message about what is expected in terms of the public mission. Consider, for example, Art. II of the Convention for the Establishment of a European Space Agency (ESA), signed in Paris on 30 May 1975[23]:

> The purpose of the Agency shall be to provide for and to promote, for exclusively peaceful purposes, cooperation among European States in space research and technology and their space applications, with a view to their being used for scientific purposes and for operational space applications systems:
>
> a by elaborating and implementing a long-term European space policy, by recommending space objectives to the member states, and by concerting the policies of the member states with respect to other national and international organisations and institutions;
> b by elaborating and implementing activities and programmes in the space field;
> c by coordinating the European space programme and national programmes, and by integrating the latter progressively and as completely as possible into the European space programme, in particular as regards the development of applications satellites;
> d by elaborating and implementing the industrial policy appropriate to its programme and by recommending a coherent industrial policy to the member states.[24]

A significant aspect of this example is, on the one hand, the exclusion of military applications, and on the other hand, the link between European-wide and national policies of the member states, as well as the indication that ESA is the implementer of an industrial policy, with a focus on satellite development.

A second formal mechanism is the instrument, developed mainly in France, of programme contracts or similar agreements between the state and public enterprises or agencies. In this case, the mission is broken down into general and specific objectives, often with the definition of indicators and implementation times.[25]

A third mechanism is the involvement of countries or members of an organisation in its governing or monitoring bodies, so as to ensure in practice the link between policies and the implementing body, although here, as we shall see later, delicate problems of balance arise in terms of managerial autonomy.

Ownership and legal form

There is a wealth of international experience in the attribution of property rights to subjects such as public enterprises, public research infrastructures, agencies, and other subjects that are formally autonomous from the state but have a public mission. At one end of the spectrum, there are public companies listed on the stock exchange, in which the state simply participates as a shareholder, sometimes as a minority shareholder, without actually exercising special rights in terms of control or due to special rules. At the other extreme, there are public bodies whose assets are fully part of the state's assets, and therefore subject to all the control mechanisms established by law for public administration, but separated from it by the attribution of a legal entity in its own right.

As regards research infrastructures, which typically derive from agreements between several states, the typical form is that of public entities that are not subject to administrative control by the individual states. Ownership is, therefore, not split up as in the case of joint-stock companies or other types of essentially private legal entities. However, ad hoc legal forms have been devised and tested in order to find solutions to the problems that arise when a supranational organisation not only has political functions in a broad sense but also activities that can be defined as public services, such as the production of knowledge as a public good. For example, for research infrastructures, the formula of the European Research Infrastructure Consortium (ERIC)[26] is increasingly used in Europe.

It is defined as a legal form aimed at facilitating the establishment and operation of research infrastructures with a European interest, without any prevailing economic purpose, whether ex novo or as a coordination mechanism of already existing entities. An ERIC has legal status recognised in the member states of the European Union, operational and organisational flexibility, a faster set-up process compared to the creation of an international body, is exempt from VAT and excise duties, and can adopt its own procurement procedures independently from those of the state in which it is established or of its individual members. It can also provide for the participation of non-EU countries, ensuring access to research results and generally contributing to the objectives of the Union.

The panorama of possibilities is actually even wider if one considers that, in principle, a public agency or a research infrastructure, having its own legal status, can in turn participate in the ownership of a company under established law. For example, the Italian Space Agency is a 20% owner of e-GEOS S.p.A.,[27] which develops, produces, and markets products, services, and applications for terrestrial observation through satellites, having selected the private partner Telespazio S.p.A. through a competitive bidding process. Telespazio S.p.A., is in turn two-thirds owned by Leonardo S.p.A.,[28] one of the main global players in the defence and aerospace sector, which is in fact controlled by the Ministry of Economy and Finance with a 30.2% share.

A very interesting example of a public entity for promoting innovation is Fraunhofer in Germany, one of the large scientific and technological associations, similar to its sister companies Max Planck, Helmholtz, and Leibniz. Fraunhofer is one of the main producers of innovations in Germany, as witnessed by the high number of patents filed annually, comparable to that of large private technology companies. An essential element of that model is the relationship between a public body and private companies in the development of applied research projects, with specific contractual solutions to the issue of intellectual property. I discuss this in more detail in Chapter 5.

The legal solution to the issue of the ownership of knowledge-intensive organisations can therefore draw on a wide range of instruments and experiences and cannot be posited abstractly. I will come back to this issue in the proposals I outline in the following chapters.

Governance

A central theme of the campaign that has been waged in past decades against state-owned enterprises, and that has underpinned often misguided privatisation policies, has been the interference of politicians in their management. In proposing, as I do here, a new generation of public intervention instruments in the form of organisations with budgetary and managerial autonomy, it is necessary to clear the field of stratification of sometimes well-founded, but often specious arguments.

For the moment, let us leave aside the historical experience of the Soviet Union and the countries that were, willingly or unwillingly, influenced by that model. In those countries, the very concept of a company with its own legal status, its own balance sheet, and a sufficiently independent management, for the most part, did not exist except in limited and particular forms. It is to the detriment of some of the literature on privatisation, especially in the United States, that its arguments have mixed criticism of the management of public enterprises in "mixed" market economies, such as those in Western Europe after the Second World War, with criticism of Soviet-type "enterprises", which were in fact units of production in the framework of crude economic planning in historical circumstances which were often marked by military priorities.

If one focuses instead on the specific issue of the governance of public enterprises in market economies, the question of information asymmetry and incomplete contracts between government and public enterprises (or even regulated private companies) has attracted much attention, especially from academic economists, but perhaps this is not the main problem.

It goes without saying that any passive shareholder, particularly one with a small share of capital, would find it prohibitively expensive to obtain the same information on the company's situation (technological, commercial, financial, organisational, regulatory, etc.) as is available to managers and directors. They live in the company's environment on a daily basis and have not only privileged access to documents but also to the mass of uncoded information that is the lifeblood of any organisation. The officer of a pension fund, an asset management company, or a financial investor will not, normally, be aware of everything that goes on in a company in whose capital his/her organisation participates, and this is broadly true of "private" companies. Since the 1930s, there has been extensive literature on the governance problems of large private companies, as well as reports of the occasional scandal showing the effects of the information asymmetry between the formal owner and the real owner.

What, then, is different about public enterprises that could justify the suspicion that governance may be worse than that of private companies in terms of efficiency and transparency? Here the argument is often expressed in two forms: even though corruption and inefficiency may exist in large private companies (in small ones everything is more under control due to the coincidence of ownership and management), there are mechanisms of "external" discipline: management that is inefficient (or worse) will sooner or later come up against the reality of the market, will present loss-making or unsatisfactory balance sheets and will be replaced by investors who ultimately expect adequate profits and nothing else. On the other hand, the institutional control provided by laws and courts will be weakened in the case of public enterprises because managers, financial police, regulators, and judges are all state employees and will tend to collude with each other and with politicians.

The first argument is certainly valid, but only if the public enterprise does not have stringent budgetary constraints. This is the concept of the soft budget constraint advanced many years ago by the Hungarian economist Janos Kornai (1992).

The argument is no longer valid if public enterprises have a sufficiently strict budgetary constraint, for example, if in the presence of losses the mechanism for covering them is not that of an automatic transfer from the state budget (or from the municipality or the owning public body). This suggests that if public enterprises (like regulated private ones) have to carry out – as part of their mission (statutory or otherwise) – activities that are occasionally or structurally in deficit, this should be provided for by instruments such as the programme contract or similar instruments referred to above. Thus, the public owner does not make ex-post reimbursements of its budgetary needs but instead plans ex-ante the financial needs arising from the performance of public service activities, such as activities performed without price compensation or with prices decided outside the market as a result of economic policy decisions overriding the economic policy undertaking. It is important to note that this control mechanism applies in a similar way to a public enterprise and to a formally private company that has a contract with the state, such as a public service concession. When this is the case, the evidence that the public enterprise is less efficient and accountable than its private counterpart is weak or non-existent.

This point is very important from the perspective of the proposals that follow, because one might think that a European public health agency could enter into a programme contract on the research and development of drugs (such as strategic drugs and those for "orphan" diseases) with private companies, reimbursing costs not covered by market revenues, but at that point, it could also alternatively consider the convenience of having its own infrastructure if the conditions were better for the taxpayer. I discuss this in the next chapter.

The second objection to public enterprise, that of collusion between the powers of the state, has often been put forward by economists in the USA or by those educated there.[29]

As is well known, in Italy and elsewhere in Europe, in our political and administrative systems we suffer, if anything, from an excess of autonomy and autarky, so that administrative, civil and criminal courts, national ministries, regions, mayors, and legislators pull in different directions, often contradicting each other. The problem of public management in Europe is not at all that regulators, judges, and politicians all collude with each other, but rather that the objectives and methods of the various components of public power tend to diverge more often than to converge, and this poses a number of problems for the administrators of public (and private) enterprises precisely because there are multiple principals. But these problems, which are typical of mature democratic systems, have nothing to do with the predominance of corruption and "political mafia", unless, on the other hand, public institutions are actually captured by various factions that corrupt their functioning. In that case, the problem is not only that of the inefficiency of public enterprise but of democracy itself: parliament, the judiciary, market regulators and "private" enterprise itself, are actually part of an autocratic state or of a pathological kleptocracy.

On the other hand, there is much to be learnt from the governance of large public research infrastructures, which – as the expression of an encounter between international scientific communities and the governments or institutions that set them up and fund them – express sophisticated models for balancing the powers of funding bodies and management.

As *The Economist* has also written, business schools should study how the management of large scientific research centres manages to be so efficient, pushing the organisation to the technological frontier, usually respecting budgetary constraints, while maintaining its strategic mission, and without the incentives of multi-million dollar salaries and stock options that are considered indispensable for managers in private companies.

But if we think about it, the secret of the governance of a public hospital, a university, or a public enterprise in general, lies in the internalisation of the mission by a professional community with which the management identifies. In all these cases, it is neither market mechanisms nor the formal separation of powers (although essential) that determine the success of the organisation, but the prevalence of intrinsic motivations: doing science, saving lives, and educating minds. It happens every day in plain sight, but perhaps we do not understand why, and how much our societies, when they are healthy, depend on these motivations, and when they are unhealthy, how much they have destroyed these motivations in communities.

Funding

The proposals I will formulate in the following chapters are ambitious and require sizeable funding in order to achieve critical mass and significant impact. Although each of the proposals may have different mechanisms, here I briefly outline some possible channels for financing knowledge-intensive European public enterprises.

Assuming – to set the record straight – that the legal form is that of a supranational public body on the model of the European Space Agency, the main channel should be that of the contribution of the member states, in the form of a transfer from the national budget to the budget of the new body. In order to ensure the soundness of the project, commitments should be of a multi-year nature, and as such entered into the budget of the member states and formalised with appropriate legal instruments between the funder and the recipient body. The ordinary contribution should not be linked to individual research or service programmes, but to the institutional activity as a whole. The governance should include mechanisms that allow representatives of member states to intervene in the strategic process that determines priorities (such a "council" exists at CERN with certain powers).

Secondly, the European Union could become one of the donors, contributing from its own budget. This scheme in which the Union, represented by the Commission, participates in major international projects together with member and non-member states is seen, for example, in the governance of ITER, the major international project to study nuclear fusion (with the participation of China, the EU – via Euratom, India, Japan, Korea, Russia, the USA, and now the UK). The funding of ESA is given by 22 member states plus, on the EU side, a framework agreement between ESA and the European Commission.

Thirdly, an indirect form of support might be the Europeanisation of dispersed national programmes, saving resources that are inadequate to achieve critical mass (e.g., the Italian Space Agency "hands over" to ESA a large proportion of the funds it gets from the state).

Fourthly, the new organisation should be able to contribute to the raising of funds for specific projects, in addition to those of general operation, partly by participating in international competitions, by attracting funds from philanthropy and private companies which, for various reasons, might wish to contribute non-reimbursable sums to the realisation of the mission.

It would then be necessary to envisage channels of recourse to the financial market, for example, through loans from the European Investment Bank (EIB) or – if it made financial sense – the issue of Eurobonds for these major projects.

Finally, as will be seen in the three examples I am going to propose in the following chapters, market revenues can be predicted on the basis of procurement contracts, such as those for national health services and public administrations, including local ones. We can also imagine some revenue coming from the licensing of patents, albeit on terms that favour maximum access.

This set of instruments would have to be studied on a case-by-case basis, but there seems to be no shortage of resources in the current conditions of the financial markets, with the extraordinary increase in the Commission's budget (Next Generation EU), with states abandoning the masochistic austerity policies that followed the 2008 recession, and with the scarcity of credible traditional financial investments for investors.

Therefore, it is an exceptionally favourable time from a financial point of view for new types of public investment, backed by an international coalition to ensure credibility.

The European Commission defines research infrastructures as follows:

> Research Infrastructures are facilities that provide resources and services for research communities to conduct research and foster innovation. They can be used beyond research e.g. for education or public services and they may be single-sited, distributed, or virtual.[30]

This definition suggests that it is possible to combine research and public service provision, a key aspect of the proposals that follow.

An example may clarify how this combination can be realised in the field of medical research. The CNAO in Pavia is a synchrotron for hadrontherapy, that is, the treatment of radio-resistant solid tumours with high-energy particle beams such as protons or carbon ions. The technology derives directly from experiments carried out at CERN (one of the founders was the well-known physicist Ugo Amaldi, who worked in the Geneva laboratory for many years). The understanding of the therapeutic effects of innovative hadrontherapy, especially the form based on carbon ions, cannot be separated from human experimentation, which is carried out at CNAO for certain types of cancer in patients who cannot be treated in any other way.

The resulting knowledge may in time lead to the approval by the health authorities of new protocols that can be delivered in the public service. Indeed, the CNAO is both a centre for scientific research and a place of treatment, thus demonstrating the possibility of merging the two roles in a single infrastructure.

I have already mentioned how other types of particle accelerators, such as synchrotron light sources, can play a role in supporting university research by the various groups working there in the study of samples of matter with very high-energy X-rays, as well as supporting companies in the analysis of applications of interest to them.

In addition to individual centres, networks have been proposed that aim to bring together large research infrastructures and companies. For example,

ATTRACT aims to "create an ecosystem of co-innovation between the basic research and industrial communities to develop cutting-edge technologies in the field of detection and imaging for both scientific and commercial uses". The fields in which these technologies are used include, to name but a few, laser technologies for manufacturing, robotics, genomics, smart power grids, wireless sensors, advanced filtration, oil recovery, cloud computing, and microelectronics. Participants include CERN, EMBL, European Southern Observatory, European X-FEL, ESRF (European Synchrotron Radiation Facility), a group of 90 companies belonging to the European Industrial Research Management Association (EIRMA), and two universities (Aalto, Helsinki, and Esade Business School, Barcelona).[31] The idea, therefore, is to act as a collective laboratory for technology-intensive companies.

A note of caution is in order. It must be acknowledged that these consortia between a number of stakeholders with different objectives and of a varied nature often have an overly complex architecture and limited resources compared to the ambitious objectives they aim to pursue.

This is a frequently observed limitation, even in some of the clusters in the form of ERICs or the likes. Although the plurality of participants may be an advantage, for example in terms of multidisciplinary research, it may not be very effective from the point of view of downstream services, since each participant plays only a limited or marginal role in the project. The following proposals, therefore, aim to propose unitary, possibly multi-centre, hubs, focusing on large-scale projects integrating research and public service, around which a constellation of other public or private entities can be brought together.

Notes

1 Meaning a good for which there is no rivalry in consumption among users, and for which exclusion of anybody is impossible or too costly. Textbook examples are national defence and lighthouses.
2 https://www.wipo.int/pressroom/en/articles/2018/article_0012.html
3 What the European Open Science Cloud is: https://research-and-innovation.ec.europa.eu/strategy/strategy-2020-2024/our-digital-future/open-science/european-open-science-cloud-eosc_en
4 The study was recently updated: Beagrie, 2021.
5 Global Wealth Report, 2021, and previous years.
6 https://www.oxfam.org/en/5-shocking-facts-about-extreme-global-inequality-and-how-even-it
7 https://www.forbes.com/billionaires/
8 https://www.forbes.com/sites/willyakowicz/2020/04/07/these-are-the-20-richest-billionaires-in-technology-in-2020/?sh=930fa9a453d0
9 Florio and Giffoni, 2019.
10 See Pagano (2014) for an excellent discussion on intellectual monopoly capitalism.
11 I will not go into the theoretical arguments that have been put forward to argue that the optimal rate of taxation of capital income is zero and that taxation of monopoly profits is inefficient as well as ineffective. These arguments are based on unrealistic assumptions.

12 Florio, 2004, 2013.
13 Gheorghiou et al., 2017.
14 See Hess and Ostrom, 2007.
15 See Malone and Bernstein, 2022.
16 For recent contributions, see *The Routledge Handbook of State-Owned Enterprise* by Bernier et al., 2020, with 57 authors from 20 countries, and, in particular, the chapter by Giuseppe Bognetti.
17 Characterised by ever decreasing costs as the quantity of product expanded.
18 Castelnovo et al., 2018.
19 Lazzarini et al., 2021, p. 562.
20 Simon, 1991. I am indebted to Giuseppe Bognetti for attracting my attention to it.
21 Mazzucato, 2018b.
22 Mazzucato, 2018c.
23 https://www.esa.int/About_Us/Law_at_ESA/ESA_Convention
24 https://www.esa.int/About_Us/Corporate_news/Articles#Art1.2
25 Thus, for example, the "Business contract 2018–2022 between the State and La Poste on the public service objectives entrusted" is a detailed 35-page document that defines for each product and service what is expected in terms of service during the contract period. http://www.collectifposte.org/wp-content/uploads/2018/01/Contrat_entreprise_Etat_LaPoste_2018_2022.pdf
26 What is ERIC?: https://research-and-innovation.ec.europa.eu/strategy/strategy-2020-2024/our-digital-future/european-research-infrastructures/eric_en
27 https://www.asi.it/en/the-agency/holdings/affiliated-companies/e-geos-s-p-a/
28 https://www.leonardo.com/en/about/profile
29 The idea that the management of public enterprises will inevitably collude with other public officials probably stems from certain features of the way the state was formed in the USA in the 18th century. For example, in the USA, federal judges, including all those on the federal Supreme Court, are appointed directly by the President and the Congress. This is not the norm in most European countries, where the separation of the judiciary from the executive, and as far as possible also from the legislature, is part of the constitution and is enshrined in law. Secondly, appointments to key positions in the police are also the responsibility of politicians in the USA. Again, things are quite different in Europe. In the United States, appointments to the heads of the main federal regulatory agencies are the expression of the incumbent President and often highly politicised. The spoil system is prevalent at all levels of government, not only at the federal level, where it affects several thousand top positions, but also at the level of the individual states of the Union. Local police corruption in the US is legendary. The judicial system is far from exemplary, and – as seen in the 2020 presidential elections – the constitutional system surprisingly convoluted.
30 https://ec.europa.eu/info/research-and-innovation/strategy/strategy-2020-2024/our-digital-future/european-research-infrastructures_en
31 https://phase1.attract-eu.com/the-project/

3 Biomed Europa

Medicines that no one else will give us

In February 2018, a committee of experts invited to Geneva by the World Health Organization identified a list of diseases at high risk to human health for which treatments are unknown or ineffective: Ebola, Zika, and SARS-CoV among them, but also a possible "pandemic X". Exactly two years later, we became acquainted with the SARS-CoV-2 virus, a close relative of the one that appeared in 2002. There are around 1400 known pathogens that can infect us. Of these only a fifth are viruses, but two-thirds of the "bad news" that has greeted the human species since 1940 has been about viruses (DNA or RNA, with a variety of replication and infection mechanisms). Several thousand are known in detail, but it is estimated that there are hundreds of thousands, perhaps millions, of viruses in nature that have the potential to set a zoonosis in motion and infect us.

The warnings of scientists have been largely ignored. Governments have totally delegated the development of vaccines, drugs, and other biomedical innovations to industry, but industry has different priorities from the public policy agenda for health. This should not come as a surprise to anyone: companies do their job of generating "value" for investors in the sense of value on the stock market.[1] It is not important to ascertain the motivations of individual board members, managers or researchers. Many of them may be convinced that they are doing their best for humankind. But if the financial returns of investing in the treatment of certain diseases are smaller and more uncertain than in other fields, those investments will not be approved by a company board, unless they are generously covered by public subsidies.

An oligopoly has been created over recent decades that protects financial investors, serial packagers" of bets around research, patents, and marketing authorisations. Governments, in turn, seem to assume that market regulation through a combination of research subsidies, intellectual property protection, and drug authorisations is more or less all that is needed to automatically align the goals of companies and health authorities. This is not the case, and so governments actually adopt the wrong policies.

The old, relentlessly repeated idea that the protection of the legal monopoly on knowledge is the only way to promote innovation in the sector has no convincing empirical basis. Historically, an important part of research in the

DOI: 10.4324/9781003381532-4

biomedical sciences, both basic and preclinical, but also clinical, has been carried out by researchers in universities, hospitals, bodies dependent on ministries of health, laboratories dealing with specific diseases and orphan drugs, and even institutes linked to the military complex. A significant example is the role of the Department of Energy in the USA, the primary funder in the 1980s, together with the National Institutes of Health, in the sequencing of the entire human genome (Science, 2001). Rea et al. (2018), in a fine book of case studies on the discovery of drugs and medical devices (from cholesterol statins to angioplasty, from hepatitis C drugs to precision medicine) conclude that innovations emerge in patterns and dynamics that vary across countries and over time, in a complex ecosystem comprising individuals, research groups, host organisations and their management, academia, and public institutions.

Hence, large companies in the sector do less and less in-house research to discover new molecules and develop new drugs, preferring to shop around for innovative projects, expenditures which are accounted for in their balance sheets as intangible assets and therefore presented as R&D. Larger companies increasingly prefer to leverage their relationships with small and medium-sized biotechnology companies and universities in order to use their innovative capabilities for the development of new drugs. The extraction can occur in various ways: through licensing agreements that hand over molecules or drugs developed by biotech companies to large companies; through the acquisition of promising start-ups or biotech companies with patent portfolios in specialised fields; or simply by large companies hiring inventors and their teams. Often large companies do not even do the initial idea selection work themselves, leaving it to venture capitalists or other specialists to hunt for companies to acquire. Once the target has been identified, the acquisition machine is set in motion, combining legal aspects, market assessments, cost forecasts, and ultimately a decision based on the business case.

For clinical trials, however, large companies often rely on intermediaries in a parallel market dominated by multinational companies, Contract Research Organisations (CROs), which deal with the recruitment of patients in healthcare facilities and other related activities. The presentation of trial results and relations with public authorities, in particular, drug agencies, is also often entrusted to specialists in various countries. Manufacturing, packaging, and even the preparation of pharmaceutical leaflets and distribution are also contracted out to service providers, including Contract Development and Manufacturing Organisations (CDMOs).

The system has produced extraordinary results in the past, but for some time now it seems to be losing steam. It has managed to devise and test vaccines for the SARS-CoV-2 virus in record time, a scientific miracle, but one that is not due to business alone. Governments poured billions of euros in public funds into the industry in 2020, both for research and for the advanced purchase agreements of billions of doses, shifting most of the risk to taxpayers. Marketing authorisations from the drug agencies came very quickly, with information that would not normally be considered sufficient. The total budget of the US government's Operation Warp Speed was 18 billion (to October 2020). The European Commission and the governments of dozens of other countries have paid out billions more Florio et al. (2023). In practice, the risk (including adverse side effects) has largely been taken on by the states, which until now have been dependent for production and wholesale distribution mostly on the few first-mover companies. They decide exclusively how much and where to produce, despite the fact that there is a whole planet to be vaccinated as quickly as possible. To do this, we need an integrated production and distribution system on a global scale for a few vaccines, not dozens of vaccines managed by fragmented processes, with major inequalities in access to them, with major inequalities of access between rich countries and others.

Little seems to have been understood by most governments about the social aspects of many diseases, including the current pandemic, an issue outside the industry's strategic horizon. Recent data from the UK Office of National Statistics show that the probability of death from Covid-19 in that country is almost four times higher for a black African adult than for a white one, three and a half times for an immigrant from Bangladesh, just under three times for an immigrant from the Caribbean. In the US, black women have the same incidence of breast cancer but a much higher probability of dying from it. There are many other examples of how little we know about the correlation between disease, economic status, ethnicity, occupation, environment, and other variables that often fail to influence the way in which samples of patients and control groups entering clinical trials are defined. There is, therefore, an important and little-explored relationship between disease, treatment, and social conditions, but the pandemic has put many of these issues on the table.

Priorities

In the midst of a largely predicted but not prevented pandemic, it is a good time to ask ourselves what our biomedical research priorities are for the next 30 years, which represent the planet's next generation.

Let us start by recalling something obvious. Human health could be much better with policies and social behaviours that do not require new discoveries so much as simple preventative and health education measures. According to WHO, of the 56.9 million deaths worldwide in 2016, more than half (54%) were caused by ten causes in all[2]: ischaemic heart disease and stroke (together causing 15 million deaths), chronic obstructive pulmonary disease (3 million), lower respiratory tract infections (3 million), Alzheimer's and other forms of dementia (2 million), lung, trachea and larynx cancer (1.8 million), diabetes (1.6 million), road accidents (1.4 million), diarrhoea (1.4 million, despite significant progress in recent years), and tuberculosis (1.3 million).

Despite advances in treatment, AIDS remains one of the most dreaded infectious diseases: an average of almost 1 million deaths every year in recent years, enough to remind us that a virus that jumps species like HIV has managed to kill 32.7 million people between 1981 and 2019. It is also a reminder of how crucial socio-economic inequality in access to treatment is: in 1996, at the height of the HIV pandemic, treatment with antiretrovirals cost 10,000 USD a year per patient, and at this price, only the very richest elite in Africa and other affected regions could get treatment. The result was a dramatic drop in life expectancy, by as much as ten years, for entire countries.

Many deaths could be prevented by improving access to safe drinking water, changing diet, reducing consumption of sugar-sweetened drinks and alcohol, and giving up smoking and unprotected sex. In Africa, 56% of deaths result from contagious diseases, nutritional problems, birth-related conditions and neonatal diseases, which can be addressed with what we already know, but with policies that are not being implemented.

In many other cases, this is not enough to save or improve the quality of life. Therapeutic innovations are needed: new antibiotics against resistant bacteria, antivirals and new vaccines for as-yet-unknown viruses, remedies for neurodegenerative diseases, robotic surgery, the use of alternative radiation to traditional radiotherapy, sophisticated imaging, molecular genomics techniques for personalised medicine, and much more. Further progress will be needed in so many areas in the face of a global trend towards an ageing population that exacerbates the spread and intensity of diseases and their causal and prognostic relationship with social inequalities.

There are also the seemingly paradoxical effects of the spectacular fall in the cost of gene sequencing following the success of the Human Genome Project (and in fields such as proteomics and other strands of molecular biology). By around 2025, it is expected that it will be possible to sequence 130 million human genomes at a unit cost of perhaps under 100 euros. Over the last 20 years, there has been a decrease in the cost of sequencing per genome of six orders of magnitude, greater than cost reductions in semiconductors for computers. It will be increasingly possible to cross-reference this data with individual information about each patient's medical history, education, occupation, and more. The increased knowledge we now have of "errors" in the coding of information that regulates or co-determines our health has led to the identification of a large number of rare diseases. In the USA alone, many diseases have been recognised with fewer (in some cases much fewer) than 200,000 patients for which the market is usually not considered profitable by companies (unless they are subsidised). For 90% of these diseases, there is no Food and Drug Administration (FDA) approved cure. According to some studies, R&D efforts are growing in the area of orphan drugs and the share that was only 6% in 2000 could reach 21% in 2022.[3] However, this increase in the share has to be seen against the background of lower overall research productivity.

It is expected that the more we know about our data, and therefore the more we move towards precision medicine, the smaller the market opportunities will be due to the decreasing number of patients for each identified disease. This is the paradox: more knowledge about ourselves, more fragmentation of markets, less expected profits, less incentive for research? The prevailing model in industry ideally needs large, stable markets with high profit margins in order to function. It may be that a traditional business model is becoming obsolete and inefficient. Let us see why.

Before Covid-19, the pharmaceutical industry's R&D expenditure was estimated at over 180 billion USD in 2019[4] against revenues of 1250 billion,[5] including both traditional and biotechnology drugs.[6] In addition, revenues in the biomedical technology sector are estimated to be around 460 billion USD in 2019.[7] These technologies encompass various segments, from in-vitro diagnostics to cardiology, imaging, orthopaedics, and ophthalmology, with an R&D expenditure of 31 billion USD. One example, among many, in the field of cardiology is the development of complete digital models of the patient's heart, which, connected with mini-sensors, would allow monitoring under any condition. An Apple Watch already allows the patient to perform and share an electrocardiogram at any time. I cite this example to show the relationship between medicine and personal digital data.

In the face of this colossal expenditure, which places the pharmaceutical and biomedical sector in general among the most knowledge and technology-intensive industries in the contemporary economy (together with aerospace, computers, electronics, software, and IT), an obvious, but sometimes curiously underestimated, aspect must be stressed. Who pays for this expensive research? Since the pharma sector is essentially made up of companies controlled by private investors, operating with profit objectives, the ultimate financiers of this enormous knowledge production effort are patients and taxpayers. We all pay, directly or indirectly, for the costs of R&D, as well as production and distribution, through the price of medicines and other products and services, or through premiums associated with health insurance contracts or other cost-sharing arrangements. Retail spending on medicines averages 2% of the GDP in the US, among the highest in the world, and is still 1.5% of the GDP in France and even higher in Germany (OECD, 2018).[8]

We also pay back to companies their gargantuan marketing expenditures. According to Gagnon and Lexchin (2008) and Lexchin (2018) the expenditures for promotion, such as advertising, organisation of conferences and costly face-to-face detailing physicians, is greater than corporate R&D spending. While the ratio between the two categories of spending is uncertain because of different definitions and data sources, there is scarce doubt that overall the industry is a big spender in marketing and specifically in promotion activities. The combined expenditure on "marketing and administration" as reported in several company patents is around 30% of revenues.

What we pay as patients must then be added to what we pay as taxpayers through taxes that fund public spending on subsidies for this research in various forms.[9]

It is difficult to quantify the direct and indirect public contribution to biomedical research through corporate subsidies, but – by doing some careful calculations – it could be as high as 50% of the total (see further discussion of the Cleary et al. (2018) study on the US government's contribution through the National Institutes of Health, NIH). Perhaps public funding is even greater when considering the role of donated knowledge from university research. According to Angelis et al. (2022), 60% of clinical trials for vaccines and drugs against SARS-CoV-2 was supported by public funds and 14% by not-for-profit entities with only 26% of such trials funded by the industry. However, these direct or indirect public subsidies do not appear to be sufficient to determine public health research as a priority. This, I believe, is the key problem of the public policy failure.

An analysis carried out by Taghreed et al. (2019) helps shed light on the issue of the priorities of the pharmaceutical sector. These authors discuss the findings of the World Health Organization's Global Observatory on Health Research and Development, established in 2017. The Observatory analysed 86,000 innovations developed since 1995, which include medicines, vaccines, and diagnostics. Of these innovative products, 14,999 were analysed and in use, of which 87% (13,004) were for non-contagious diseases, 9% (1319) for infectious diseases (1047), and the rest for conditions related to maternity, neonatal diseases, and others. Of the products for non-contagious diseases, almost half relate to cancer. Less than 0.5% of the products in use relate to the WHO list of neglected tropical diseases and only 0.4% relate to diseases which are included in the WHO priority list.

At the conclusion of this systematic analysis, the researchers write that:

> These findings and other recent analysis of the observatory's data show little indication that decisions on new investments on health research and development are evidence-informed or prioritized, or that they reflect the public health needs of people living in low- and middle-income countries.[10]

According to the authors, an analysis of the distribution of grants by the ten largest public agencies funding research reveals that in 2016, 72% (40,035 funding allocations) were for non-infectious diseases, followed by 20% (11,123) for infectious, nutritional, maternity, and neonatal diseases, and 6% for trauma. However, the proportion is reversed when looking at priority destinations in low- and middle-income countries. To put it simply: existing drugs and public funds for new drugs go mainly to treat diseases in markets that can directly or indirectly repay the investment and are disconnected from the public health agenda, in particular, from the priority research areas suggested by WHO itself.

Particularly worrying is the weakness of research into infectious diseases given that these account for 37% of deaths globally (21 million people each year). As the current pandemic shows, not only are these diseases already a significant global risk factor, but they could be part of the imminent future. Immunologist Sergio Abrignani (2020), looking at the sequence of years 2002 (SARS-CoV), 2012 (Mers), and 2019 (SARS-CoV-2), wrote that:

> [...] and as the social contexts that favour species jumps continue around the world, the question is not "if" there will still be a jump of a coronavirus from animal to human, but "when" this will happen; the succession of years in the sequence suggests that a new coronavirus infecting humans could appear in this decade.[11]

Recent research by Testoni et al. (2021) shows that the academic research agenda is skewed in the same way as the industry R&D priorities. They have studied 95,415 articles published between 1998 and 2018 in the 30 highest impact factors (in the Web of Science database). They find that only 1% or less of the articles deal with such categories as pathogens, microbiology, or environment. In contrast, 40% of the articles are associated with molecular biology, 15% are associated with cancer, and 8% with cardiovascular diseases. They also discover, looking at affiliations and co-authorships, that:

> [...] the research agendas of large pharmaceutical firms are intertwined with those of leading academic institutions concentrated in specific countries [...] it is significant that research on pathogenic viruses, bacteria or other microorganisms, and biological vectors (for example, bats) is marginal. [...] research on prevention, social determinants of health, and assessment of socio-environmental factors influencing disease onset or progression is negligible.

Industry

In what follows, for the sake of simplicity, I will refer to the pharmaceutical industry, but as I mentioned in the previous section, the non-pharmaceutical biomedical technology industry has a market size of hundreds of billions of USD annually.

At the top of the pyramid are the big pharma companies. Prior to the current pandemic (which will change the numbers), the top companies in terms of sales value included Pfizer, Roche, Novartis, Johnson&Johnson, Merck, Sanofi, AbbVie, GSK, Amgen, Gilead, Bayer, Sinopharm, Takeda, Astra Zeneca, and BMS, some of which also have very large revenues in other sectors (this is the case with Johnson&Johnson and Bayer).[12]

The cumulative revenues of the top 10 in 2019 amount to approximately 40% of the total market value. In itself, this does not indicate the extent to which the market structure is dominated by an oligopoly. There are certain sectors, such as automotive to give a classic example, where the concentration is higher (well over 50%) and at the same time the possibility of new entry is lower. However, what is characteristic of the pharmaceutical industry is a peculiar combination of monopolistic legal protection of intellectual property (patents), exclusive marketing authorisation regime (by drug agencies), long gestation times of innovations, high risk in the early stages of research, economies of variety (it pays to have a portfolio of products), and market power over the individual drug even after the patent has expired (due to a certain degree of inertia in the system induced by advertising and promotional expenditure in general). In market segments defined in relation to specific diseases, the concentration is higher than the aggregate data on the drug market would indicate.

The sector is a large aggregate of markets. In each market, a few companies with a few drugs compete with each other. Often, the treatment protocols adopted by healthcare systems or recommended by consensus among experts provide for only one drug of first choice for a disease and type of patient, and only if this cannot be administered for certain reasons will other drugs be used. This strict segmentation of the market is a peculiarity of the industry, which makes it very different from other sectors with a high concentration of market shares: for each type of car, computer, or refrigerator – to mention other examples of oligopoly – the customer still has several alternatives.

I will come back to patents later, but here I would like to point out that the long time from idea to commercialisation is in itself a favourable element for oligopolistic market dominance. According to EFPIA (2020), the European Federation of Pharmaceutical Industries, it typically takes six years after filing a patent to study acute toxicity risks, chronic toxicity risks and pharmacology in phase 1 and another two years in phase 2 clinical trials. Once phase 3, which requires larger samples of participants, is completed, ten years have elapsed since the initial patent filing before crucial authorisation, and a further year is needed to establish post-marketing prices and contracts. At that point, pharmacovigilance for possible adverse effects begins and at year 20 (in some cases, 25) the patent expires.

Obviously, such a long cycle (although not always so long in practice in all fields) of investment and economic return is not sustainable for a small company that seeks to enter the market with a single innovation or with a family of related innovations, whose risk of failure is, therefore, mutually correlated. The capital needed to go beyond the early stages would not be easy to come by, even in contexts where venture capital helps inventors. It is, therefore, optimal to have a large organisation that builds up a portfolio of patents and development projects over time, each at a different stage of the cycle, so that proven and profitable projects finance new and initially riskier projects. Hence the economies of variety.

If we add to this policy of accumulating projects (above all by means of acquisitions and mergers on the part of the major companies) the optimisation of relations with national regulators, financial investors, component suppliers and distributors, we can understand why Big Pharma and the oligopoly prevail in the structure of the industry, in a way that complements start-ups or companies that specialise in a single drug or a single phase of the process.

It is therefore not surprising that, given the effective concentration by segments, the profitability of the sector is abnormally high compared to other industries. Oligopolistic market segmentation and high profits almost always go together. According to a specialist in company accounting analysis, Prof. Aswath Damodaran (NYU Stern Business School),[13] the after-tax operating margin for the pharmaceutical industry (with appropriate accounting adjustments for the capitalisation of multi-year components, such as R&D expenses and leases) is in the range of 24% of revenues, among the highest ever. More significantly, a study by the Government Accountability Office (2017), the US government's most authoritative agency for accounting analysis, reported that the average profitability of large pharmaceutical companies is double that of the world's top 500 companies.

Governments

A not insignificant, and in many ways disconcerting, aspect of government policy is the large flow of public subsidies that the pharmaceutical industry receives, despite its high profitability. Governments seem to go to great lengths to ensure that companies receive an abnormal return on their investment, primarily by co-financing research, generally without imposing strict conditions on the intellectual property of innovations and economic returns. While private investors, for example, venture capitalists, exercise their acumen in squeezing their share of profits out of the support they give to innovative companies in their early stages, governments seem uninterested in offering taxpayers a fair return, despite the fact that they have co-funded company R&D through general taxation as well as through drug prices. This policy is even being touted as progressive and pro-competitive.

In OECD countries, the pharmaceutical industry reported spending around 101 billion USD on R&D in 2016, while governments in 31 OECD countries collectively contributed around 53 billion USD to health-related R&D. Health research is a broader category than drug research, but on the other hand, government expenditure data underestimate total government support because they exclude most tax incentives and funding for higher education and others.[14] Focusing on the leading country, and only looking at NIH grants, in 2019, each US citizen paid just under 120 USD per year to support biomedical research. A study from a few years ago based on a report by the Battelle Institute,[15] suggests this division of labour between government and industry in the US: the public sector through NIH contributed 31.8 billion USD each year to support mainly basic research, to a lesser extent "translational" research, and to an even lesser extent clinical research, while the private sector contributed 51.8 billion USD with an inverted priority structure. If the numbers in the study cited above were taken literally, the NIH channel alone would account for 38% of total R&D expenditure in the sector. A similar percentage would be reached by considering the detailed work of Cleary et al. (2018) on 210 active ingredients (new molecular entities) approved by the Food and Drug Administration, the US drug agency. These authors calculated that NIH contributed an average of 840 million USD (2010–2016) to research on each of these 210 active ingredients.

Wouters et al. (2020) studied the R&D costs for 360 FDA-approved drugs from 50 companies over a decade and found a median value per new drug (out of a sample of 65 products placed on the market between 2009 and 2018) of 985 million USD and an average of 1336 million USD, but with great variability: costs were approximately double the average for oncology and immunology, average for infectious diseases and gastrointestinal diseases, and below average for the nervous system and dermatology.

The values are adjusted to take into account the frequent failure of projects. Thus, taking the Wouters et al. (2020) estimate of corporate spending on the one hand, and the NIH contribution estimated by Cleary et al. (2018) on the other, we would have 840 million USD per drug in public funds compared to 1336 million USD in corporate R&D funds. Adjusted for duplication in company budgets, if public and private funds were to be combined to bring the drug to market, the public contribution would be 39% of the total. However, the actual proportion is probably higher for the following reasons.

Public funding of R&D is often underestimated[16] and corporate funding is overestimated. In addition to NIH funds, there are also funds from other US agencies such as the National Science Foundation and BARDA,[17] and from public funders (including those from other countries) and non-profit organisations (such as the Bill and Melinda Gates Foundation), which in turn often benefit from tax exemptions on upstream profits. Grants flow generously to universities and other bodies, but then, directly and indirectly, trickle down to businesses. On the other hand, as mentioned above, companies tend, for obvious public relations reasons, to overestimate the amount of their R&D expenditure.

Combining these two sources of underestimation of the public contribution and overestimation of the private contribution, and considering that, especially in Europe, it is the taxpayers who directly pay for the structural functioning of university departments of pharmacy, pharmacology, biosciences, and other disciplines which contribute to drug research, the public contribution to research could account for at least half of the total research expenditure. Although some universities (e.g., MIT and the University of California in the US) and other institutes hold or co-hold pharmaceutical patents, in general, the public and non-profit sectors do not hold a patent portfolio commensurate with their contribution to research.

The taxation of profits is notoriously kind to multinationals, such as Big Pharma, which can generally choose the most favourable tax regimes in the different states in which they operate. This, too, is essentially an incentive, in addition to other tax benefits.

All this might still be politically acceptable if research took the path of the public health agenda and if there were no adverse consequences in terms of inequality. As mentioned above, corporate R&D takes – as is necessary for such a context – the route of "value" for the private investors, with serious implications for inequality of access to care. In essence, governments offer all kinds of incentives (regulatory, direct, indirect, fiscal) to drug companies in the hope that they will give us the means to save our lives or improve their quality. But they are not charities: they cash in and pursue their strategies, which include the pricing policy to be expected when demand is rigid and supply is oligopolistic or – for individual drugs – monopolistic, with legal protection and/or structural barriers to entry throughout the cycle. So, the priorities of governments and industry may or may not coincide, but the system is not effectively governed in this direction. Moreover, it is not efficient.

Particularly worrying is the decline in the industry's productivity in terms of innovation: while in the 1950s–1960s, the FDA approved around 50 new molecules as active ingredients of a drug per billion USD of R&D), in the 1980s–1990s it fell to around five molecules and after 2000 to less than one molecule per billion USD per year. SSR Health (2016) analysed R&D productivity for the 22 largest publicly traded companies in the US over the years 1990–2014, looking, in particular, at patents and patent citations (a crude but useful indicator of impact) and found evidence of a clear downward trend over time.

In the face of declining productivity, the average unit price of new drugs is rising with unpredictable effects on the expenditure of public and private healthcare systems, particularly where insurance models prevail.[18]

According to a study by the OECD, retail expenditure on drugs in member states was worth on average 1.4% of GDP in 2017 but (as reported above) over 2% in the US. The total value of expenditure on pharmaceuticals would then have to be supplemented depending on the country (between 9 and 30%) for supplies to hospitals and other healthcare facilities. Whereas in real terms, expenditure on pharmaceuticals in the OECD area has been declining for a decade due to the high number of patents that have expired and the cost-containment policies of purchasers, there have been sharp increases in areas such as cancer and rare diseases.[19]

Apart from egregious cases, such as the cost of treating a patient with a particular haematological disease with a gene therapy provided by Bluebird Bio at a cost of nearly 1.8 million USD, or the 2.1 million USD price of Novartis' gene therapy for spinal muscular atrophy, the average price of new drugs is rising fast. Some studies on the cost to private insurance systems (widely prevalent in the US and elsewhere) predict a doubling of retail spending on drugs over the period 2013–2027, partly due to the growing influence of marketing expenses that sometimes appear in companies' budgets and annual reports mixed in with true R&D spending.

Lessons from the pandemic

I ask this question: instead of subsidising private companies in the hope that their research agenda might coincide with that of public health, would it not be better for governments to directly fund entities that focus exclusively on the public mission?

I am not proposing that pharmaceutical companies stop doing their business or be nationalised,[20] but I am questioning the fact that governments continue to rely exclusively on subsidies to companies, on patents, and on the regulation of oligopolistic markets for drug policy.

As we saw in the previous chapter, governments intervene directly in sectors of general interest, from energy to telecommunications, from transport to hospitals: why should they not do so in biomedical research and drug development? What is the taboo against this? My proposal[21] is to create a public, supranational biomedical research infrastructure in Europe, comprising one or more R&D centres linked (in appropriate legal forms) with production and distribution units. This infrastructure could also invite selected pharmaceutical companies to collaborate on specific projects, with transparent contracts. In some market segments, this infrastructure could however also compete with companies in order to rebalance prices and accessibility of medicines and to send a signal that governments are not powerless.

Before looking at the idea in some detail, let us look at some previous experiences and some proposals already in the field. Public enterprises in the pharmaceutical sector have existed in the past, especially in the field of vaccines, but they were then dismantled almost everywhere in the years of rampant privatisation. Not everywhere: China, India, Indonesia, Thailand, and Brazil have state-owned companies which produce and export the active ingredients of medicines all over the world, which are then mixed, compressed, packaged, and distributed in Europe, the USA, and elsewhere. In the EU, there is talk of a growing dependence – in this as in other fields – of developed economies on the manufacturing sector of third countries.[22] Cuba, a country in severe economic difficulty, nevertheless has a rather innovative public pharmaceutical sector, with BioCubaFarma (a network of companies and institutes), 1500 employees and a portfolio of 2430 international patents and 2640 pending patent applications, and a successful track record on Covid-19 vaccines.[23]

It would be wrong, however, to think that public pharmaceutical companies are only present or feasible in less developed economies. I will give a few illustrative examples.

In the USA in 2018, Senator Elisabeth Warren proposed to Congress the creation of an Office of Drug Manufacturing under the Department of Health and Human Services. This office would aim to reduce costs, improve access, and reduce shortages of essential drugs. Another broader project of public intervention in the drug cycle has been presented by the think tank Democracy Collaborative (Brown, 2019).

A US practical example is CivicaRx, a non-profit manufacturer founded in 2018 that has the mission to reduce the shortage of generic drugs and, in particular, to stabilise the supply and price of 50 products including insulin for sale to participating hospitals and for wholesale distribution. The project proved to be attractive and created a network of 1400 hospitals, attracting 30 million USD in donations.[24]

Remaining in the United States, it should also be considered that centres of excellence in public biomedical research are not just funders of others' research: the NIH (National Institutes of Health) have very significant resources for in-house research, in the order of about 4 billion USD each year, 1200 principal investigators and 4000 post-doctoral fellows.

In Europe, the picture is in many ways more fragmented and drug R&D expenditure is lower in absolute and relative terms than in the US.[25] There are few public or non-profit drug organisations. One very particular example is the Swedish public company APL,[26] which is now one of the largest producers of certain types of extemporaneous and individualised drugs (2000 products), those that used to be prepared by pharmacists on targeted prescriptions and are essential for patients with certain allergies, particularly in paediatrics. By definition, these drugs are not supplied by the pharmaceutical industry.[27]

The example certainly relates to a niche market (1–2% of the Swedish market) not covered by pharmaceutical companies, but it also represents a case to be studied.[28]

What could we do in Europe with a large public infrastructure? The view of several experts[29] is that, first and foremost, there should be preparedness for future pandemics, whatever their aetiology. An issue that is well known to specialists, but apparently not sufficiently to the public, is the health risk associated with the long-standing selection of bacterial strains that are resistant to currently available antibiotics, for example for diseases such as tuberculosis. Already today, in some European countries, such as Ukraine and Russia, multi-resistant tuberculosis (i.e., not treatable with any of the first-choice antibiotics) is in the order of 20%: a probability that for every five infected, one cannot use the antibiotic mix that normally saves lives. These percentages are increasing for various infectious diseases. According to one study,[30] around 20% of infections are currently due to antibiotic-resistant pathogens in the EU, and twice that proportion in countries such as Romania and Greece. The Review on Antimicrobial Resistance, a study for the UK government coordinated by Lord O'Neill, predicts that worldwide bacterial infections will cause around 10 million deaths per year by 2050. By comparison, there are 8.2 million deaths from cancer and 1.5 million from diabetes. The O'Neill report proposes a 2-billion-dollar Global Innovation Fund to finance research at an early stage, which is not the most expensive stage, although it is the one most at risk of failure.

He also proposes a system of incentives and disincentives (a pay or play system) to penalise pharmaceutical companies that decide not to invest in the R&D of new antibiotics, or to reward companies that decide to "play" the game. O'Neill envisaged a premium of 1–1.5 billion USD for each new antimicrobial drug successfully brought to market. The system is bizarre and shows a certain subservience to the idea that nothing can be done without pharmaceutical companies.

For several years, the European Union has contributed with grants to some studies on the topic.[31] In 2017, the European Commission adopted a new European Action Plan against antibiotic resistance.[32] An earlier decision of the European Commission already included the topic in the list of serious cross-border health threats.[33] Among the various initiatives currently underway is a collaborative research platform (JPIAMR) that coordinates national and European funding to support transnational research and activities on the topic of antibiotic resistance.[34] Since 2011, JPIAMR has supported 99 projects and 1221 researchers, with funding of around 80 million euros, which is small compared with what would be needed to find solutions.

There are several lessons to be learnt from (the lack of) preparedness for the current pandemic, as discussed by a Lancet Commission, among others.[35]

Firstly, there is a need for coordinated monitoring systems at the supranational level, which implies not only effective mandatory data provision systems (the current systems have not worked well for either the European ECDC or the US CDC) but also standardised diagnostic protocols, supported by research into tests for known and new pathogens. It has been demonstrated how important early tracing of outbreaks is, but we are still unprepared for future outbreaks in terms of information systems. We have seen how inefficient the improvisation and lack of coordination between states has been in having individual tracking and alerting software, even in an area where the density of smartphones and other devices per capita is the highest in the world.

Secondly, as trivial as it may seem, we have bitterly discovered that we did not have the production capacity in Europe to manage the emergency, both in terms of personal protection equipment and certified disinfectants, and in terms of ventilators, oxygen cylinders, and other countermeasures, not to mention vaccines after their marketing authorisation by the European Medicines Agency. More than research, it is a question of having a European authority that can coordinate the emergency response, an aspect that has been blatantly lacking on this occasion and that is to a certain extent taken into account in a recent initiative by the European Commission to create the Health Emergency Response Authority (HERA, see Appendix).

Thirdly, we need to prepare for future vaccines, antiviral drugs and antibiotics, and, in general, those therapies that are of little interest to industry, by focusing on objectives in order of danger for public health and riskiness of research, not in order of profitability. Perhaps we have lost our collective memory: as the famous US infectiologist Peter Hotez reminds us, it was only thanks to 14 key vaccines in the past that potentially lethal diseases, such as tetanus, diphtheria, smallpox, polio, and others, were eradicated or greatly limited. Measles, for example, still killed 180,000 people in 2018.[36]

How to prioritise? It could be the scientific community itself, freed from the exclusive dependence on pharmaceutical companies for research, which defines the agenda of research priorities with the governance of a European public infrastructure, in an open dialogue in which researchers and health systems participate together. I will discuss this later. These are not easy goals, but they are not impossible either. In Europe (including the UK, Switzerland,

and other non-EU countries) we have all the tools to meet the challenge, but there is a lack of coordination, critical mass, and public mission-oriented approach. For basic and early-stage research, there are centres of excellence, both in universities and in public or independent institutes, such as the Karolinska Institutet in Stockholm, the European Molecular Biology Laboratory in Heidelberg (with sites in other countries), several units belonging to the Max Planck Gesellschaft and other German scientific societies, the Robert Koch Institute in Berlin, the Institut Pasteur in Paris and elsewhere, and the Wellcome Sanger Institute and other centres at the Wellcome Genome Campus in Hinxton (near Cambridge, UK). Italy, in addition to hosting independent facilities such as the Mario Negri Institute for Pharmacological Research in Milan and other locations, has excellent university departments in the biomedical area, the Istituto Superiore di Sanità, and hosts the ambitious Human Technopole project in the Milan Expo area, with centres dedicated to genomics, computational biology, neurogenomics, structural biology, and data science.

As with many other aspects of the European landscape, the wealth of structures is combined with duplication and loss of energies resulting from national projects, only very weakly networked by European research funding programmes such as Horizon Europe. These programmes often generate consortia motivated by access to EU funds through participation in calls for proposals, usually without a stable supranational identity and mission, with few exceptions. There is a further funding channel offered by the EU Health Programme (EU4Health). The programme is implemented through annual work plans agreed with the countries on a set of priority actions defined each year and criteria for financing actions under the programme. On this basis, the Consumers, Health, Agriculture and Food Executive Agency (CHAFEA[37]) organises calls for proposals for projects and operating grants, as well as calls for tenders and soliciting joint action. CHAFEA, specifically for the health programme, has managed a budget of 449.4 million euros (2014–2020), which is set to increase more than tenfold with the pandemic. 5.1 billion (2021–2027), with the following objectives: Accelerating preparedness for major cross-border health threats by stockpiling medicines, creating a reserve of health personnel to be mobilised as needed, increasing surveillance on possible threats, strengthening national health systems to deal with epidemic crises, long-term health challenges, prevention and health promotion in relation to ageing populations, digital transformation of health systems, access to care for vulnerable groups, making medicines and medical equipment available and affordable, promoting prudent and efficient use of antibiotics, and promoting pharmaceutical innovation and "green" production of medicines.

While these objectives are perfectly worthy, the main limitation of this intervention model, as well as that of Horizon Europe for research, is that it is based on a system of calls for proposals and subsidies that is de facto aimed at individual states and organisations, this approach is unlikely to achieve a critical mass and a genuinely European scale of activity.

Opportunities are thus wasted. In contrast to the US, access to health care in Europe is predominantly based on public health services, albeit with considerable variation in national organisational models. This potentially offers considerable opportunities for the establishment of a public mission. Clinical research on drugs is in fact largely carried out within this framework and is characterised by contracts for the various trial phases between public hospitals and private companies. Pharmaceutical companies increasingly use private intermediary companies, the CROs, for this purpose. These companies can offer a wide range of services from preclinical research to – crucially – clinical trials, to accompanying the pharmaceutical company to the final stages of obtaining authorisation from the European Medicines Agency.

According to some estimates, the global CRO services market in 2018 was over 38 billion USD with such high growth rates that it is expected to exceed 90 billion by 2026. Although there may be as many as a thousand companies in the market, the top ten have over 50% of the market and the trend is for even greater concentration.[38]

In practice, these companies offer contracts to hospitals and other organisations in direct contact with patients in order to enrol them in trials. This has created a marketplace whose focus is on data regarding the response of patients to the therapies to be investigated, collected by medical and paramedical staff. For hospitals, payments from CROs or other subjects for trials are a source of additional income compared to public funding, which is increasingly inadequate to meet needs. In Italy, for example, cuts before the pandemic have been particularly severe. For CROs, a clinical trial is a business; for pharmaceutical companies, it is an indispensable information base to support the application for authorisation to drug agencies. For university researchers, clinical trials, with large budgets offered by pharmaceutical companies, are the experimental database that allows them to publish in international journals, possibly those with the highest reputation. Indirectly or directly, pharmaceutical companies thus also have a certain influence on the scientific journals themselves, because a paper from a group that can claim a large-scale trial for various reasons is more likely to be accepted. Contracts with hospitals for trials can take various forms but essentially involve the recruitment of patients at a price of perhaps several thousand euros per patient enrolled, with payments to the hospital based on price lists and negotiations. The system involves double intermediation because the profit margin of CROs enters into the costs declared as R&D by pharmaceutical companies on which they calculate their margins. This whole ecosystem could be made more efficient, fairer, and better oriented if there were, on the one hand, a public drug R&D infrastructure to conduct trials at all stages from preclinical to clinical, focusing on a few priority areas, and, on the other hand, public health systems. From this perspective, it would be necessary to effectively counterbalance the sometimes aggressive policies of pharmaceutical companies and CROs which, when there are relatively few patients available for recruitment, offer high fees to hospitals for each patient enrolled, perhaps partly in order to displace possible competition.

The current market solution in this area appears to be particularly inefficient, generating an unjustified rise in costs, with some ostensible benefits only for hospitals, which, while in the short term, they may benefit from revenues from CROs and pharmaceutical companies for their provision of patient data, will sooner or later face the ever-increasing price of new drugs that they will have to buy from the very same pharmaceutical companies.

As can be seen, it is not just a question of regulating the market in this context. Companies in the sector have their own business models that appear to be relatively impervious to public incentives and regulation (except occasionally). Rather, Governments need to intervene structurally to prevent the formation of rents in the financial chasm between public research, public funding of private research, the pharmaceutical cycle and public health. In our economies, few things are more essential than the efficient integration of biomedical research and healthcare systems, so there is no reason why an effective public infrastructure should not be tried, as has been the case in other sectors.

A proposal

The proposal, which – to give the concept a name – I will call Biomed Europa here, consists of the creation of a biomedical R&D infrastructure integrated with the entire cycle of research, development, production and distribution of new medicines. For simplicity's sake, I am referring here only to drugs, but innovations in the biomedical field not adequately offered by the sector might also include, for example, new diagnostic technologies, radically innovative surgical approaches, telemedicine, digital health information management, screening, and prevention systems, and more, with a list of priorities being selected.

It is necessary to think both about future emergencies that are more or less predictable, and also about services that serve to avoid having to resort to drugs, in a long-term perspective, which may require advances in basic research and digital information systems. I lead below the discussion of the proposal from various angles: public mission, technological and human resources, organisation and legal basis, interaction with other public and private actors in the system, and financial foundations.

As far as the public mission is concerned, the strategic objective of Biomed Europa could be defined as follows: to build up a portfolio of innovative R&D projects in the biomedical area within a time horizon of 20, or better still 30 years. In general, this means selecting projects of critical importance for human health in the 21st century on the basis of an agenda of priorities established by the consensus of the scientific community and the public health systems of the participating countries, including by drawing on the guidelines of various European institutions and the WHO, guidelines that already exist but have often not been implemented. What these priorities are can only emerge from a careful periodic process of bottom-up consultation in the typical style of research infrastructures, reconsidering from the perspective of a public investor the recommendations made by individual experts, state bodies and public institutes, non-profit organisations, and patient associations, as mentioned above. Research on certain aspects of human nutrition should not be excluded from this mission, since according to some estimates the availability of food must be increased by 50% in the next 30 years in order to cope with the increase in per capita income and population. We still know too little about the interactions between human health, human medicines, and products used in agriculture and animal husbandry (including veterinary medicines).

One might wonder if WHO itself could not be the reference point for the project. Today WHO, more than 70 years after its creation in 1948 in Geneva, is a large organisation with more than 160 member states, 7000 employees, and 150 local offices. It has an annual budget (2020–2021) of 5840 billion USD, partly in the form of regular contributions, the rest being linked to specific programmes.[39] The role of research, however, is not preeminent there, essentially WHO produces recommendations and data, but its impact, even in terms of influencing publications, does not seem to be adequate.[40]

Luigi Ferrajoli, a jurist whose vision of a constitutionalisation of fundamental rights on a planetary scale is very interesting, has suggested that an attempt should be made to relaunch the WHO, but he himself acknowledges that "it does not even have the means and institutional apparatus necessary to offer poor countries the 460 life-saving drugs that, as the WHO itself established 40 years ago, should be accessible to all, and the lack of which causes 8 million deaths every year".[41]

Without detracting from this prospect, which is perhaps now less impossible after the inglorious end of Trump's term of office in the White House (having withdrawn the United States from the WHO, accusing it of being in the service of China), I do not believe that this institution – even if reformed – can serve the purpose of a structural change in the delivery of medical innovation. This is partly because it is too conditioned by powerful industry interests through certain governments and donors, but mainly because it has never set out to intervene directly in the entire drug cycle, not even in life-saving drugs whose patents have expired. Only recently has the WHO appointed a chief scientist. Despite early warnings about the risks of unknown pathogens, as mentioned at the beginning of this chapter, it has not been able to follow up the warning. WHO had already been criticised for not issuing timely warnings for the Ebola outbreak in Congo and on several other crucial occasions.

In addition to the primary mission of creating a portfolio of innovative projects in the biomedical area on the basis of an agenda of priorities established by the consensus of the scientific community and the public health systems of participating countries, the proposed Biomed Europa could usefully carry out certain types of clinical studies related to already authorised drugs, which are not of interest to pharmaceutical companies. One example is comparative studies of the real-life efficacy of existing drugs. For obvious reasons, the industry is not interested in such comparative clinical studies, which could be very important from a public health perspective. Moreover, patent-expired drugs that have been approved by the authorities for certain specific uses may often be used to treat other diseases. But to prove their efficacy, they need to be tested in clinical trials with the same rigorous standards as new drugs.

The comparative assessment of the efficacy, risk–benefit ratio, and cost-effectiveness of different drugs is an area in which, for obvious reasons, the patent or market authorisation holder of a drug has no interest in investing if it suspects that the outcome may be unfavourable. Most drug agencies do not have this mandate and capacity for analysis, so the field is relatively unexplored (occasionally studies are commissioned by third parties).

An ancillary task could be to oversee the supply of raw materials, which are often imported from outside the EU in the case of traditional medicines, and the selection and supply (possibly entrusted to selected CDMOs) of generic medicines that have created an unsatisfactory market balance, with unjustifiably high prices or unverifiable quality because they are produced outside the European Union.

Finally, as I have already mentioned, it is not only some drugs that should be dealt with, but also vaccines – of course – and any other product of research in the above-mentioned fields of diagnostics, imaging, computer systems for managing and sharing biodata, including tracking during epidemics, with a selective strategy investment.

There would also be great utility in studies on how strategies to contain environmental, nutritional, and social risks (inequality is a disease that kills more than any other) could be implemented in the most effective and efficient way, minimising the use of drugs. Again, this is not the typical pursuit of investor interest in the industry, but it would be crucial. The current system, whereby a drug with even a limited therapeutic profile is marketed and huge resources are spent on promoting its use, should be validated by independent social benefit–cost studies.[42]

Studies on the medium- to long-term effects of drugs would also be useful since the expectations of studies done at the time of registration are not always fully confirmed by clinical practice after 10 or 20 years.

As far as technological resources are concerned, once the general mission and policy objectives have been defined and the specific objectives have been set, the investments involved need to be discussed. According to the logic of the proposal, only an in-depth study could define the set of technological instruments to be activated. Unlike physics, biomedical research requires less expensive equipment, even if it is often not accessible everywhere. Modern cryo-electron microscopy, which enables resolution at the level of a single molecule (e.g., of a single virus or even smaller objects without using X-ray crystallography), requires instruments costing several million euros. Synchrotron light sources for certain types of research at the molecular level cost hundreds of millions of euros in investment. There would be clear economies of scale to manage the latest generation of instruments in a coordinated way through a technological hub that in turn coordinates a distributed system of centres, not least by enhancing existing centres that adhere to the same principles.[43] It would therefore be necessary to envisage a functionally integrated complex of various laboratories, including not only facilities of the highest security level for the study of lethal pathogens but also units accessible in rotation to different groups according to the general model I have set out in the previous chapters.

The downstream activities of basic and pre-clinical research could be managed either in-house or through agreements with one or more CROs, and similar arrangements could be made with organisations that contractually manage the manufacture of the final product (CMO) or aspects of its development (CDO). Some pharmaceutical companies or their consortia could be invited to co-develop certain projects, without giving them unconstrained intellectual property rights.

The definition of the technological basis would therefore depend on the configuration of the use of existing public and private structures. In the Biomed Europa model, innovation could be both demand-driven (based on the identification of the needs of public health systems) and technology-driven (based on the interdisciplinary research opportunities offered by cutting-edge platforms). Thus, the mix of instrumentation and technological investments depends on the combination of innovative trajectories suggested by the scientific community and health authorities.

Perhaps the most important point of the Biomed Europa proposal is the large-scale attraction to a public mission of excellent human capital. Worldwide, the life sciences community arguably accounts for the largest share of the approximately 8.8 million researchers estimated by UNESCO by 2018, with more women participating than in other fields.[44] Hundreds of thousands of young researchers in the life sciences in general, and in the biomedical area in particular, have essentially two professional outlets for their long-term careers: pharmaceutical/biotechnology companies and their service providers or the university (including university clinics) and some public or independent institutes. Salaries and employment contracts in general are considerably more generous in companies than elsewhere. Almost everywhere, the logic of careers is unrelated to public health priorities. In the case of business, this is obvious for the reasons already explained. Inevitably, a young scientist entering the world of pharmaceutical companies becomes a cog in a machine that is designed to make a profit and although he/she may have his own ideas about what should be a priority, the means available will be directed towards the potentially more lucrative research projects, with exceptions that do not change the overall effect.

It is perhaps less obvious how things are for young people entering universities. Here, the imperative is to publish and possibly publish in the most prestigious journals, which are usually those with the highest impact factor.

The career of a young researcher may, in essence, depend on how much and where he/she publishes, rather than on what is relevant to human health: the two may or may not coincide, but often do not for two reasons. Firstly, some research topics and methods of investigation, although they may relate to fundamental human health issues, may be less fashionable than others. There is a process of topic selection that starts as early as doctoral studies, where the students' topics are often guided by the professors' preferences. They inevitably follow the currents of scientific thought due to reputational reasons or even just because their curiosity leads them in certain directions as opposed to others. There is nothing wrong with this, it is often how it should be, but it is not necessarily the best system for the health agenda. There is a second distorting mechanism and that is the direct or indirect influence of the pharmaceutical industry on the university research agenda itself. To publish at a high level in the medical area it is often essential to have participated in double-blind clinical trials with randomised samples of treated patients and control groups, and this requires high numbers of patients with certain characteristics and above all accurate and standardised data collection. Notoriously, this is the most expensive step in research and requires funding which, at least for large-scale trials, can usually only be offered today by pharmaceutical companies developing a drug.[45] For a university researcher, being involved in these trials often gives the only opportunity to obtain the kind of data needed to publish at a high level. In other words, the human capital of universities often ends up being drawn into the orbit of market-driven research. At any rate, it is not prioritised in the orbit of research oriented towards public health priorities.

The system is not effectively corrected by public research funding. Consider again the case of the NIH, which has a budget of some 49 billion USD (2023) is surely the largest biomedical research body in the world under a single public institution. But essentially, the NIH selects who it gives grants to on the basis of the proposals it receives from external scientists, despite having its own substantial intramural research agenda.

More than 80% of the budget supports 50,000 grants per year, allocated to 2500 universities and other organisations.[46] The allocation of funds sees a very significant weight of research on the diseases of ageing[47]: for example, dementia currently affects 50 million people, 30–50% of those aged 85, and so far no effective treatment has been found. The cost of care is estimated by the WHO to be 1 trillion USD per year and 152 million people are expected to be affected by 2050.[48] NIH intramural research, moreover, is endowed with some 4 billion USD per year, with over 6000 researchers working in the laboratories of the 27 institutes housed on the campus (75 buildings) in Bethesda, Maryland. There is much to learn from this experience.[49]

Biomed Europa would serve to counterbalance the labour market for researchers by offering in-house research opportunities in the form of international collaborations to a large scientific community. To illustrate this, the Biomed Europa community should be at least of the same order of magnitude as the NIH intramural research community in terms of internal permanent staff and external researchers recruited on project-specific contracts. Once more, as a point of comparison, consider that EMBL (which covers only some of the topics that would be needed for Biomed Europa) employs 1700 people in 80 research groups in six locations (Heidelberg, Hinxton/Wellcome Genome Campus, Rome, Grenoble, Barcelona, and Hamburg), with a budget one-tenth of the NIH intramural program (with a very different scope). An essential aspect in terms of human resources would be to have project managers capable of guiding drug research and development up to the stage that follows approval by the drug agencies, that is, from basic research to clinical trials, development, production, distribution, and surveillance, although several of these stages can – if economically viable – be purchased by Biomed Europe on the services market.

What hope is there of attracting bright, young scientists and experienced project managers? I am optimistic. We saw with our own eyes during the pandemic that something significant was happening. Medical, nursing, and technical staff, as well as tens of thousands of researchers, were engaged in a daily battle against the pandemic to save lives directly, to analyse data and samples, to test therapies and vaccines, and to publish a vast amount of work available through open access. Of course, this was an emergency, and not everything was done well, but the mobilisation was impressive. Biomed Europa should work to avoid the next pandemic and to tackle the health crises of the future, which will almost certainly arise from the fields left uncovered by industry: many young people (and not so young people) would flock to a project that could become the most important in the world in the biomedical area.

Turning to the organisational model and the legal basis, in a context as rich in centres of excellence as Europe, the model could presumably be that of a polycentric body, but I am inclined to the idea that there should be a central hub, a reference campus, to which distributed sites are linked, provided they are well integrated. A loose confederation of institutes, as a European Research Infrastructure Consortium (ERIC) often is, would not work. Staff, wherever they are physically located, should be full-time on the new project and not contribute fractions of their time while maintaining their main loyalties to their university or group. An important aspect is that Biomed Europa should not only have its own legal status but also all the necessary requirements to enter into the patenting and marketing authorisation procedures for drugs on its own or through its own controlled organisation. Whatever organisational model is adopted, it should adopt the lesson of research infrastructures: the effective combination of bottom-up creativity and mission orientation.

Various legal issues would have to be carefully resolved, but the study of the statutes of supranational bodies with their own legal status, such as EMBL or even ESA, could provide good ideas for founding treaties and governance design. Then there is the issue of the public enterprise status that some of the activities would take on, and thus the possibility that some might see a risk of "state aid" and violation of competition, especially if the pharmaceutical companies were to get in the way. But first and foremost, public funding to Biomed Europa could essentially concern research and would not be dissimilar to the funding that already exists, perhaps in a less transparent way, for private companies themselves. Secondly, in this case, it would not be a single state supporting a "national champion", and various European funds do not fall under state aid when they are directed to projects of supranational interest (see Chapter 4 regarding the Innovation Fund set up by the European Union for projects on climate change). Thirdly, and decisively, there is the argument of the overriding public interest in health over the abstract protection of market conditions, when the areas of intervention are precisely those in which there have been significant failures in terms of efficiency and fairness.

The governance of the project should provide for appropriate mechanisms for consulting the various stakeholders in the system: the health authorities of the member states; the pharmaceutical agencies; the public health systems and their professional organisations; the patients' associations; and the private companies in the various segments of the chain. The aim is to build a coalition that is strong enough to convince the pharmaceutical companies themselves that the elements of complementarity between the public and private sectors could prevail over those of competition; to convince political decision-makers that chasing after a hundred projects on a relatively small scale on a national basis is inefficient and in the long run politically unprofitable; and to convince civil society and patient associations that Biomed Europa could be a valuable ally in containing the costs of treatment, in prevention, and in preparing for future emergencies.

Regarding the financial resources, if the ambitions of the project were on the scale I have indicated above, I believe that the resources involved each year could be as mentioned, at least roughly equal in order of magnitude to the in-house research share of the NIH budget, to which the costs of downstream clinical trial activities up to the final stages of the drug cycle and other innovations would be added. In the broadest version of the project, this could be an annual budget of approximately 0.1% of EU GDP, or proportionally less if third countries such as Switzerland, the UK, Norway, and others also participate. This financial basis should not, when fully operational, be entirely, and perhaps not even predominantly, based on multiannual transfer commitments from the budgets of the member states (which could, incidentally, represent savings compared to scattered national funding). There would be income from the not-for-profit sale of medicines and other products and services, or from the assignment of economic rights to a portfolio of patents (which should, moreover, be of overriding public interest).

Social benefits and costs

Reasoning about the benefits and costs of the project might be useful. Even before the pandemic, Fan, Jamison, and Summers (2018) wrote that there was little doubt about the recurrence of pandemics and our unpreparedness to deal with them. It turned out shortly afterwards that they were right, as were those who had preceded them in their prediction by at least 20 years. To get an idea of the economic cost of such an event, they cited a World Bank study[50] according to which a pandemic comparable to the Spanish flu could reduce global GDP by 4.8%, an order of magnitude that – when added to monetary value of the years of "statistical life" lost,[51] not counting the suffering that losses entail in those who survive – would be of the same magnitude that various models estimate for the risks deriving from climate change. According to the World Bank[52] itself, the global contraction of GDP in 2020 could have been −3.3% and −4.9% in advanced economies (−9.9% in the UK). We do not know what the long-term effect will be, because it is difficult to foresee the recovery in subsequent years after a shock of the size of the current one. Some forecasting models do not have reliable parameters on which to base assumptions about how quickly one can recover, but for the time being it seems that it will take at least two years to recover the annual product loss.

If the scientists are right, there is a high probability of a pandemic every ten years (between 2010 and 2019 there were two potential pandemics and one "successful" one). Just to set the record straight, let us assume that the cumulative economic value of the production lost permanently in the European Union (compared to the long-term trend) in a decade was one percentage point of GDP, and let us also ignore the economic value of the "statistical lives" lost and the psycho-physical suffering and bereavement associated with the disease itself. In such a case, public spending of around 0.1% of GDP each year on research and development of vaccines, drugs, and any other tool useful for preventing or managing a pandemic episode would be fully recovered in terms of avoided risk, without counting the impact in sectors other than infectious diseases not covered by the industry, or the benefits for consumers of a price reduction effect. For the reasons I have explained, this can scarcely be achieved by subsidising industry or by increasing the tasks of existing institutions such as WHO and others.

The 2022 budget of the NIH in the United States combined with BARDA is 45.5 billion USD, compared with a GDP of around 24.9 trillion USD, so that the public expenditure of the federal government of that country on its core public infrastructure for all kinds of pathologies, not just infectious diseases, is in the order of 1.8 per 1000 of GDP. For various reasons, I believe that the budget of Biomed Europa could be significantly less: in the case of the USA, most of that budget, as already mentioned, is spent on grants, which should be a minor item in the project proposed here (they are mostly funded in the EU by the Horizon Europe Program and other mechanisms). For the reasons I have explained above, grants are ultimately a way of subsidising drug research, which, on the one hand, are dispersed in tens of thousands of small funding streams in the laboratories of universities and individual groups, and on the other, end up being concentrated downstream in companies with their selective agenda on the basis of profit criteria. A great deal could be saved by having an in-house project selection system, with the support of the international scientific community. In addition, perhaps the UK, Switzerland, Norway, and other non-EU countries could contribute to the budget, not least so as not to lose out on the opportunity.

Let us assume that all activities downstream of research and development (production, marketing, distribution) are carried out under normal contracts with public or private organisations (such as public health systems, and logistics manufacturing companies) with prices equal to marginal cost, as Biomed Europa does not have to remunerate financial investors. What would one actually "buy" with one per 1000 of European GDP, that is, with just over 15 euros per capita per year (similar to the ESA budget)?

If we take as an indicative reference the data on the average cumulative cost (with a much lower median) of research and development of a drug mentioned above of around 1 billion euros, an infrastructure such as Biomed Europa could launch and support over 100 innovative projects in two or three decades, including the phases that include clinical trials, patent filings, approvals by drug agencies, monitoring, long-term comparative studies. There would be inevitable failures, precisely because of the high-risk research, it would have the potential to accumulate a large portfolio of innovations of high social interest, to be distributed at affordable prices in areas not prioritised by private industry. This size would make Biomed Europa the world's leading centre for biomedical research, with an R&D investment size comparable to the leading companies in the sector. In addition to catching up with the US, Europe would make a globally significant contribution to the challenges of human health and equality of access to care.

Appendix: some proposals from the European Commission

In 2020, during the Covid-19 pandemic, the European Commission made several proposals to strengthen the Union's capacity to act in the field of health.[53] It was proposed to create a European Health Union based on several pillars. While the landscape is still changing, I will briefly recall the main ones here, to underline some similarities but also the differences with the proposal in the chapter. The main difference is in the nature of an immediate and contingent response to the health risk of the European Commission's proposals, whereas my proposal is for a systemic intervention, in other words, a structural and long-term perspective because the issues at stake seem to me to go largely beyond the management of occasional emergencies.

European Centre for Disease Control (ECDC)

The Commission noted that the ECDC currently lacks the mandate and capacity[54] to analyse health data in a timely manner that would allow for evidence-based decisions in real time. It is proposed to strengthen the mandate in the following areas:

1 epidemiological surveillance through integrated systems enabling real-time surveillance;
2 preparation and planning of the response, communication of information and monitoring;
3 development of non-binding recommendations and risk management options;
4 ability to mobilise an EU health task force to support local responses in member states;
5 establishment of an EU network of reference laboratories and a network for substances of human origin, such as organs for transplantation, bone marrow or cord blood for transplantation.

European Medicines Agency (EMA)

The Commission stated in relation to EMA:

> The COVID-19 pandemic has shown that EMA lacks a strong system to monitor and mitigate shortages of critical medicines, as well as a solid framework for crisis response. As a result, the Agency's ability to fast track scientific advice, procedures and obligations on Member States and developers has been hampered.[55]

The mandate of the EMA will be strengthened so that it can facilitate a coordinated EU-wide response to health crises mediated by the EMA:

1 monitoring and mitigating the risk of shortages of essential medicines and medical devices;
2 scientific advice on medicines with the potential to treat, prevent or diagnose crisis-causing diseases;
3 coordination of studies to monitor the efficacy and safety of vaccines;
4 coordination of clinical trials.

To strengthen the role of the EMA, it is proposed to set up:

1 a permanent coordination group on medicine shortages;
2 a new permanent coordination group on shortages of medical equipment;
3 a permanent EMA task force on emergencies;
4 new expert panels on medical equipment;
5 a stronger European infrastructure for clinical trials;
6 the creation of a vaccine monitoring platform.

Health Emergency Response Authority (HERA)

According to the Communication from the European Commission:

> The authority's mission will be to enable the EU and its Member States to rapidly deploy the most advanced medical and other measures in the event of a health emergency, by covering the whole value chain from conception to distribution and use. To that effect, it will, for example, undertake horizon scanning and foresight to anticipate specific threats, identify promising potential countermeasures and underpinning competencies, and generate and disseminate knowledge on these. It will monitor and pool production capacity and development facilities, raw material requirements and availability, and ensure that supply chain vulnerabilities are addressed. It will support the development of cross-cutting technologies and solutions sustaining multiple potential future threat responses (e.g. vaccine platform technologies, or the application of digital tools and artificial intelligence) as well as the development of specific countermeasures, including through clinical trials and data infrastructure. It will ensure that sufficient production capacity will be available when necessary, as well as arrangements for stockpiling and distribution. The European authority will plan, co-ordinate, and assemble ecosystems of public and private capabilities that jointly enable a rapid response when the need arises. When an EU health emergency is declared, it will acquire specific additional resources required to adequately react in the interest of all Member States.[56]

In order to achieve the above policy objectives, the Commission assessed different scenarios for HERA with different levels of ambition and complexity[57]: Policy option (0) this option assumes the continuation of ad hoc solutions in the event of a crisis, as seen during Covid-19; Policy option (1) foresees enhanced coordination for threat assessment and knowledge generation based on common commitments and other mechanisms; Policy option (2) envisages the establishment of an autonomous authority with a permanent structure, different degrees of operation and related infrastructures (option(2) includes two sub-options); Policy option (3) envisages the establishment of an end-to-end authority that will also deal with streamlining existing initiatives and funds at EU level to counter serious cross-border health threats.

Currently, the HERA is not a self-standing agency, but a Directorate-General, under the commissioner also in charge of the European Commission.[58]

Health and Digital Executive Agency (HaDEA)

In addition to the actions described above, the Commission established the European Health and Digital Executive Agency (HaDEA) in Decision No. 2021/173 of 12th February 2021.[59] This is an executive agency that until

December 2028 should be dedicated to the implementation of programmes and all health-related activities, including the new EU health programme (EU4Health), the health research intervention axis of Horizon Europe as well as the health components of the single market programme.[60] Some contracts to support HERA are in fact signed by the HaDEA from their own budget.

Notes

1 Lazonick, Hopkins, Jacobson et al., 2017.
2 https://www.who.int/data/gho/data/themes/mortality-and-global-health-estimates
3 OECD, 2017.
4 https://www.statista.com/statistics/309466/global-r-and-d-expenditure-for-pharmaceuticals/
5 https://www.statista.com/topics/1764/global-pharmaceutical-industry/
6 https://www.statista.com/statistics/309471/randd-spending-share-of-top-pharmaceutical-companies/
7 https://www.statista.com/statistics/309297/worldwide-medtech-research-and-development-spending/
8 The data refer to expenditure in 2018 on prescription and self-medication medicines, often referred to as over-the-counter products. It excludes pharmaceuticals consumed in hospitals and other healthcare facilities. Post-pandemic data are higher.
9 Taghreed et al., 2019.
10 Taghreed, Ambinintsoa, Soumya, 2019.
11 Translated from Italian, https://www.corriere.it/salute/malattie_infettive/20_novembre_24/necessita-realizzare-vaccino-tutti-coronavirus-0170b80a-2e47-11eb-9814-5d0b7c9bd2b5.shtml.
12 The ranking according to various sources differs in relation to the criteria used for unbundling diversified activities.
13 https://aswathdamodaran.blogspot.com/search?q=Divergence+in+the+Drug+Businesses%3A+Pharmaceuticals+and+Biotechnology
14 OECD, 2018.
15 Chakravarty et al., 2015.
16 According to OECD (2022), in 2020 there was a significant jump of 15% increase of government budget allocations for R&D (GBARD) for the OECD area (followed in 2021 by a limited decrease of 4.4%) compared to 2020). The available evidence suggest that such increase was driven by public expenditures on R&D for health, which in any case is the sector where the overall increase of yearly budgets has been highest: + 300% in constant PPP USD between 1991 and 2020, a major driver of the 200% increase of total GBARD.
17 https://aspr.hhs.gov/AboutASPR/ProgramOffices/BARDA/Pages/default.aspx
18 Scannell et al., 2012.
19 https://www.statista.com/statistics/280572/medicine-spending-worldwide/; https://www.oecd-ilibrary.org/sites/9789264307391-3-en/index.html?itemId=/content/component/9789264307391-3-en
20 A topic mentioned in a debate on the subject hosted by the *British Medical Journal* in 2020 (Mazzucato, Li, Darzi, 2020).
21 Reflected in the study for the Science and Technology Panel (STOA) of the European Parliament: https://www.europarl.europa.eu/RegData/etudes/STUD/2021/697197/EPRS_STU(2021)697197_EN.pdf
22 According to EFPIA, 9% of the active ingredients come from Asia: https://www.efpia.eu/news-events/the-efpia-view/blog-articles/eu-strategic-resilience-in-phar

maceuticals-global-value-chains-and-innovation/. See also: https://www.fda.gov/news-events/congressional-testimony/safeguarding-pharmaceutical-supply-chains-global-economy-10302019
23 https://www.nature.com/articles/d43747-020-00522-5
24 Dredge, Scholtes, 2021.
25 Bouillon et al., 2015.
26 https://www.apl.se/in-english/about-apl/our-history.html
27 APL is also one of the largest suppliers, on the basis of specific contracts, in the life sciences sector (in the form of a CDMO, Contract Development Manufacturing Organization), particularly in materials required for clinical trials, but also in the development and manufacture of specific drugs. In 2018, it had revenues of 140 million euros and 489 employees with locations in Gothenburg for supply management, logistics, and some preparations; in Umea, for preparations in sterile environment and materials for clinical trials; in Malmö, for preparations in a non-sterile environment; and in Stockholm, for other types of preparations and customer service. It exports to 35 countries.
28 In Italy, there is the Stabilimento Chimico Farmaceutico Militare in Florence, which deals with certain orphan drugs, those of little interest to private pharmaceutical companies, and cannabis for therapeutic use. There are sporadic but insignificant other experiences. Almost everything is left to private industry.
29 Some of whom I recently interviewed as part of the above mentioned study for the European Parliament, Florio et al., 2021.
30 OECD, 2019.
31 https://health.ec.europa.eu/antimicrobial-resistance/research-projects-studies_en
32 https://health.ec.europa.eu/system/files/2020-01/amr_2017_action-plan_0.pdf
33 https://eur-lex.europa.eu/legal-content/EN/TXT/HTML/?uri=CELEX:32013D1082&from=EN
34 https://www.jpiamr.eu/about/
35 Sachs et al., 2022.
36 https://peterhotez.org/
37 https://ec.europa.eu/chafea/index_en.htm
38 https://www.fortunebusinessinsights.com/industry-reports/contract-research-organization-cro-services-market-100864
39 https://www.who.int/about/accountability/budget
40 World Health Organization, 2016.
41 Ferrajoli, 2020.
42 Studies of this kind go beyond the relationship between benefit and risk, because they include the relationship between social benefit and social cost. See Florio, 2019.
43 Examples of instrumentation are genomics and proteomics platforms, cryo-electron microscopy, synchrotron light sources with specialised beamlines for biomedical research, frontier resources for handling very high-intensity data for computational biology, advanced distributed bioinformatics systems, sample biobanks and much more to be managed in the style of large research infrastructures.
44 UNESCO, 2021.
45 Grants by public funds on charities will usually cover small-scale trials.
46 Li, 2017.
47 https://report.nih.gov/funding/categorical-spending#/
48 https://www.who.int/news-room/fact-sheets/detail/dementia
49 Georghiou et al. (2017) mention that

> An analysis of the benefits associated with medical research in terms of reductions in the direct costs of illness due to new drugs and treatments, reduction in indirect costs of illness due to a healthier workforce, and the reduction in

intangible costs due to increases in longevity and better quality of life was estimated to be USD 240 billion, i.e. 15 times the annual investment.

(United States Senate, 2000)

50 Jonas, 2013; GPMB, 2019.
51 Monetary values of a statistical life is provided by several studies in cost–benefit analysis, health economics, and environmental economics (Florio, 2019).
52 https://www.worldbank.org/en/news/feature/2020/06/08/the-global-economic-outlook-during-the-covid-19-pandemic-a-changed-world
53 https://ec.europa.eu/info/sites/default/files/proposal-mandate-european-centre-disease-prevention-control_en.pdf, https://ec.europa.eu/info/sites/default/files/proposal-mandate-european-medicines-agency_en.pdf; https://eur-lex.europa.eu/legal-content/IT/TXT/HTML/?uri=CELEX:52020DC0724&from=EN
54 The ECDC budget 2021 is about Euro 74,7 million (2021). The US CDC budget was about 6.5 billion US USD.
55 European Commission, 11.11.2020 COM(2020) 724 final, p. 4. https://ec.europa.eu/info/sites/default/files/communication-european-health-union-resilience_en.pdf.
56 Communication from the European Commission, Building a European Health Union: Reinforcing the EU's resilience for cross-border health threats, pp. 20–21, https://ec.europa.eu/info/sites/default/files/communication-european-health-union-resilience_en.pdf
57 https://ec.europa.eu/info/law/better-regulation/have-your-say/initiatives/12870-European-Health-Emergency-Preparedness-and-Response-Authority-HERA-_en
58 https://ec.europa.eu/info/departments/health-and-food-safety_en
59 https://eur-lex.europa.eu/legal-content/EN/TXT/HTML/?uri=CELEX:32021D0173&from=EN
60 In addition, the HERA will be responsible for implementing digital programmes to ensure that Europe enters the digital age, including programmes for industry and space.

4 Green Europa

Science and technology for saving the planet

Climate change will have a wide impact on inequality. There are complex interactions between global warming and inequality when considering its different dimensions: political, social, economic, environmental, territorial, cultural, and in terms of access to knowledge.[1]

We can easily identify unidirectional impacts ranging from global warming to scarcity of drinking and irrigation water to threats to food security and the spread of infectious diseases. Other impacts are more complex to analyse and go in the opposite direction: changes in inequality can set in motion conflicts, migration, depopulation of areas, changes in crops, elsewhere excessive anthropogenic pressure, and unsustainable consumption of natural resources. These phenomena can in turn have an impact on the biosphere and trigger cumulative processes. The inequality and the biosphere interact significantly in many ways, given the interconnected nature of social and ecological systems and their large-scale impacts on global environmental change.[2] The warming of the planet is therefore a crucial aspect of inequality and vice versa. The current economic model has an unsustainable impact on climate change, starting with energy production and consumption.

Currently, around 85% of the energy we live on (not including biomass) comes from burning fossil fuels: oil (34%), coal (27%), and gas (24%). The rest comes from nuclear and renewables. We release 9.5 billion tonnes of carbon dioxide (CO_2) and other carbon residues from combustion into the atmosphere annually. In the last 40 years, the atmospheric concentration of CO_2 has risen from around 330 parts per million (ppm) to over 410 ppm. If it were not for this bonfire we build out of the remains of past organic life (and present life when we burn biomass), the natural carbon cycle would be roughly in balance between emission and absorption. This had been the case for thousands of years before the industrial age. We have altered this balance.

Nick Stern (2007), the author of the famous report *The Economics of Climate Change: The Stern Review*, called global warming and its link to the carbon-based economy, the greatest market failure in history. Unfortunately, it is also the greatest failure of public policy on the environment. Conference after conference, governments are only partially succeeding in adopting and

DOI: 10.4324/9781003381532-5

implementing policies that could prevent us from going beyond the 2-degree Celsius temperature increase in the last century, the threshold beyond which experts predict a catastrophic vicious cycle will begin.

A large part of the problem is the lack of international policy coordination when it comes to a public good like the health of the planet. As with human health, much could already be achieved with what we know how to do but fail to implement. But the argument I am making here is that not enough is being invested in scientific and technological research and in the adoption of radically innovative solutions, not only in relation to climate change but more generally to the difficult game of assessing the health of the planet and making it safe, an issue of unparalleled scale and complexity in human history.

Here too, as in the case of biomedical research, existing oligopolies – old and new – such as oil, gas, and electricity companies, the car industry, air and sea transport, multinational agri-food companies, and other polluters are doing their job investing for profit.

Decarbonising the economy and, in general, cleaning up and preserving the environment in which we live would, for some sectors, mean radically changing activities, investing colossal sums in reconversion with current technologies, and possibly jeopardising the bottom line. Similar considerations apply to carbon "capture" technologies downstream of existing processes. In some of these sectors, moreover, the research and development expenditure of most large companies has been gradually decreasing in real terms for at least three decades.

In addition to the political will to tackle the problem, a new player would be needed, given the stated ambitions of the green economy, most recently in the 16 September 2020 State of the Union address by European Commission President Ursula von der Leyen. I propose the creation of a supranational public entity that combines scientific research and development of new technologies with zero or minimal impact on carbon emissions with the implementation of downstream innovations, in agreement with the public sector of the member states and the most far-sighted private and state-owned enterprises. Let us see why such a player is needed.

What's wrong with the planet? And why we don't know enough about the cure

The main facts mentioned in the European Commission's 2019 communication on the Green Deal[3] are simple and at the same time shocking. Year after year, we observe a parallel warming of the atmosphere and changing weather patterns; one million living species are at risk of extinction, more than 10% of those known to us; the remaining natural forests are visibly thinning every year, replaced by areas of lesser biodiversity. The Amazon forest alone absorbs 3% of plant carbon emissions, but since 1970 it has shrunk by an area equivalent to the whole of France, and is still shrinking.

According to the WHO, 90% of the world's population lives in places where air pollution is dangerous, with the effect that – in 2016 alone – 4.2 million people, including 290,000 children, died prematurely from respiratory diseases and millions more suffer from chronic conditions that reduce their quality of life.

The oceans are increasingly polluted by plastics and waste of many kinds. Between now and 2050, the European Union will still contribute to the release of significant quantities of greenhouse gases into the atmosphere, despite their planned reduction; 75% of emissions still come directly from energy production. The goods we import from third countries, as part of a globalisation of trade with inadequate environmental protection rules, are themselves produced with carbon emissions so that the adoption of stringent rules within the Union could be thwarted by the relocation of polluting production elsewhere. Today, there is also a problem of poverty induced by energy consumption because of the price paid by low-income consumers, and this problem is exacerbated by the adoption of renewable technologies whose unit production cost is higher than polluting ones, a cost passed on in the electricity bill.[4]

Industrial processes contribute significantly to environmental problems:

> From 1970 to 2017, the annual global extraction of materials tripled and it continues to grow, posing a major global risk. About half of total greenhouse gas emissions and more than 90% of biodiversity loss and water stress come from resource extraction and processing of materials, fuels and food. The EU's industry has started the shift but still accounts for 20% of the EU's greenhouse gas emissions. It remains too "linear", and dependent on a throughput of new materials extracted, traded and processed into goods, and finally disposed of as waste or emissions. Only 12% of the materials it uses come from recycling.[5]

The interconnections between sectors are significant. A first example concerns construction:

> The construction, use and renovation of buildings require significant amounts of energy and mineral resources (e.g. sand, gravel, cement). Buildings also account for 40% of energy consumed. Today the annual renovation rate of the building stock varies from 0.4 to 1.2% in the Member States. This rate will need at least to double to reach the EU's energy efficiency and climate objectives. In parallel, 50 million consumers struggle to keep their homes adequately warm.[6]

A second example concerns a central aspect of the consumption model of the last century: mobility. Zero-emission mobility, as the Commission proposes, therefore concerns not only the combustion engines of road vehicles but also ships and aircraft:

> Transport accounts for a quarter of the EU's greenhouse gas emissions, and still growing. To achieve climate neutrality, a 90% reduction in transport emissions is needed by 2050. Road, rail, aviation, and waterborne transport will all have to contribute to the reduction. Achieving sustainable transport means putting users first and providing them with more affordable, accessible, healthier and cleaner alternatives to their current mobility habits.[7]

A third issue concerns food production. This entails reducing the use of chemical pesticides, fertilisers, and antibiotics, that is, today's essential ingredients of agricultural production.

A fourth item is related to biodiversity and the protection of natural capital (forests, water bodies, etc.), on which the European Commission admits that several targets that were set were not met in 2020. I will discuss the proposed strategy in the next section, but first I would like to mention the estimates that are made of the investments needed:

> To achieve the ambition set by the European Green Deal, there are significant investment needs. The Commission has estimated that achieving the current 2030 climate and energy targets will require €260 billion of additional annual investment, about 1.5% of 2018 GDP28. This flow of investment will need to be sustained over time. The magnitude of the investment challenge requires mobilising both the public and private sector.[8]

Widening the perspective to a planetary scale, I recall below some other facts and predictions.

Much of the damage that can result from climate change will not come from average atmospheric effects but from their variance, that is, the increased occurrence of extremes, such as intense phenomena, floods or episodes of drought or intense cold. A hurricane can cause 100 billion USD in damage (Harvey in Houston, Texas, August 2017) or kill thousands of people (Puerto Rico, September 2017). It is estimated that with an average temperature increase of more than 2.5 degree Celsius, destructive hurricanes will become frequent in the subtropical belt of the planet. These phenomena, combined with other climatic effects, such as heat waves, will make areas that are now densely populated uninhabitable, not least because of drought and damage to the agriculture currently practised, which is very sensitive to temperature and the pest attacks usually associated with mild winters. All this can lead to mass migrations and conflicts over the control of territories and water bodies. One example: after Lake Aral, which has now practically dried up, the Caspian Sea is also at risk.

One phenomenon that is now certain is the rise in the level of the oceans due to the combined effect of an increase in the temperature of sea water, which then expands; the inflow of water from melting glaciers; and the melting of the polar ice caps. These phenomena are now taking place in front of our eyes, leading to coastal erosion and increased storm surges.

Putting together droughts and crop damage, destructive storms, economic damage from local climate variations, coastal damage, migration, and conflict, the costs of inaction seem very high. If the worst-case scenario of changes in major ocean currents and desertification of vast areas were to occur, the costs would simply be incalculable, because human beings would literally find themselves living on a different planet, one that is altogether more hostile than the one we have known for centuries or perhaps thousands of years, albeit with natural climatic fluctuations.

An example of a knock-on effect is the damage caused to freshwater bodies by saltwater infiltration, which can in principle be remedied by desalination, but this in turn requires energy.

The scale of the energy transition that would be required to achieve the goal of stopping global warming from rising by well below 2 degree Celsius compared to pre-industrial times can only be grasped by thinking historically. According to Smil (2021), between 1850 and 2000, the use of energy by mankind as a whole increased 15-fold. Since the symbolic date of the industrial revolution, James Watt's patent for the steam engine (1769), it took another 130 or 140 years for coal to replace traditional energy sources: human labour, biomass, and animal labour. Even in the 1950s, oil accounted for only 25% of the primary energy required by human activities, while the use of biomass in developing countries has decreased in share but increased in absolute terms. To reach the target I mentioned above, in the next 50 years, 90% of the energy now produced by fossil fuels would have to be replaced by renewable sources, by nuclear power, or by combustion processes with carbon capture.

In the meantime, the population could grow further (depending on the demographic model chosen) by between 1 and 3 billion people by 2100 (up to a total of 10–11 billion). The 800 million people who still burn biomass could increase or, in any case, aspire to be connected to the electricity grid. The required transition would need to be much faster than the centuries-long transition that replaced biomass and human and animal energy with coal, and then coal with oil.

Ultimately, what matters is the comparison of costs (standardised according to plant lifetimes and other elements), which have actually fallen dramatically for renewables over the last ten years: according to some studies,[9] by 87% for solar, by about 60% for wind (more for offshore than onshore). These cost calculations are not easy,[10] but without adequate energy storage, the penetration of renewables cannot progress very far, so the cost should be calculated including the (very significant) costs of investment in energy storage and structural changes to electricity grids.

It is true that in windy areas, wind power could have significant potential for expansion. It may be that solar can expand further, while coal continues to decline (27% of supply in 2018). For example, in Vietnam, which relies mainly on coal (43%), solar played virtually no role until 2017. With a subsidy of 0.09 USD per kWh, 850 MW of solar was expected, but by the end of 2019, 5 GW had been installed, more than in Australia. Within five years, solar could compete with coal in much of Southeast Asia. There is also hope for the hydrogen cycle, mentioned below.

But solar is highly discontinuous, as is wind, not only daily but especially between seasons. The electricity grid would require radical changes to accommodate generation from renewable sources, regardless of their variability.

The key factor is that the new renewable power plants are distributed across the territory according to completely different criteria than fossil fuel and nuclear power plants. Further progress is needed in the various electricity storage technologies, despite significant progress in recent years with lithium batteries. The potential of hydrogen and carbon capture in processes such as cement production and agriculture needs to be further explored.

According to some estimates,[11] between now and 2050, 800 billion USD per year will be needed for investments in renewables, compared to 250 billion USD in 2019. These estimates do not take into account the fact that the energy oligopoly is not sitting on its hands. Oil and gas companies still invest twice as much in fossil fuels (including fracking) as they do in renewables, so the prices they can charge to offset these investments are likely to be aggressive. The big companies in the oil oligopoly, before the 2022 spike, have been hit hard by the pandemic, but also by a trend that began in the years before the price decline (the worst sector in terms of share price performance among those in the S&P 500, an index of the largest 500 listed companies compiled by Standard & Poor's). However, large companies such as ExxonMobil, Chevron, Total, BP, Equinor (Norway), and ENI, thanks to investments and rationalisations in recent years, can make profits at half the prices needed to balance the budget in 2013. Some companies have – somewhat reluctantly – set themselves targets to cut production and emissions in view of more aggressive decarbonisation policies, but with their own timeframes and budget constraints, that is, too slowly.[12]

For example, China is currently home to half of all coal-fired power plants, and although the share of the total is declining, in 2019, the overall capacity grew by 37 GW net of decommissioned plants, with a strong localist push from provincial governments for political reasons, despite the fact that on average only 50% of capacity is used.

Large infrastructure investments have been directed towards China, now the largest importer of oil and gas, including a major pipeline from Siberia and a 20-year agreement with Exxon to supply liquefied gas. Saudi Arabia is stepping up its efforts, including through the use of price discounts, to penetrate the Chinese market. The International Energy Agency (IEA) predicts that, with unchanged policies, demand for fossil fuels will grow by 30%

between 2018 and 2040 without stabilising, although some think tanks are more optimistic (not least because of the pandemic[13]) that it could permanently change some habits, for example by increasing video conferencing and remote working.

Nor can the attitude of the oil-rich countries be ignored. At 2020 prices (around 40 USD for Brent crude) almost all of them were in an unsustainable situation (with the exception of Qatar). They will initially have to run up budget deficits and then drastically cut public spending. Saudi Arabia itself, which has on several occasions deliberately reduced prices to eliminate competition from countries with higher extraction costs, has a "Saudi Vision 2030" of oil diversification. Some producing countries have accumulated large budget surpluses in the past and will be able to hold on for a few years, but the adjustment will be painful for them and for their neighbours on whom they depend for migrant labour. If the governments of these countries resort to tax increases, redundancies, and spending cuts, further political destabilisation cannot be ruled out in areas that are already plagued by civil wars, conflicts between states, and the financing of terrorism. The implications for this situation for oil prices are unclear, if and when the market turmoil of 2022 will end. Governments desperate for cash are unlikely to be able to restrict quantities produced to raise prices in the longer term, and, of course, this is not conducive to the substitution of fossil fuels by alternative sources. On the gas front, the investments in Europe that have been made in the past few years in liquefied gas as an alternative to Russian gas and the new pipelines as an alternative for Russia from its dependence on passing through hostile Ukraine have made the market more diversified, not least because of large-scale storage. However, the demand boom in 2021 and the Russian invasion of Ukraine have created an unexpected price spike, with the spot price of brent oil close to 100 USD per barrel.

Russia still has large reserves and will certainly fight to maintain a large supply. Moreover, in January 2020, the European Parliament voted in favour of 32 new projects in the sector that will be eligible for public funding. The Russian–Ukraine war in 2022 has radically changed the price and supply scenario again, for the worst in terms of sustainability.

We are, therefore, far from a policy framework that is unambiguously geared towards a smooth energy transition. Paradoxically, governments subsidise fossil fuels (by some estimates to the tune of 420 billion a year), spending much more than they do on investments and subsidies for renewables. The history of international agreements is littered with disappointments, from the 1988 Toronto conference, through the first agreement in 1992, to the more recent Paris Agreements. In 1992, the Intergovernmental Panel on Climate Change (IPCC) was created, according to which emissions in 2005 should be 20% lower than in 1988. However, they were 34% higher and in 2017, they were a further 22% higher. In fact, policies have more often been national rather than based on international agreements, despite other conferences such as Rio de Janeiro in 1992 and especially Kyoto in 1997 (including developed countries only and not ratified by the US) and Copenhagen in 2009. In contrast to the successes achieved against chlorofluorocarbons (CFCs), a gas believed to be co-responsible for the ozone hole discovered in 1985 in the Antarctic, but whose production and use were limited to identifiable industrial sources, emissions of CO_2 and other greenhouse gases affect hundreds of thousands of large production units and many millions of smaller units. The economic interests at stake have been effective in combating the energy transition, even financing research and pseudo-science aimed at denying the anthropogenic origin of global warming, or even its existence.[14] This was spectacularly seen with President Trump's decision to withdraw the US from the Paris Agreements (the first to have clearly established targets), a decision fortunately reversed by President Biden in one of his first acts the day after taking office.

It seems certain that even in moderately optimistic scenarios on the adoption of public policies by the end of this century the increase in the planet's temperature could be 3 degree Celsius, an increase that guarantees huge problems of adaptation on a planetary scale. The battle seems to have been lost.

What can be done?

The European Commission's strategy and its limitations

The President of the European Commission Ursula von der Leyen, elected by the European Parliament in July 2019 by a cross-party coalition (European People's Party, Party of European Socialists, Liberals), has a pro-active approach to environmental policies, summarised by the proposal for an ambitious Green Deal. This strategy aims to make the EU the first region in the world with zero greenhouse gas emissions by 2050 and whose growth will not be based on the consumption of natural resources.

After 2020, as a result of the approval of the Next Generation EU budget, the strategy will have more resources than initially planned. Let us look at some aspects.

1 The aim is to reduce net emissions by more than 50% in 2030 and to zero in 2050. This will involve various measures regarding the current Emissions Trading Scheme (ETS) and its possible extension to other sectors. It will also cover changes to land use rules, taxation of energy products, climate change adaptation investments, as well as – to counter relocation – a system that increases the EU border price of imported goods in relation to their carbon content.
2 The European Commission is requesting energy and climate plans from the member states to be assessed by the Commission, starting in 2023. These plans should dedicate ample space to energy from renewable sources, smart grid integration, transnational infrastructure, carbon capture systems, hydrogen networks, and combating energy poverty resulting from socially unsustainable tariffs.
3 The EU's industrial strategy should be based on green and digital transformation. An action plan for the circular economy (still rather nebulous) should be developed. Special attention should be paid to the reconversion

of the steel, chemical, and cement industries. In addition, there will be measures to make resource-intensive industries such as textiles, electronics, construction, and plastics more circular, and a more comprehensive approach to packaging recycling by 2030. There is a proposal to tighten waste regulations, to adopt a strategic plan on the battery value chain, partly in view of the development of electric cars. Finally, the contribution that can come from the digital economy is considered essential: "The Commission will examine measures aimed at ensuring that digital technologies, such as artificial intelligence, G5, cloud and edge computing and the Internet of Things can accelerate and maximise the impact of policies to tackle climate change and protect the environment".[15] Environmental monitoring systems based on the digital economy, environmental compatibility of telecommunication systems, and recycling of mobile phones, tablets, and chargers will be encouraged in the context of the Green Deal.
4 The European Commission intends to take a rigorous approach to assessing the building standards adopted by the member states, particularly with regard to the energy balance of the sector. It also proposes offering incentives for large-scale public and private building renovation projects.
5 With regard to the sustainability of transport, it is proposed to encourage multi-modality and a major shift from road to rail and waterways. The proposal for a single airspace to optimise routes will be relaunched. There is a proposal to revise the pricing and subsidy system to penalise polluting fuels and encourage alternative fuels. There is a plan to extend to the transport sector the CO_2 emission permit trading system already in use in other sectors.
6 In the food sector, "the Commission's proposals for the Common Agricultural Policy for 2021–2027 foresee that at least 40 per cent of the total budget of the Common Agricultural Policy and at least 30 per cent of the Maritime and Fisheries Fund will contribute to climate action".[16] Measures are envisaged that discourage the use of antibiotics, chemical fertilisers and pesticides, and that favour recycling waste and packaging.
7 A biodiversity strategy with quantifiable objectives will be proposed, starting with the Natura 2000 network, a revival of forestry policies and protection of the seas, the so-called "blue economy".
8 The Commission will adopt in 2021 an action plan for zero pollution of air, water, and soil. This objective will call for more effective monitoring and sanction mechanisms, with a particular focus on certain sectors such as chemicals.

In terms of instruments, these can be condensed into two mechanisms: on the one hand, a regulatory role or the issuing of directives to the member states; on the other a direct role for the European Commission. The latter would involve integrating climate objectives into the EU budget (now increased by Next Generation EU), with a minimum of 25% of funds linked to the environmental strategy. The Union's own resources would then be based on a Community share of the revenue from environmental taxation and emissions trading (ETS, discussed below). Thirty per cent of the InvestEU Fund should be oriented towards environmental objectives, and the European Investment Bank should increase the share of projects related to environmental objectives in its lending policy to 50%. Environmental objectives should specifically be found in the various EU funds, such as the ERDF, the ESF, and the Fair Transition Mechanism, in the governance of private companies, in the functioning of financial markets, in national budgets, including by reviewing the structure of taxation and the rules on state aid for investment projects in a "green" direction (encouraging "green" projects).

As mentioned in the previous section, the role of research and innovation appears to be peripheral to the strategy.

The Commission recognises that further knowledge is required and entrusts the task primarily to Horizon Europe, the research support programme:

> New technologies, sustainable solutions and disruptive innovation are critical to achieve the objectives of the European Green Deal. To keep its competitive advantage in clean technologies, the EU needs to increase significantly the large-scale deployment and demonstration of new technologies across sectors and across the single market, building new innovative value chains. This challenge is beyond the means of individual Member States. Horizon Europe, in synergy with other EU programmes, will play a pivotal role in leveraging national public and private investments. At least 35% of the budget of Horizon Europe will fund new solutions for climate, which are relevant for implementing the Green Deal.[17]

At the time the Commission's communication was published (December 2019), it was assumed that Horizon Europe might have a budget of €100 billion (2021–2027). The agreement one year later (December 2020) stands at 95.5 billion at current prices, which includes 5.4 billion from Next Generation EU. This is an increase of 30% (at constant prices) compared to the previous Horizon 2020 programme.

In this framework, the European Commission states that:

> Four "Green Deal Missions" will help deliver large-scale changes in areas such as adaptation to climate change, oceans, cities and soil. These missions will bring together a wide range of stakeholders including regions and citizens. Partnerships with industry and Member States will support research and innovation on transport, including batteries, clean hydrogen, low-carbon steel making, circular bio-based sectors and the built environment. The knowledge and innovation communities run by the European Institute of Innovation and Technology will continue to promote collaboration among higher education

> institutions, research organisations and companies on climate change, sustainable energy, food for the future, and smart, environmentally-friendly and integrated urban transport. The European Innovation Council will dedicate funding, equity investment and business acceleration services to high potential start-ups and SMEs for them to achieve breakthrough Green Deal innovation that can be scaled up rapidly on global markets.[18]

In essence, the impetus should come from internalising the environmental R&D objectives entrusted to funding instruments such as Horizon Europe and bodies such as the European Research Council, the European Innovation Council, the European Institute of Innovation and Technology, and the new Innovation Fund. I will discuss later why this strategy is too fragmented and not fully convincing.

As with other aspects of EU policies, there is an obvious tension between desires and concrete possibilities, which results in making a virtue out of necessity. Without taking into account the extraordinary and therefore non-structural increase of the Next Generation EU, the EU budget is around 1% of the GDP of the member states, about 2% of their public expenditure, two-thirds of which is for agricultural and regional policy, and the rest for competitiveness, administration, policies towards third countries and more. For comparison: in Germany the central government budget is 60% of total public expenditure despite the federal form of the state, in the USA it is over 50%. In other countries where the regions have a lot of weight, such as Spain, Belgium, and Austria, the central government has well over 50%.

In this sense, the European Union's own resources that can be deployed for the environment are minuscule, far less than those of individual states. Hence the emphasis on regulatory aspects, on which the Union has undoubtedly had important successes in the past, for example in setting limits on car emissions, the management of solid urban waste in landfills, the pollution thresholds allowed for industry and many other fields. The results have been more controversial in the field of the Emissions Trading Scheme (ETS), which sets a cap (decreasing over time) on the amount of greenhouse gases that can be emitted by certain industrial plants and sectors, and then allows trading of these unused permits by those who have met their targets. The system started in 2005, is currently the most extensive in the world and effectively sets a "market" price for CO_2.[19]

In 2020, the reduction in emissions will be 21% compared to 2005 and is expected to be 43% in 2030 (a limit that the European Commission wants to raise by at least ten points). In this regard, the results are apparently quite good, but it is not entirely clear to what extent the downward trend in emissions (not only of carbon dioxide but also of other greenhouse gases) is due to the ETS or would not have occurred anyway due to a number of other circumstances, in particular, the century-long downward trend in the energy intensity of industrial products, a phenomenon that was clearly visible even before 2005, the change in the mix of sources in electricity production, the effect of other types of regulatory constraints or even simply the increasing tertiarisation associated with the relocation of manufacturing activities outside the EU. Indeed, since the 1970s, the correlation between economic growth and energy consumption has ceased to be significant.

The idea that you can do a lot with the "price" of carbon is one that most economists like. The Pigou tax to correct environmental externalities is taught, and I also teach it to students as a simple mechanism to change firms' incentives. The idea of making private agents internalise the social costs of pollution so that they adjust their behaviour accordingly is not wrong, but – for it to work – how high should the corrective tax be? Currently, only 20% of the world's emissions are taxed. According to Nick Stern and Joseph Stiglitz (2017), the carbon price had to be set immediately and structurally between 40 and 80 USD per tonne and on all emissions. Others say it should go up to 100 USD by 2030.[20] The median price is currently 15 USD in non-EU countries where these schemes are in place and 6 USD or lower in many countries. Increases are expected, and before the pandemic, a UN ETS scheme for 70% of aviation emissions was due to have been implemented. China has launched its own scheme. However, the pandemic has forced some countries to postpone or dilute these programmes.

In general, progress is most relevant when there are clear technological alternatives, for example, combined-cycle gas technology, which can efficiently replace coal in electricity production and at the same time reduce emissions.

In the automotive sector, despite high fuel taxes, the lack of alternatives has in fact curtailed demand at the pre-tax price. In any case, resistance from entrenched interests has to be overcome, especially if, as in the Commission's proposal, the ETS scheme were to be extended to transport in general, maritime traffic, and heating of buildings. Various solutions have been imagined to "purchase" consensuses, such as creating funds for reforestation, paying a tax dividend to citizens, or others. But the most serious problem is the relocation of entire production chains since it is unthinkable to imagine a global ETS market. The Commission's proposal for a carbon border adjustment tax mechanism (a duty that is de facto proportional to the significant amount of carbon in goods) would probably give rise to international disputes, for example, with China, which would be difficult to manage, even if US president Joe Biden were to introduce a regulation along the same lines. It is easy to imagine the bureaucratic muddle and cheating that would arise if all goods were subject to a customs declaration of carbon content.

Moreover, as I said, the Green Deal strategy has limited direct firepower in terms of EU public spending and can only rely essentially on regulatory instruments. These instruments in turn may or may not be effective, but – as we have seen transparently in the USA with the Trump presidency – they are an easy target for powerful lobbies that base their profits on a traditional production model.

Although less strong today than in the past, especially in relative terms, oil and gas companies are still part of the scene, remaining at the top of the world ranking of companies by market value. The broader energy sector also includes electricity and gas transmission and distribution companies, which have huge past investments to pay back. At least two other major sectors are tied to a traditional industrial paradigm: transport, including cars, and a large part of chemistry and metallurgy. Other sectors mentioned in the EU Green Deal, such as agriculture and construction, however readily they might respond to fiscal and other incentives, are overall conservative, politically influential and have a problematic relationship with environmental policies. Subsidies in the EU to fossil fuels amounted to 56 billion euros (2019),[21] a figure which is higher than the revenues of carbon taxes. Once more, subsidies to fossil fuels in the world amount to as much as 423 billion euros per year.[22]

Above all, the Green Deal strategy should be measured according to what it proposes: on the one hand, combating climate change, and on the other hand, combating the depletion of natural resources.

In terms of the first item, the consensus around setting a limit of 2 degree Celsius on the increase in the average temperature of the planet already poses an extremely difficult target to achieve. During the 20th century, and especially since the 1950s, the average temperature (with large geographical differences) has risen by 0.6–0.9 degree Celsius. The increase is expected to be 2–6 degree Celsius in the 21st century (compared to the beginning of the last century). Against this background, it is unclear to what extent EU policy could make a global contribution to stabilising the planet's temperature. The phenomenon of temperature increase due directly or indirectly to human activity is certainly related to a complex set of interacting factors. Without a radical break from the prevailing technological model and the economic factors that determine it, the Commission's strategy risks being only marginally useful if viewed from a global perspective, which is only relevant because climate change, like the current pandemic, does not respect political boundaries.

Secondly, the decrease of anthropogenic pressure on natural resources is also linked to the abandonment of production and consumption patterns that can hardly be achieved by mere marginal incentives and disincentives. Much could be done with good environmental education, but who can truly make the calculation of the natural resources used by a smartphone? Who can ultimately calculate the impact on the planet's resources of switching from a petrol car to an electric car? One can only ask what contribution the Green Deal can make to a circular economy if one does the maths against a benchmark, otherwise, one is left in the realm of laudable intentions, which however – if essentially perceived as prohibitions and costs by producers and consumers – can contribute to fuelling populist and neo-nationalist reactions, as is clearly visible in Trump's USA.

From this dual perspective, only a radical paradigm shift in science, technology, and consequently socio-economics can rise to the challenge. And so, one comes to ask whether European institutions could not play their cards better.

To put what the European Commission is proposing into perspective, consider Chinese President Xi Jinping's similar announcement (22 September 2020) that he wants to stabilise carbon emissions in 2030 and make China net-zero in 2060.[23] The goal for China is much more difficult, as its annual CO_2 emissions in recent years have hovered around 10 billion (for comparison, US emissions are around 5 billion).

In contrast, the EU target for 2050 seems to be formulated in terms of carbon-neutrality. Certainly in relative terms, the Chinese contribution would be large and would lead to a revision of the forecasts until 2100, which, according to various models, would – if the commitments of the Paris Agreement sub-writers were fulfilled – still lead to a temperature increase of 2.7 degree Celsius above the pre-industrial reference average.

This trend remains catastrophic according to many experts. Should China keep its commitment, the trend could be mitigated by 0.2–0.3 degree Celsius, still too little. If Biden were to concretely reverse the US position and the EU were to seriously play its part, between 2050 and 2060 the three areas responsible for 45% of emissions would finally be synchronised and the goal of keeping warming below 2% would be within reach.

However, it is necessary to reflect on the trends. As mentioned above, the EU stabilised CO_2 emissions around 1990 and has since reduced the amount emitted by 21%. The US peaked around 2005–2007 and has since reduced by 14%, on a much slower trajectory than the EU. China would have to do much better than both Europe and the US to reduce net emissions to zero. To achieve this, among other things, China would have to decarbonise electricity production, which is still 60% dependent on coal, while continuing to invest in the sector. Even if nuclear energy were to be used on a large-scale, many experts believe that this would still require carbon capture technologies that are not yet available on the necessary scale. Cutting emissions from the transport and industrial sectors would also require technologies that do not yet exist.

This seems to me the key point of the whole policy. The greatest contribution that Europe could make to the health of the planet is not only, and not even, to set goals on its own territory, but to create and donate to the world the scientific and technological knowledge necessary for the transition. The necessary research and innovation are more likely to be catalysed in the European Union than elsewhere. The whole European strategy would be of little use if China, India, and other countries failed.

The emphasis for the Union should be on the creation of public knowledge for the planetary ecological transition, fostering equal access to new "green" technologies.

According to the estimates of the Stern Review and others, 2.5% of the world's GDP (i.e., over 2 trillion USD) would need to be invested *annually* to contain and adapt to climate change.

The Economist convincingly writes that such a colossal mobilisation requires two levers: political and technological. The first is risky because of the strength of the hostile interests at stake (as seen in Trump's US). The other lever seems relatively more promising:

> In technology, progress will come from putting large amounts in well-chosen areas outside the mainstream. There is little point in ploughing money into solar and wind power, or electric vehicles. Better to focus on taking the risk out of things which the world needs but markets will not yet invest in. Building full-scale pilot plants for emissions-free steel-smelting and concrete-making would be helpful. So, too, would creating farms that maximise both crop yields and carbon storage, becoming sinks for greenhouse gases instead of sources.[24]

These three examples are not necessarily the right ones, but the logic is flawless. It is to focus on the demonstration effect that new technologies, that are potentially competitive, could have in disrupting and displacing old ones, but on which investors do not invest because they are too risky or are too long-term. Let us look at a few examples.

The role of cutting-edge research and innovation

One could therefore ask what progress in knowledge is needed to finally tip the scales in the direction of a green transformation of the economy.

Again, to be clear: good results can certainly be achieved by incentivising energy saving in some way, for example, greater use of renewables, and even through more conscious consumer behaviour. Even in Texas, the US oil state par excellence, 20% of electricity needs are met by Danish-made wind turbines. However, the social cost of subsidies, especially in the form of tax credits or preferential tariffs, cannot be underestimated. In the long run, this is not the solution.

Stabilising the global warming phenomenon, if it succeeds, would be a global public good, but the world does not seem to be on course to meet the challenge at all, despite the fact that in recent years CO_2 emissions from energy production (electricity, heating, transport) have, according to IEA (2021), stabilised at 33.3 billion tonnes, thanks to the decline in the use of coal. But only 20 years ago, emissions were 30% lower. It is by no means certain that when the pandemic and the Russia–Ukraine war are over, there will be no new increase. A break is needed, which can only come, as has happened in other fields, from a leap in scientific and technological knowledge. According to Mairate (2023):

> In its World Energy Outlook (2021), the International Energy Agency shows that the transition to cleaner energy sources is occurring at a rapid pace, but it also highlights that it is still not aligned to a path that would stabilize global temperature increases at 1.5°C and achieve other

> energy-related sustainable-development goals. Current technologies do provide solutions to decarbonise the economy at the required pace between now and 2030. However in 2050, "almost half the reductions in CO_2 emissions will come from technologies that are currently only at the demonstration or prototype phase. [...] The emerging "cleantech" sector could provide substantial scope for innovation-driven economic growth. In the EU, clean tech investment in venture capital has doubled in 2021, thereby closing the gap with the US but bringing it to scale will be difficult and rely on EU policy to accelerate the green transition. Despite these opportunities, current levels of energy R&D remains very low compared to other sectors such as defence, health or space exploration. Public R&D spending on energy is also minimal compared with the deployment of renewable energy, although the latter can stimulate private innovation and bring down production costs.

The latter issue is, in my opinion, critically important.

Here are a few examples, entirely illustrative, and not necessarily in order of relevance of potential disruptive change.

a *Nuclear fusion.* For decades, the idea of replicating on earth the process that generates the energy released by the sun (instead of using the energy that comes to us naturally by exploiting the photoelectric effect) has been the "holy grail" of the planet's most advanced energy efficiency research. Unlike controlled nuclear fission technology, which has been used for decades to produce electricity, this does not involve "breaking" atoms, but "fusing" them. The most widely studied reaction is the deuterium–tritium reaction (hydrogen isotopes fusing to form helium). As a side effect, this reaction produces fast neutrons and makes the reactor components radioactive, but on the other hand, it produces much less waste than nuclear fission reactors (and zero greenhouse gas emissions). Another reaction, which constitutes a strategic goal, is the deuterium–deuterium reaction, which requires more activation energy, but does not produce any neutrons. With this reaction, there would be no creation of radioactivity. The technological challenges of creating confinement – magnetic or inertial – of the fusion plasma to "crush" the atoms against each other are formidable. The ITER (International Thermonuclear Experimental Reactor) project, conceived in 1985, with 35 participating countries, including the European Union, the USA, Russia, China, Japan, Korea, and India, and under construction in France, has revised its investment costs and start-up times several times, moreover with the objective of creating a positive balance between energy produced and used, but not of generating electricity (the objective of the later DEMO project). In 2018, the construction cost was estimated at 22 billion USD, but the US Department of Energy, which contributes to the project, made public its own estimate of 65 billion (disputed by ITER management). The completion date was moved to 2035, with initial experiments in 2025. In turn, the DEMO project will not succeed in producing electricity at competitive costs, but only in demonstrating the feasibility of the technology. In essence, although fusion power generation could be the ultimate solution to the energy transition problem, we will not know for several decades whether this path will lead to cost-effective solutions. This time horizon is too long in comparison to the urgent need to keep global warming below the 2-degree Celsius threshold, beyond which irreversible planetary damage is created. We must therefore continue with ITER and DEMO, but in the meantime, more is needed, and quickly.

b *Hydrogen*. Much shorter-term hopes lie in hydrogen technology. Since hydrogen as such is not available in nature, it has to be produced, but if in turn it is efficiently produced from renewable sources, it would allow energy to be stored and transported while limiting greenhouse gas emissions. Fuel cells exploit electrochemical reactions. In this case, the scientific and technological principles are known, but the main limitation is the cost of producing the batteries or, for large-scale systems, the cost of the infrastructure for transporting hydrogen, although, to some extent, the infrastructure used for transporting methane could be converted. Hydrogen is considered by some to be most promising for motor vehicles and trains, but the decisive application would be the possibility of storing energy in a way that complements renewable sources such as wind or solar power. As we know, the problem with these sources is their unpredictable variability (or the fact they cannot be planned), whereas an autonomous hydrogen system could be designed with electrolysers, hydrogen storage, fuel cells, and batteries, which would be activated when required, with the system being powered by these intermittent sources when in operation and discharged when not in use. The abundance of hydrogen in nature in the form of compounds and the possibility of extracting it with a variety of energy sources leads to the hypothesis that we could finally abandon fossil fuels for a hydrogen economy with either large, centralised generators or decentralised fuel cells. What has hitherto slowed down the use of hydrogen is the question of its efficient conversion into electricity, since direct use in endothermic engines, as is done with methane, has never been considered feasible. Safe storage and transport seem more solvable problems, but research should focus on the development of efficient and economical hydrogen fuel cells.

c *Photovoltaics*. The technology has a long history, starting in the 1950s at Bell Laboratories. The efficiency was relatively low (6%), the cost of the panels was initially very high and the only customer willing to pay was NASA for use in satellites, as there were practically no alternatives. The main factor in the current increase in the use of photovoltaics, especially on a small scale, is the drastic reduction in the price of panels rather than the improvement in their efficiency. This limits large-scale applications. Today, efficiency is around 17–20%, but the physical principle has remained the same as it was 70 years ago: two sheets of ultra-pure silicon, suitably "doped" to make them semiconductors. Apart from that, the physics is the same as that of various contributions in the 19th century, with a new theoretical interpretation by Einstein of the photoelectric effect in the 1905 article that won him the Nobel Prize, and a vast strand of subsequent studies. Current applied research concerns the use of other elements instead of silicon, such as aluminium, gallium, indium, phosphorus, and arsenic. In satellites, gallium is generally used. In the laboratory, using a mixture of elements and processes, an overall efficiency of 47.1 % has been achieved.[25] The efficiency of these cells increases if sunlight is concentrated with mirrors or lenses. Other materials are certain types of perovskites, which were tested by OxfordPV on the basis of research conducted at that university (efficiency of 28%) and a plant under construction in Germany. In this case, it would also be possible to work with fairly low light intensities such as domestic light (studies at Tor Vergata University and Fraunhofer Dresden) with an efficiency of 22.6%. The pandemic lockdowns revealed that if the skies are clean due to less pollution, electricity production from photovoltaic cells can increase significantly. In Germany, for example, in one week in April 2020 (due to the partial lockdown) it reached 23% of the total, compared to an average of 8% in 2019. The technology could therefore be favoured by advances in other fields, triggering a virtuous circle: less pollution, more solar, less pollution. This requires further research, not least because some pollutants actually have protective screen functions and reducing them may be desirable in some ways, but in other ways may make warming worse.

d *Electrical networks*. Until the viability of economically and universally producing electricity from nuclear fusion is proven (perhaps by the end of this century), realistically, in the coming decades, electricity will be produced from a variety of sources in both decentralised and centralised systems, both intermittent and continuous. The grid of the future is "smart", capable of fine balancing in real time with a greater speed of response than what current dispatching systems have been doing for decades to balance supply and demand. An intelligent grid requires that information in time and space is exchanged between nodes. In practice, this requires an ICT (Information and Communication Technology) infrastructure to be integrated into the grid, and there are several possible solutions in this regard. The electrical infrastructure could in turn be made dramatically more efficient, particularly in terms of energy dissipation, if superconductivity could be used in the transmission of current. It is known that electrical resistance becomes zero with certain materials maintained at extremely low temperatures. The technology underlies the magnets in use in particle colliders such as the LHC but also, with much lower field strengths, in nuclear magnetic resonance imaging in hospitals. So far there are only a few local power line experiments, but the research is ongoing because the key issue concerns how to achieve the effect at room temperature.

e *Batteries*. Currently, an electric car can cover more than 300 km before needing a recharge and this distance is sufficient for many daily activities, but not for all, and it is thus not conducive to the adoption of a new type of propulsion that would contribute to the reduction of urban pollution. The batteries that changed the scene are the lithium-ion batteries with liquid electrolyte, introduced by Sony in 1991. Their modern version has a capacity of over 200 W per kg and is critically dependent not so much on lithium, which is abundant, but on cobalt, which mostly comes from mines in Congo. There are alternatives to using nickel and manganese. The price of lithium batteries has fallen sharply, from 1160 USD per kg in 2010 to below the 100 expected by 2024. This seems to be the threshold to make electric cars truly competitive. This could also be achieved with further studies at Samsung, which uses a solid electrolyte consisting of silver, germanium, and sulphur, offering more than double the capacity of current models and a corresponding increase in the vehicle's range. However, the technological problems of large-scale production seem far from resolved due to the required characteristics of the solid electrolyte (a special polymer or ceramic material). The other problem with the development of electric cars is the widespread infrastructure for recharging batteries. The solutions are manifold and deserve to be the subject of extensive research and development.

f *Transport*. The recent jump in Tesla's market value would say that financial investors are "voting" for the future of the electric car. Volkswagen will invest 60 billion euros between 2020 and 2025 in the electric car and other technologies, although consumer response is uncertain. In China, the government has heavily subsidised electric vehicles and consumer response has been good. In general, further mergers are expected after the one between FCA and Peugeot-Citroën, so that ultimately the key choices are in the hands of an increasingly concentrated automotive oligopoly. While vehicle manufacturers may be interested in, or at least incentivised to, a change of propulsion system, they cannot be asked to imagine logistics that minimise the need to transport people and things, replacing physical movement with data. We have discovered with the pandemic that certainly not all, but many work and study activities can be carried out remotely, albeit in an inconvenient and in many ways qualitatively inferior way. This is partly due to the fact that ICT technologies were unprepared to handle the traffic of hundreds of millions of people using remote communication systems. This is also true for 3D printing, which could allow certain types of artefacts to be produced where, and in the quantities, needed, instead of moving millions of containers of objects by sea, sky, and land, burning both fuel and time.

g *Earth observation*. Satellites, originally developed for military applications, can observe how the planet is changing in real time. Just one example among many: the research organisation TRASE observed the retail production chains of 5570 municipalities in Brazil, tracking the likelihood not only of illegal deforestation but also the production processes that rely on illegally deforested areas, including animal husbandry and soya cultivation, even in distant locations. It could be seen that 95% of the tree felling for soya production in Mato Grosso between 2012 and 2017 was illegal. It was thus revealed how much of the multinational soya companies' production comes from a supply chain that uses illegally logged areas, despite what the companies themselves claim. The European Union with the European Space Agency is engaged in the Copernicus programme with its Sentinels, a fleet of earth observation satellites, providing detailed and continuous information on the state of the planet. The problems in this field are mainly the under-use of data, even when it is freely accessible, due to the difficulty for public administrations to process the data themselves, which is by no means always trivial. Information Technology (IT solutions) and research on data integration from different sources are needed. More generally, satellite earth observation could be fundamental for monitoring a broad class of environmental risks, including natural ones (such as volcanic eruptions), as well as anthropogenic ones (such as methane emissions and nuclear weapons tests). In addition to satellites, some projects aim to use the atmosphere as a large sensor by exploiting the movements of free electrons in the ionosphere, observed by instruments on earth, which can see the waves created when destructive natural phenomena, such as hurricanes, earthquakes, and eruptions, as well as man-made ones such as nuclear explosions, missile launches, and other military activities, occur on the earth's surface. The AtmoSense project, funded by DARPA – the agency famous for supporting the birth of the Internet and much more – aims to exploit certain physical properties that transmit signals from the earth to the ionosphere and from the ionosphere back to the earth.

h *Negative emissions*. According to some simulation models,[26] there is considerable inertia, combined with natural climate variability (such as cyclical El Niño). In practice, improvements may take a long time to manifest themselves: if CO_2 were reduced by 5% per year from now, there would only be a statistically significant effect on the planet's temperature in 2044. A reduction in emissions was only achieved in 2020 with the pandemic, otherwise, the trend is still upwards, not downwards. The underlying reason for inertia is that it takes decades, if not centuries, to fix the excess carbon already emitted and for heat exchange between the oceans and the atmosphere to take place. Furthermore, interactions between various types of emissions, for example, those from methane and sulphur compounds, can complicate the transition. This may justify investing in research into technologies that generate negative emissions, either as a side effect or as a main effect. Thus going beyond carbon capture towards carbon-free processes. The way forward is reforestation, but on an unprecedented scale, which also requires a leap in understanding how to manage the planet's green canopy. The first model of the impact of greenhouse gases on temperature dates back to Arrhenius' studies in around 1850. His equations predicted that doubling the level of CO_2 in the atmosphere would warm the planet by 5 degree Celsius. One hundred years later, a computer was programmed for the first time to solve climate models. Climate models divide the atmosphere into millions of cells and study the centuries-long evolution of the atmosphere using probabilistic approaches. A prediction comparison exercise on 56 models carried out in 2013 by the Coupled Model Intercomparison Project[27] predicted that a doubling of CO_2 would generate a warming of 1.5–4.5 degree Celsius, that is, with a large uncertainty. The models needed should combine ocean dynamics, atmospheric dynamics, and anthropogenic and biological scenarios, with complex feedback effects. This requires more advanced calculation tools than the currently available, as well as a myriad of standardised observations repeated over time. Without more accurate modelling, public policies risk making inappropriate choices either way, depending on which hypothetical scenario is adopted. This is another important field of research. Moreover, given that weather conditions in the coming decades will favour extreme phenomena, it is necessary to develop not only observation technologies but also forecasting technologies that require complex weather models, which must then be followed by effectively managed procedures. This requires communication systems that reach individuals and organisations in good time, but also protective systems that can be quickly activated. According to the Global Commission on Adaptation,[28] a non-governmental organisation, the risk by 2050 of disruption of water supplies, loss of crops, and thus disruption of the food chain – which would have to increase production by 50% in 30 years to cope with population growth and per capita income – is inevitable unless we find ways adapt (e.g., with types of crops that are more resistant to changes in temperature, salinity, and precipitation). Large-scale investments are needed. A UN Environment Programme estimate suggests a need for between 130–300 billion USD per year over the next decade; these investments in turn require new scientific and technological studies, which are anything but trivial (as the example of the MOSE flood barriers in Venice shows).

These eight examples suggest that a broad range of scientific and technological advances are needed to win the game. They are far from exhaustive. Technological change in transport, steel, and construction materials, CO_2 capture, environmental sustainability of the food chain, and alternative manufacturing processes in some of the other areas I have mentioned, are other examples that are often discussed, and there may be others yet to be explored because they are only at the basic research stage. The key point is that we should not subsidise with public funds the solutions that are relatively more expensive than polluting alternatives, as is partly happening with some of the renewables, but we need to introduce new "green" technologies that displace the old ones because they are inherently cheaper.

The role of the European Union and a proposal

How can we sustain a scientific and technological leap that literally changes the world and does it in time? The European Commission's approach, although it sets out significant goals and identifies various instruments to achieve them, does not yet seem adequate for two reasons.

First of all, the use of competitive bidding mechanisms under Horizon Europe is essentially a scheme to offer non-reimbursable grants to groups of researchers, modelled on the previous Horizon 2020, albeit with a statement of strategic missions. This is primarily a question of scale. Horizon Europe and mechanisms, such as the calls of the European Innovation Council and, even more so, the European Research Council, have a budget and funding arrangements, which are essentially aimed at individual groups of researchers.

Such schemes fail to generate projects that range from basic research to the development, not only of experimental prototypes but also of radical innovations that change technologies adopted on a large-scale with global demonstration effects. These results can hardly be achieved with the typical system of calls for tenders that put up resources in the order of a few million euros, spread over several years. In fact, these tenders typically attract consortia of universities and research institutes and only occasionally companies. In turn, these research consortia only rarely give rise to permanent organisations with a public mission. In fact, the EU offers non-reimbursable contributions to the budgets of universities and other institutes with their own strategies and projects, which are chronically in need of funding. At best, EU funds, therefore, help to accelerate certain studies or to carry them out better and involve more people. To put it bluntly, they are not oriented by strategic missions: they do not "send people to the moon", they do not sequence the human genome for the first time, they do not give rise to projects that radically change scientific and technological knowledge by demonstrating that something can be done on a large-scale. The fact that the new Horizon Europe programme has thematic missions, including the fight against climate change, does not seem sufficient to correct this defect, because these missions are defined in terms that are too broad.

Secondly, although the systems for awarding funds are competitive, with peer review systems by panels of experts, the vagueness of the missions has an impact on the actual choices, which award scores on a series of characteristics of the projects that also end up rewarding the good packaging of the projects, the reputation of the participants and various other collateral aspects that ultimately do not enter into the merits of what is proposed, or at least not in the same way that an organisation with a mission to be accomplished within a certain timeframe would. When envisaged, the negotiation phase hardly has a role, simply because those who manage it on behalf of the European Commission do not have this mandate. *Funding* research by third parties is not the same as *commissioning* research by third parties.

In general, European institutions have a tendency to disperse resources in a plurality of initiatives and organisations that are not likely to have the critical mass necessary to achieve the programmatic objectives within their missions. For example, the European Institute of Technology and Innovation (EIT), created within the framework of Horizon 2020, based in Budapest, also has competences in the fields of energy and the environment. The name of this institute is ambitious, but an examination of its mandate, structure, and budget reveals certain limitations. The EIT states its mission in general terms: "Increase Europe's competitiveness, its sustainable economic growth and job creation by promoting and strengthening cooperation among leading business, education and research organisations".[29]

As can be seen, the emphasis is on cooperation between stakeholders and the creation of an environment that stimulates innovation. For 2021, the EIT Strategic Innovation Agenda included the following themes:

a increase the regional impact of Knowledge and Innovation Communities (KICs), which should involve universities, enterprises, and research institutes;
b stimulate the innovative capacity of universities: it is stated that it wants to support 750 institutions, especially in countries with less innovative capacity;
c launch new KICs, and the first example mentioned concerns the culture and creativity industries.

Climate-KIC[30] is presented as having the objective of accelerating the transition to a zero-carbon economy in 2050. This community comprises more than 370 partners including universities, cities, large companies and SMEs, and non-governmental organisations. Focal areas include cities, sustainable production systems, decision-making metrics and finance, and sustainable land use, which in turn are broken down into programmes: in-depth demonstrations, transformative capital, education, research, and innovation (along the lines of the knowledge helix, which envisages "knowledge flows between governments, academia, industry, civil society"). The EIT claims to have achieved the following results so far: more than 550 million euros of investment in more than 1000 innovative start-ups; creation of more than 2000 full-time jobs; 3.4 billion euros leverage on investments; 367 new products and services; 25 climate impact assessments, with an estimated reduction of 911,000 tonnes of CO_2.[31]

Perhaps all of this makes sense in terms of creating collaborative relationships between different European organisations, so that at least some of the hundreds of organisations involved in some way may have improved their capabilities.

The EIT's financial model, with a 2014–2020 budget of 2.4 billion euros, provides for an average contribution to projects of 25%, which in some cases can reach 100%. Given that there are a dozen KICs (there is also one on the subject of energy) and each of these can involve hundreds of actors and dozens of projects, it seems clear that the average annual funding that reaches the individual participant is not such as to have a significant effect. As for the possibility of a multiplying effect through financial "leverage" and a demonstrative follow-up, it is too early to draw conclusions, but the impression from reading the documents is that this type of initiative is more useful for raising awareness on issues rather than for radically changing knowledge and shifting the scientific and technological frontier.

The ambitions of the European Innovation Council (EIC), also part of Horizon Europe, seem greater, pointing to identifying and supporting radically innovative and game-changing technologies with the potential for ever-wider international applications and to become market leaders; 70% of the entire budget is allocated to small and medium-sized enterprises.[32]

The cumulative budget available in the years 2018–2020 is in the order of 3 billion euros, which is significantly more than the EIT's budget (the two organisations also aim to collaborate). The system is again that of calls for proposals. For example, on the topic of "radically innovative technologies for zero-emission power generation for full decarbonisation", the Commission will consider proposals requesting a contribution of EU funds of up to 4 million euros for a duration of up to four years (with some flexibility on amounts and duration).

The priority allocation to SMEs and the amount considered reveals, as in the case of the EIT, an orientation that is not exclusively focused on the target, nevertheless with amounts and procedures that envisage relatively small-scale R&D activities.

The work of the European Environment Agency, headquartered in Copenhagen, with a budget of approximately 54 million euros in 2029, and a staff of 200, does not seem to be integrated with the monitoring of the results of these activities. This agency has existed for 30 years, with informational tasks:

> The European Environment Agency (EEA) is an agency of the European Union, whose task is to provide sound, independent information on the environment. The EEA aims to support sustainable development by helping to achieve significant and measurable improvement in Europe's environment, through the provision of timely, targeted, relevant and reliable information to policymaking agents and the public.[33]

For this activity, it cooperates with Elionet, a network of observation points in 32 countries, hence including non-EU members. A specific role in the Union's innovation strategy is not mentioned.

On a different scale and timeframe, as I mentioned earlier, there are more long-term large projects such as ITER for nuclear fusion, but also a number of scientific projects (e.g., at CERN and elsewhere) that could be relevant to the goal, partly with other funding channels, both European and national (such as Fraunhofer in Germany). Furthermore, the orientation of the EIB, the world's largest investment bank, which will devote a large part of its future project portfolio to the environment in a broad sense, cannot be overlooked. But there are no effective coordination mechanisms for the various instruments.

DG Climate, the Directorate-General for Climate Action, is maybe one place where we can obtain an overview of what is being done in the European Union to move towards the ambitious targets set by the Commission for 2030 and 2050 respectively. It has a staff of about 220 people and its main policy mission concerns greenhouse gas emissions and the ozone layer, with a particular emphasis on the European ETS, its national implications, international negotiations, but also the promotion of technological change. Its main instrument is the Innovation Fund, whose legal basis dates back to a 2003 directive.[34]

The fund will presumably be endowed with 10 billion euros for the period 2020–2030 for the commercial demonstration of innovative projects in the field of low-carbon technologies in four fields: energy-intensive industries, renewable energy sources, energy storage, and carbon capture, use, and storage. The fund is financed with revenues from the auctioning of emission rights and will allocate grant funding on the basis of calls for tenders. It is proposed to focus on highly innovative technologies and large flagship projects that can lead to significant emission reductions in Europe. It is proposed to share the risk with project promoters to help obtain highly innovative projects with demonstration effects in all eligible sectors in the EU, Norway, and Iceland, which have adequate maturity in terms of planning, business model, and legal and financial structure. Small-scale projects with a capital cost of less than 7.5 million euros may also be considered, and 30 were selected at the end of 2021, with average funding of 3.6 million.

Given that the first announcement was in July 2020, only at the end of 2021 it was known, after a two-stage process, which of the 70 projects selected for the first stage was eventually selected, on which topics and with what funding. Here, the resources at stake and the funding mechanisms seem more promising.

With this in mind, let us take a closer look at how the Innovation Fund works. The management of the fund is entrusted to CINEA (European Climate Infrastructure and Environment Executive Agency),[35] an agency of the European Commission that also manages calls in other sectors, in particular, in the trans-European transport networks. The Innovation Fund will provide up to 60% of the capital and operating costs of large projects and up to 60% of the capital costs of smaller projects. Grants will be disbursed flexibly according to progress made during the project's life cycle. INEA will decide on advances, provide support for applications, manage calls for proposals and evaluations, be responsible for signing contracts, disburse grants, monitor project management, including ex post, provide technical support, ensure initiatives to make results visible, and report regularly to the

Commission. In turn, the EIB will contribute with technical support and possible loans. Grants from the Innovation Fund will not be considered as state aid, which is a very important point from the point of view of EU law, and can be combined with private capital and funds from other channels, such as InnovFin Energy Demo Projects, Connecting Europe Facility (subsidies for infrastructures including telecommunications), Horizon 2020 and Horizon Europe, InvestEU (financing also with venture capital), Modernisation Fund, Just Transition Fund, and Enhanced European Innovation Council (EIC).

As can be seen, there is no shortage of Community instruments and initiatives at the scientific and technological level, some with a long history behind them, such as ITER and Horizon Europe, and others as recent as Innovation Fund. What seems to be missing is an organisation that assumes as its sole mission that of meeting the scientific and technological challenge of climate change, and thus of the energy transition and the environmental sustainability of production and consumption processes, a mission against which to measure its own success and failure with a vision that extends from Europe to the entire planet, with a timeframe of 2050, if not 2030 as well, as set out by the Commission itself.

Tender mechanisms such as those of Horizon Europe and the Innovation Fund, the granting of loans by the EIB at modest interest rates, undoubtedly have the advantage of being flexible and open to proposals in a way that is not predetermined by the research community and business. But they also have a disadvantage. Once the grant or loan is awarded, be it on a large or small scale, there is no place to accumulate the kind of vision that one might have within an organisation that has co-ownership of projects in some form.

In essence, the implementation of the mission stated in the EU climate change policy is entirely left to universities and companies, whose goals are not necessarily aligned with the mission itself, for reasons similar to those we have seen in the case of the biomedical sector. Academic communities are made up of researchers who pursue their career goals: publications, reputation, influence, as well as having teaching missions. They can do excellent basic and applied research, including on climate change issues, but they cannot be expected to do work that is radically different from what they already do by offering them subsidies on a necessarily small scale. And if the subsidies were on a very large scale, the university is not the right institution to manage them independently.

The same applies to companies that usually, apart from varying strengths of "green" public declarations, do not have a public mission, but rather that of obtaining an adequate return for the financial investors that control them. Partial exceptions can be made for some state-owned enterprises,[36] which, however, often respond to a "mixed" logic in terms of objectives, when they do not behave exactly like private ones, except in secondary aspects. These companies are also subject to the influence of governments at a national, and sometimes even local level, so they do not have a global or even a European perspective: unless they are entities such as Airbus (38% German, 38%

French, 20% British, and 4% Spanish) or to some extent such as the European Space Agency (in which 22 countries participate), which conducts research in-house but also has industrial objectives. It is to these truly European models that I think we should look.

A European public infrastructure, largely open to non-EU collaborations, based on its own autonomous research and development capacity could build up a portfolio of showcase projects, partly in collaboration with third-party companies and research centres. To really learn, things must be done, or at least commissioned, in the form of calls not to obtain subsidies, but for innovative supply (known as procurement for innovation), just as CERN and ESA do with thousands of high-tech suppliers, qualified through appropriate procedures (such as those in use in the nuclear and aerospace industries).

The basic difference to what is already envisaged by the EU institutions is that the resources would not be allocated as grants to third parties, but in the form of contracts for the joint development of projects. The ownership of investments and results (i.e., of tangible and intangible assets) would remain directly with the agency, or would possibly be transferred to project companies in the form of joint ventures (if the participants have invested their own capital). This implies that the intellectual property of technological innovations would also remain with the agency. The agency itself (or its co-owned public–private companies), would then have to implement a licensing policy on patents in the public interest, including in favour of developing countries, given the planetary nature of the topic. This is a fundamental issue from the point of view of breaking oligopolistic models and countering social inequality.

The Agency's own capital should be based on a combination of transfers from the budgets of the participating states, and the EU, including through ETS revenues or other sources, as is currently the case for the Innovation Fund, and be invested, in combination with EIB loans, in the development of projects with scientific and industrial partners, with a view to also having a demonstrable financial return when the projects enter the market phase.

To this end, there should be a solid central infrastructure staffed by scientists, technologists, and managers, supported by professional resources capable of assessing and aggregating risk capital according to the degree of maturity of projects. Over time, this should result in a portfolio of fully functioning demonstration projects on which to build the dissemination policy.

By project portfolio, I mean both internal projects and a set of participations in project companies that are capable of demonstrating the technical feasibility, environmental benefit, and market sustainability of alternative ways of producing goods and services, not through more or less hidden subsidies, but through superior technological efficiency.

The idea is not as heretical as it might seem, not least in light of the evolution of the European Innovation Council itself, which in January 2020 announced its intention to make direct investments, in the form of equity stakes, in 42 innovative start-ups and some SMEs, totalling 178 million euros,[37] ranging from a minimum of 500,000 to a maximum of

15 million euros, combining with other funds in the usual form of capital grants. Out of 293 companies selected by EIC as of December 2019 (for a total of 563 million euros in subsidies), 159 companies will be able to become participated companies, gradually making EIC a large investment fund. If the same logic were applied to the Innovation Fund, on a much larger scale and without limiting operations to start-ups and SMEs, but also extending it to industrial partners, we would be very close to what I am proposing, provided that the logic of participation is strategic and not purely financial.

It is possible, as with the other proposals I make here, that one of the centres already existing in Europe could be the hub on which to build the project portfolio strategy. This would be preferable to starting from scratch, but only careful reconnaissance could identify the subject and location of one (or more) campuses that relate to the science and technology of environmental sustainability, in the same way that ESA relates to space research, development, and industrial policy. In the Appendix, I highlight some features of ESA that might be interesting for "Green Europa", a European Agency for Ecological Transition.

Appendix: The European Space Agency model

The European Space Agency is an international organisation founded by convention in 1975, currently with 22 member states (Austria, Belgium, the Czech Republic, Denmark, Estonia, Finland, France, Germany, Greece, Hungary, Ireland, Italy, Luxembourg, the Netherlands, Poland, Portugal, Romania, Spain, Sweden, Switzerland, and the United Kingdom) and various associates. This membership base does not coincide with that of the European Union, with whose institutions there are, nevertheless, close collaborative relationships in various programmes and which contribute around 20% of ESA's budget.

The purpose of the Agency is to design and implement the European space programme, excluding military purposes, partly in cooperation with other agencies, with projects concerning the knowledge of our planet, the solar system and the universe, but also to develop technologies, satellite services, and the European industrial capacity in the sector, which employs around 40,000 people directly. Industrial contracts are awarded to companies in each country in proportion to their contributions. ESA develops its own launchers (Ariane 5, Vega, and new projects) and spacecraft.

The Agency is also involved in satellites for telecommunications, earth observation (Copernicus), navigation (Galileo), and meteorology (operated by EUMETSAT) and is developing a new generation of nanosatellites. Overall, it has designed, launched, and operated 80 satellites since 1975. In the earth observation sector in particular, there are 15 operational satellites, 40 in development, and 13 in preparation.

Research programmes include those for the study of climate change, asteroid and comet impacts, gravitational waves, extraction of raw materials and energy generation outside our planet, robotisation applied to space exploration, deep space probes, and participation in the crews of the International Space Station. It collaborates with NASA and the space agencies of various other countries.

The ESA has its headquarters in Paris and specialised branches in other countries: EAC, the European Astronaut Centre, in Cologne, Germany; ESAC, the European Space Centre for Astronomy, in Villanueva de la Cañada, Madrid, Spain; ESOC, the European Space Centre for Operations, in Darmstadt, Germany; ESRIN, the ESA Centre for Earth Observation, in Frascati, near Rome, Italy; ESTEC, the European Space Centre for Research and Technology, in Noordwijk, The Netherlands; ECSAT, the European Space Applications and Telecommunications Centre, in Harwell, Oxfordshire, UK; ESEC, the European Space Centre for Security and Education, in Redu, Belgium; offices in Belgium, the USA and Russia; a launch base in French Guiana, as well as control stations in various countries. A total of 2200 people work there, including scientists, engineers, computer scientists, and administrative staff.

The financing mechanism is as follows: each member state makes an annual contribution in proportion to its GDP to the regular budget and with optional additional contributions if it joins additional specific programmes. In total, the 2022 budget was 7.15 billion euros.

In terms of governance, strategic decisions are taken by the Board in which each member state has one representative and one vote, regardless of its financial contribution. The Board appoints a director general, to whom the directors of each sector are accountable.

Characteristic of ESA is the combination of a research organisation in the form of a "mission-driven" infrastructure together with the promotion of an industrial policy. In particular, Art. VII of the founding Convention[38] specifies that this industrial policy must consistently support the European space programme and that of the member states, enhance the global competitiveness of the European space industry, develop space technology on the basis of the existing potential in the individual countries, ensure that each state can participate equally in the implementation of the space programme with reference to its financial contribution, and exploit the advantages of competitive tenders unless this is incompatible with other industrial policy objectives. The criterion of *juste retour* (which is also partly applied by CERN) obviously facilitates the cohesion of the member states because it basically means that as far as possible, the financial contribution of each country "returns" to the industry of that country, with a focus on small and medium-sized companies.

Notes

1 Hamann et al., 2018.
2 Hamann et al., 2018.

3 https://ec.europa.eu/info/sites/default/files/european-green-deal-communication_en.pdf
4 Sustainable Development Goal 7 of the United Nations states that the whole population (especially low-income households) should be guaranteed access to sustainable and clean energy, eliminating energy poverty. However, at present, low-income population groups remain excluded, while higher-income and better-educated population groups can invest in clean technologies and achieve an economic return.
5 European Commission, 11.12.2019 COM(2019) 640 final, p. 7
6 European Commission, 11.12.2019 COM(2019) 640 final.
7 European Commission, 11.12.2019 COM(2019) 640 final, p. 10.
8 European Commission, 11.12.2019 COM(2019) 640 final, p. 15.
9 https://about.bnef.com/new-energy-outlook/
10 The oil and gas price spikes in 2022 show the volatility of some predictions.
11 International Renewable Energy Agency.
12 Albeit with a lively debate, see, for example, the website and blog of the Energy Institute at Haas (the executive training school of the University of California at Berkeley). https://haas.berkeley.edu/energy-institute/.
13 https://www.iea.org/
14 Coll, 2012.
15 European Commission, 2019.
16 European Commission, 2019.
17 European Commission, 11.12.2019 COM(2019) 640 final, p. 18.
18 European Commission, 11.12.2019 COM(2019) 640 final, p. 18.
19 The EU ETS operates on the principle of cap-and-trade. A cap is set on the total amount of certain greenhouse gases that can be emitted by plants covered by the scheme. The cap reduces over time so that total emissions decrease. Within this limit, companies receive or buy emission allowances, which they can trade if necessary. They can also buy limited amounts of international credits from emission reduction projects around the world. Limiting the total number ensures that the available allowances have value. At the end of each year, companies must surrender enough allowances to cover their emissions if they do not want to face heavy fines. If a company reduces its emissions, it can keep the unused allowances to cover future needs, or sell them to another company that is short of them.

Source: https://ec.europa.eu/clima/eu-action/eu-emissions-trading-system-eu-ets_en

20 There was a 100 USD price spike in February 2022, in part related to the Russia–Ukraine war. See Mairate (2023) for an update of the potential impact of carbon pricing.
21 https://www.reuters.com/business/energy/fossil-fuel-subsidies-face-tighter-eu-scrutiny-2022-01-31/
22 https://www.cnbc.com/2021/10/29/world-spends-423-billion-a-year-to-subsidize-fossil-fuels-un.html
23 However, a distinction must be made between carbon-neutrality and climate-neutrality: in the latter case, it is not only a matter of cutting CO_2 emissions, but also other greenhouse gases such as methane.
24 The Economist, 22 February 2020, p. 10.
25 Geisz et al., 2020
26 Samset, Fuglestvedt, Lund, 2020.
27 https://www.wcrp-climate.org/wgcm-cmip

28 https://gca.org/about-us/the-global-commission-on-adaptation/
29 https://eit.europa.eu/who-we-are/eit-glance/mission
30 https://eit.europa.eu/news-events/news/snapshot-eit-climate-kics-innovation-portfolio
31 The detailed report mentions 59 projects. As is inevitable, given the premises and numbers mentioned above, these are essentially small-scale projects, such as the improvement of energy efficiency in a few hundred social housing flats in the south of Milan, the transformation of Amsterdam's "red light" district into "green" (an amusing colour association), reducing energy poverty in Bologna's "Pilastro" district, rainwater conservation and treatment systems in Rotterdam's stadium, a combined electric quadricycle, IoT technology to improve irrigation systems in vineyards and vegetable gardens, tools for measuring nitrogen and CO_2 in the soil, development of a complement to soya in animal feed, recycling of beer waste, recovery of mangroves in French overseas territories, recycling of used lithium batteries, raising awareness on the use of disposable plastic objects in the Mediterranean, "circular" design of the domestic kitchen, and so on. These are hardly radically innovative projects.
32 https://ec.europa.eu/commission/presscorner/detail/en/ip_20_2530
33 https://www.eea.europea.eu/it/about-us
34 https://eur-lex.europa.eu/legal-content/EN/TXT/HTML/?uri=CELEX:32003L0087&from=EN
35 https://cinea.ec.europa.eu/index_en
36 Rikap (2022) offers an impressive case study about a state owned enterprise that is now an intellectual monopoly, building on the national innovation system: the State Grid Corporation of Chine (SGCC). This firm has developed a strategy of applications of Artificial Intelligence in the energy sector, particularly, initially in the Ultra High voltage technologies, and then in clean energy and smart grids more in general. As part of the Chinese government strategy to become the leader country in green technologies, SGCC has a clear innovation mission. The company is the second in the world by revenues in the Fortune 500 ranking, the most important utility in the world, with 1 million employees. In 2017, it invested 1.15 USD billion in R&D on energy and other fields, has been granted 17,000 patents and filed 100,000, while published over 4000 scientific papers in the 15 years to 2018. AI applications for to enable clean energy lead this performance, with strong in-house capacity (similarly to Huawei in telecommunications) but also with important relations with both a large number of national and foreign universities and research organizations.
37 https://ec.europa.eu/commission/presscorner/detail/en/IP_20_2530
38 https://www.esa.int/About_Us/Business_with_ESA/How_to_do/Industrial_policy_and_geographical_distribution

5 Digital Europa

How to get our data back

Introduction

Several times in the history of technology, the adoption of an innovation by public authorities has created opportunities for private investment: the water systems in the Eastern empires, the Roman consular roads, and the postal and telegraphic service. In the last century: telephone, electricity, the Internet, space-based radio-navigation systems, and much more.

States in the past retained some control over technological innovations, if only for military reasons. Today, national governments are struggling to exercise sovereign power over technology, except for the occasional use of repressive powers. New technologies make the borders between nations permeable. It is not a question of lamenting the passing of customs charges, taxes, and stamp duty. It is a question of understanding what the quid pro quo is. On the one hand, this relinquishment of virtual borders has enabled billions of users, individuals, and businesses, to develop their private activities. But paradoxically, on the other hand, global oligopolies of companies based on the digital economy have been created, clubs of investors and managers who effectively expropriate data and knowledge as raw material for capital accumulation. In the process of oligopolistic concentration, structural dynamics are at play: according to Autor et al. (2020), the emergence of superstar firms (such as digital platforms) is correlated with the falling share of labour in incomes, the most relevant aspect of growing inequality in our societies.

The convergence of electronic communication networks of various kinds (from cable TV to mobile telephony, from social media to Voice over Internet Protocol or VoIP) as associated with the oligopoly on personal data with all kinds of Big Data (including government data and data on human health) is accompanied by an imbalance of power and concentration of wealth. This imbalance may, in the long run, be incompatible with democratic political systems and open societies, due to the enormous disproportion of influence resulting from the control of information. How can we counteract the undesirable effects of digital capitalism, the accumulation of wealth and influence based on the effective ownership of data?

DOI: 10.4324/9781003381532-6

The key companies in the digital oligopoly are mainly based in the US and China, with some others in Europe, Japan, and other Asian countries. The European Union is now waking up to this imbalance. In the already mentioned State of the Union 2020 address, von der Leyen announced that 20% of the Next Generation EU funds (i.e., 150 billion euros) would go to projects for a digital Europe, which would include a European cloud for industrial data (actually all those not directly managed by people, as the competition for consumer-to-business data was now deemed by the EC as lost); 8 billion would go to the supercomputers of the future, to investments in 5G and 6G technologies, to a broadband infrastructure, to a European e-identity, to investments in artificial intelligence and in digital common spaces. An e-identity would potentially mean connecting people's data in such a way as to greatly simplify the systems for issuing certificates, collecting taxes, paying pensions and other forms of assistance, managing emergencies, and tracking health, with time savings that with the pandemic have come to the fore. These are unprecedented resources and a perhaps unrepeatable opportunity for a project of shared sovereignty in the digital economy, even if its contours are still hazy.

What is missing, however, is a clear identification of the stakeholders, an analogue of the European Space Agency for the shared policy in that field. If these resources end up subsidising private ICT companies, there is a risk of strengthening their oligopoly. Having a European public agency for the digital economy could make the difference between a heterogeneous set of projects and grants, with the risk of capture by vested interests on the one hand, and an effective strategic policy of regaining public sovereignty over the digital economy on the other.

A short history of bits

The idea of reducing information to simple signs is as old as the invention of writing and numbers. The adoption of a binary code (0/1) that matches two logical alternatives with two states of a physical system, such as the open/closed configuration of an electrical circuit, is more recent. There are various 19th-century antecedents to the idea of a binary signal, such as the Morse code for the telegraph (short/long), punched cards for the Jacquard machine and calculating machines, and punched tapes for teletypewriters. The bit appears for the first time in a famous article by Shannon (1948), *A Mathematical Theory of Communication*. The article, by no means coincidentally, was published in the *Bell System Technical Journal*, the journal of Bell Telephone Laboratories. These had been founded in 1925 jointly by AT&T, the then-dominant telephone company in the USA, and Western Electric, the equipment supplier, itself controlled by AT&T. Signs are at the heart of any formal system of both communication and computation, and Bell Laboratories were at the forefront of many crucial innovations, including the three-terminal transistor version on semiconductor material that enables the transfer of an electric current and translates signals into physical signals.

Seventy years later, we live in a world of digitised information on a binary (and therefore transistor) basis. Many everyday objects and services have a size defined in terms of bytes (a sequence typically of eight bits, i.e., 2^3) and in multiples growing in orders of magnitude as information flows and memory grows. From the smartphone to the supercomputer, from the radio telescope to the television, from the robot to the video game, and from the dishwasher to the electron microscope, everything has a dimension of encoded information.

The use of the byte as a unit of measurement originated at IBM in 1956 (during the design of one of the first computers) and has also become the standard in commercial communication.[1]

Research infrastructures, from particle physics to radio astronomy, from supercomputers to biodata banks, generate a quantity of digital information that forces us to use units of measurement of a surprisingly large order, but which may in the future prove to be inadequate to measure data flow and storage: petabytes, exabytes, zettabytes, yottabytes (10^{15}, 10^{18}, 10^{21}, 10^{24} bytes, respectively). Many examples can be given of the size in bytes of the information circulating (as a stream per unit time) or accumulating (as a memory stock) on our planet. A DVD-ROM usually has a capacity of 4.7 gigabytes, an episode of a high-definition Netflix series corresponds to 7, and the memory of the MacBook I am writing on corresponds to 16. Someone calculated that the videos uploaded to YouTube in 2016 corresponded to 24 terabytes, about 2.5 times the data transmitted by the Hubble Space Telescope; 10 billion photos on Facebook correspond to 1.5 petabytes. It is said that the data held by Google (a few years ago) was in the order of 15 exabytes.

A few examples can help visualise these orders of magnitude. The first sequencing of a human genome (1990–2003) by the Human Genome Project can be seen as the production of information on 3 billion DNA bases, approximately 3 gigabytes. The first time it took about 3 billion USD and over 12 years. Now, the same operation can be completed at a cost of well under a 1000 USD and in less than an hour, thanks to the technology developed with the HGP by a small group of specialised companies. In the past decade, one of the world's leading research centres in this field, the Broad Institute (Harvard and MIT), produces a sequencing operation every 12 minutes, thus accumulating information on 100,000 individuals in ten years, with a database of 70 petabytes of genetic data. The same exponential trend in the accumulation of genetic information is being recorded at other centres with a research scope that includes thousands of living and extinct species. A private company (23andMe), that offers partial sequencing (for just 99 USD), has ten million customers and, therefore, data on their genomes. It is predicted that by 2025, genome data will amount to more information than the accumulated data of Facebook, YouTube, and other social media (as speculative as these predictions are).

The future SKA radio telescope, with 130,000 antennas at 500 stations in Australia and other types of antennas in South Africa, could generate raw data (unfiltered and compressed) of 159 terabytes per second, or 4.9

zettabytes per year in Australia and 62 exabytes in South Africa. This scale is roughly that of the current annual data traffic on the entire web and will require inventing new techniques for filtering, processing, storing, and transmitting data (the control node will be in the UK). According to a report from a few years ago (COST European Cooperation, 2010):

> The SKA is more than a science project. It is a laboratory for innovations in radio communications, data transport, intelligent analysis, storage, and world-wide dissemination of knowledge [...] The team of scientists working on the SKA will inevitably come up with new ideas that could change the way we do things. If these ideas can be developed and their organizations receive patents and industrial partners, then SKA innovations could spread to the marketplace with considerable profit potential.[2]

Two other examples in the field of astronomy are the Large Synoptic Survey Telescope (LSST) in Chile, which, around 2025, will begin optical scanning of 37 billion galaxies and stars over ten years, corresponding to handling 30 Terabytes of data every night, and the James Webb Space Telescope (NASA, ESA, Canadian Space Agency), heir to the Hubble Telescope, which travels into deep space 1.5 million kilometres from Earth's orbit, at a cost of 9 billion USD, covering distant galaxies not visible from Earth, exoplanets, and other celestial objects. It is expected that complex problems of computer-aided image classification, the creation of a catalogue crossing different signal wavelengths, the temporal evolution of observations, the calibration of interpretative models, as well as, of course, the problems of reliable data communication from the space telescope to ground stations will have to be solved.

It may be useful to compare Facebook's data archive with that of CERN. In the former case, an estimate from a few years ago estimated that around 300 petabytes of content were stored on Facebook's various servers (HIVE)[3] with a daily flow of 3–4 petabytes and perhaps over 2 billion active users. I will come back to the implications of these data flows later. The CERN Data Centre has 10,000 servers with 174,000 physical processors and handles 1 petabyte per day of data, the equivalent of 210,000 DVDs. After filtering operations, 500 petabytes of data are currently stored, while 10 gigabytes per second are sent to the Worldwide LHC Computer Grid, the heir to the WWW, which connects 170 nodes in 42 countries that are in turn connected to thousands of other computers. In other words, CERN, with its relatively small community of scientific users (perhaps 10,000 people) generates and manages more data than Facebook with its more than 2 billion users and with economic resources in terms of annual revenue (2020) that are about 70 times those of CERN.

Research infrastructures, Internet companies, as well as public administrations and digital communication companies (from telecoms to online content managers) therefore handle data flows on the petabyte scale and, with a view to the future, on a scale that will be orders of magnitude higher, such as exabytes and zettabytes, with seemingly limitless growth. Some estimates[4] of the world's data production in 2019 are in the range of 33 zettabytes in 2018, or 7 trillion DVDs[5] and 40 zettabytes in 2019, with a forecast of 50 zettabytes in 2020 (not counting the effects of the pandemic that will increase the amount).

This amount of information would not be manageable if various technological revolutions had not occurred sequentially, or sometimes in parallel, apparently independently of each other, almost always with the important role of public agencies in triggering the process. Several authors have emphasised the role of ARPA in the creation of the Internet and of CERN as the place where the World Wide Web was invented. These are interesting episodes but, as we will see in a moment, the history of the role of the public sector in ICT is much broader.

In 1957, the USSR launched Sputnik and the US felt threatened. The then-senator – and future president – Lyndon Johnson declared: "Soon they will be dropping bombs on us from space like kids dropping rocks onto cars from freeway overpasses". Former General Eisenhower launched the Advanced Research Projects Agency (later renamed DARPA by adding Defense at the beginning, so that there would be no doubt about the mission), with an initial budget that, expressed in present-day euros, would be around 3.74 billion euros, to be spent on funding research projects potentially useful for defence. Although ARPA had neither laboratories nor a campus (but a generous budget and capable management), as *The Economist* writes: "The agency shaped the contemporary world, helping to create missile defence, stealth technology, the internet and the personal computer, lasers and GPS".[6] As far as we know, management had a great deal of autonomy and according to the agency's history,[7] the decision to create ARPANET, the precursor project to the Internet, was made in a half-hour meeting. DARPA, at the end of 2019, had a budget of 3.4 billion USD, not much less than the initial budget, with a staff of 220, that is, it remained essentially an agile structure with a large budget with which to fund cutting-edge projects.[8]

The history of the World Wide Web at CERN is well known to the non-specialist public and has been told himself by the inventor Tim Berners Lee, a young CERN employee who had observed the waste of time incurred by the world's particle physicists using incompatible computers and software, meaning that they could not interface their systems and share data, except by ad hoc procedures. The initial idea of the WWW (a series of codes and protocols including http and HTML) did not attract much interest and started modestly by putting the CERN telephone directory onto the fledgling WWW. Later, outside CERN, the protocols of the WWW were adopted for the electronic document archive of another particle accelerator: SLAC in Stanford (USA). Given CERN's own initial lack of interest in the development of the project, Berners Lee moved to MIT in 1991, while in 1993 CERN – despite holding the rights to the WWW – decided to give them up for free, as did Berners Lee himself. These "fateful" decisions created an incalculable positive impact on billions of people and companies. Indeed, CERN soon realised that the potential was enormous and the first global WWW conference was held at CERN in 1993, with the fundamental contribution of Robert Caillau (whom many consider to be the co-inventor of the web). DARPA is also part of this history because it supported the World Wide Web Consortium created at MIT, with the co-sponsorship of the European Commission. The consortium still pursues a policy of open and free access regarding the technologies and standards that it develops.

Despite the fact that, initially at least, commercial uses of these codes were apparently prohibited, e-commerce was born as early as 1995 with Amazon and eBay. Within a few years, there would be hundreds of start-ups and stock market listings of Internet companies, including Google, founded in 1998. Speculative valuations led to the notorious dot.com bubble (the fledgling Internet-based companies) in 2001, but the companies that survived are today at the peak of world economic power. According to some estimates, there are 4.66 billion users of the WWW, or 59% of the world's population (95% in Europe), including more than 4.1 billion social media users, of which Facebook, Instagram, Messenger, and WhatsApp accounted for 2.3 billion in 2019. In ten years, Facebook has grown from 2000 employees to 45,000, and Google from 24,000 to 119,000.

If we look further East, China's Tencent reached in 2021 (March,2) a market value of 862 billion USD,[9] is the leader in online video games (which it mostly gives away and then sells connected goods), controls a dozen companies in the sector, including in the US, Finland, and elsewhere. Its app (WeChat) has 1.2 billion users and it is estimated that two-thirds of Chinese play online video games from their smartphones (in the US it is one-third of the population). Unknown to most, the fourth largest European company is in terms of value the Dutch Prosus (online betting, e-commerce), which owns a 31% share in Tencent and is active in many developing countries.

The TikTok app (one of the targets of Trump's anti-Chinese policy, which he implausibly accused of spreading Communist Party propaganda or espionage) has been downloaded 2 billion times. ByteDance, the company that developed it, could be worth (it is not yet listed on the stock exchange) up to 100 billion USD, has 60,000 employees and over 100 million users in both China and the US. Incidentally, the market for video games in general (Nintendo and others) thanks to the pandemic is estimated at 175 billion USD in 2020 (Newzoo data) and requires rather sophisticated technologies.

If each of the users of the services of these Internet-based companies paid the inventors a royalty of two euro cents per month, CERN would have its budget entirely financed by the WWW, without the need to rely on the member states.

While the tales of the role of public agencies in creating the digital world we know are certainly evocative, they do not tell the whole story of the chain of events and forces at play. The story is more complicated, but perhaps also more interesting than how it is sometimes popularised.

First, as I mentioned above, the very idea of using binary signals to transmit information had already been applied on a large scale with telegraph systems in the 19th century. Morse himself had the support of the US government (Congress funded the first line). The importance of the electromagnetic telegraph for military purposes was very soon grasped everywhere, just as had happened previously with postal systems. This was the origin of the public postal and telegraph service, which for example in Italy dates back to 1862. If the subsequent evolution of analogue telephony for voice was based on a different principle, with the transition from analogue to digital there was a return to the use of binary codes. Something similar has happened (or is happening) for television and radio with digital signals. In the vast majority of countries, post, telegraph, and telephone have been seen by governments as part of a public communication infrastructure. This infrastructure is often operated directly by companies or entrusted to private companies with concession mechanisms. It is difficult to underestimate the innovative role in the last century of the largely public telecommunications companies throughout Europe. These companies, together with computer and semiconductor manufacturers, have been the driving force behind the evolution of information science and technology, gradually seeing the transmission of digital signals as the outcome of a branched bundle of trajectories. I do not believe, therefore, that one can reduce the history to only ARPA and CERN because the Internet and the WWW should be seen as the development of more than a century of ideas on the communication of electric or electromagnetic signals encoded in various ways.

Secondly, the birth of the computer, even though mechanical calculating machines of various types had existed in earlier centuries, was initially linked to military uses for encrypting and deciphering messages during the Second World War, that is, ultimately linked to the need to hack (we would say today) coded radio communications. The best-known and most emblematic case is the Colossus machine, based on Turing's ideas and built for the Royal Navy to decipher the German Enigma code towards the end of the Second World War (1944), secretly replicated in numerous examples, with the employment of thousands of technicians, and capable of deciphering thousands of enemy messages on a daily basis. Without a concatenation of antecedents, perhaps the first computer "for market" (UNIVAC, 1951), developed by the same designers who had worked on military projects, would not have existed. If IBM first, and Apple second, seem to us the archetype of private enterprise in the USA, we now know how much of their history is due to research conducted, essentially for military purposes, in government-funded laboratories and universities.

The US Army started the large computer programme that would result in several machines, first with the adoption of thermionic valves and then transistors. Transistors (developed, as I mentioned, mainly at Bell Laboratories in 1947–1948) work as "switches" of an electric current. They are based on semiconductor materials and by switching on and off billions of times in integrated circuits, they are the physical counterpart of almost all the data economy of our time. They show the relationship between different strands of research, from solid-state physics to computers to telecommunications. Incidentally, the transistor is considered to be the single most produced artefact in the world, as several billion of them are produced every day. A million transistors could be housed in a chip in the 1980s, in 2005 over a billion, currently up to 50 billion in some cases. One of these objects might measure seven nanometres, a billionth of a metre, a 1000th of the diameter of a red blood cell, and, to improve it further, it might be possible with new materials such as graphene or with films of "white graphene" (amorphous boron nitride).

The third pillar of the convergence between telecommunications and computers occurred, as I have already mentioned, with the Internet and the World Wide Web, both of which were developed within public research projects. The network and the universal language that allows the network nodes (in fact computers) to connect to each other are at the basis of the transformation of digital information into a planetary phenomenon. Paradoxically, given all the talk about it, we do not fully understand and cannot predict the extent of this phenomenon. The totality of instantaneous information, from our planet and potentially from the universe (whose signals reach us), that is, every word, number, image, sound, colour, and much more, can be transformed into digital data that is processed virtually by algorithms and physically by semiconductors (and perhaps tomorrow by quantum computers) and can be transmitted over a single network and with a single universal metalanguage at a marginal cost that is close to zero.

Finally, the digitisation of signals is at the basis of the fourth element of the information society, the possibility of using very different networks for their transmission, from the old copper telephone pair to optical fibre, from radio waves to satellites. It is as if one and the same vehicle could transport billions of packets and their contents (almost) unhindered over highways, mule tracks, sea and air routes, retrieving them and getting them to their destination with minimum loss and delay.

Therefore, the science and technology of information, the technology that makes it possible to transform any content into a digital signal, store it, transmit it, process it, and make it available to users, developed at the instigation of governments for strategic purposes, has become the foundation of global economic and social progress, both in market and non-market transactions, in the same way as electricity was, and before that, the steam engine, but with a considerably greater degree of abstraction, and thus of universality.

All this has happened in the space of a generation or so. To take some emblematic dates: the TCP/IP protocol and the word "Internet" itself appeared in 1982, while the http protocols, the HTML language and the World Wide Web date from 1990–1991. The information society, as we know it today, is little more than a generation old. We need only go back a few more decades to find a world with no computers, no television, no mobile telephones and even few landline telephones, few radios, and no household appliances, all of which currently incorporate a logic board based on binary codes.

This tumultuous process, in which political-military interests, scientific and technological trends, transformative cultural mechanisms, capitalist economic forces and public administrative apparatuses have converged, has resulted in a global socio-economic dynamic that still eludes us today and that governments are unable to control. I will try to argue two theses: the first is that the digital oligopoly is an unforeseen but somehow inevitable outcome; the second is that this outcome – despite appearances – creates, but also destroys, social value while it generates disproportionate financial value for investors.

The digital oligopoly

The socio-economic effects of the innovations I have mentioned can be read in various ways. For example, one could try to estimate what the benefit is of using email instead of physical mail, for passengers and airlines of being able to make online bookings, what the impact of connecting even small hotels and restaurants to the web is, what it meant for all of us in 2020 during the Covid-19 lockdown and still today to be able to use services such as Skype, Zoom, Teams, and many others in a situation where billions of hours of business meetings, lectures, and family gatherings could not be held in person because of the pandemic. Given the pervasiveness of information and communication technology, this is probably an empirically impossible account, as would be the social accounting of the effects of electricity or writing. But this is not just an empirical problem. There is also a conceptual problem related to the cumulativity of knowledge, for example, Internet without electricity and without the invention of an alphabet is useless, so ultimately, I cannot say how far back one should go in establishing cause–effect relations in the presence of such widespread global public goods and externalities.

But on a more modest scale, there are facts that we can observe. One of these facts is that in a market economy, the value of enterprises, prices of goods and factors of production are determined by demand, supply, and expectations of benefits for the participants. The market has voted for this message: the benefits of the ICT technology revolution are not being distributed evenly between industries and factors of production, but in a highly unequal manner. The profitability of restaurants does not seem to have increased significantly because they can now promote themselves with a website on which they display a menu, location, and biography of the chef, or because TripAdvisor publishes reviews. While the productivity of airline reservation services can only be improved with online-booking services, the wages of airline employees have not enjoyed the same improvement.

In the future, it may be that the benefits will spread with artificial intelligence techniques, which we discuss later. But it is not so obvious. A McKinsey survey in 2019 reveals that among managers in various industries, those who say that artificial intelligence (AI) will improve their company revenues by more than 10% are a minority, with a large majority expecting no effect or an effect of less than 5% in sectors such as manufacturing, supply chain management, human resources and others. Similar or smaller percentages are found for the expectation of cost reduction. For example, in manufacturing almost 60% of the respondents expect no or less than 5% effect in increasing revenues or decreasing costs.

On a global scale, we have little evidence that there has been an overall effect of information technology (IT) on the income of the worker or even the median income from investments in the last 30 years. But we have abundant evidence that a rather small club of Tech Giants has been created at the top of world capitalism to whom the market has attributed the potential to disproportionately reap the benefits of change.

Let us look at some facts. Before the pandemic (1 February 2020), Amazon and Alphabet each had a market value of about 1 trillion USD, Apple 1400 billion, Microsoft 1300 billion, and Facebook 575 billion, a similar value to China's Tencent and Alibaba. For all of these companies, the value would have greatly increased with the pandemic, reaching for the five US companies 40% total market value (share value and dividends) at the end of November 2020, compared to the stagnant performance of the remaining top S&P500 companies. Even other tech companies like Netflix, Salesforce, and Paypal have market values between 130 and 160 billion USD. To make some comparisons: Toyota, BYD, NIO, Volkswagen, Daimler, General Motors, BMW, Ferrari, Honda, and Saic, the top ten automotive groups in the world (excluding TESLA due to its peculiarities but including the two largest Chinese companies) have a cumulated market value of less than 75% of Amazon. Tesla, the leading bet in the field for the self-driving car, basically an AI product rather than a manufacturing one, is worth several times more than traditional car manufacturers. It is estimated that every eight hours of driving a Tesla will produce 30 Terabytes of data, making it one of the world's leading information producers.

Even before the pandemic (2019), the increase in the stock market value over the previous year of the five US Tech Giants was 52%, bringing them to represent one-fifth of the value of the SA&P 500 index, 5600 billion USD. Revenues in that year increased by 17%, with great scope for further expansion, for instance, only 20% of enterprise data is stored in the cloud. This group of five companies employs 1.2 million people and invests 200 billion USD each year.

The Amazon case is the most remarkable. The founder, Jeff Bezos, a Princeton graduate, founded an online bookshop in 1995 after having worked in finance. Amazon was able – in response to the pandemic – to hire 170,000 employees in a few months and increase its fleet to 82 aircraft. Although it is not a monopoly (it controls 40% of US e-commerce but only 6% of all retail sales), it has accumulated tangible assets of 104 billion and generates 11,000 USD per second of transactions, handling 3.5 billion parcels (2019). The price/earning ratio, which somehow expresses the expectation of future profit in mid-2020, is 118, three to four times as high as Microsoft and Apple, respectively. What is striking is the dynamic: the market value has roughly quadrupled since 2016. The advertising revenue alone is 11 billion per annum, 7% of the online market, (still far behind Google 38% and Facebook 22%, but climbing rapidly). Amazon's Cloud services (AWS) have a revenue of 35 billion in 2021.

In terms of geographical distribution (one of the aspects of global inequality), 90% of the market value of the 70 largest tech companies is attributable to US or Chinese companies, while Africa and Latin America together account for only 1%. The rest of the world, including Europe and Japan, count for only 9%. The five largest Indian software companies are worth 200 billion USD cumulatively, employing cheap digital labour: Tata Consultancy Services, the largest, has as many employees as Microsoft, Apple, Alphabet, and Meta put together. Overall, India's software industry employs 4.4 million people, and has a turnover of 180 billion USD in 2019, or 6% of India's GDP. One million people work in subsidiaries of multinationals that have relocated software development to India, mainly of large US companies.

New value chains are being created, playing on wage differentials, with a digital proletariat in developing countries. This fact has geostrategic, as well as economic, implications. For instance, Europe gives most of the data it generates to entities outside national jurisdictions. Governments, for a variety of reasons, may not be keen on the idea of not being able to guard their virtual borders in terms of data movement: hence the blocking of some social media and other platforms in several countries. The issue of cybersecurity is becoming an increasingly hot topic. Ninety per cent of US companies have appointed a cybersecurity officer. There is growing evidence of attacks on corporate and even hospital government servers in recent years, but potentially all of a country's technological systems, from the power grid, transportation, and telecommunications – to give three examples – could be subject to devastating attacks. From this perspective, the concentration of data control in a few companies, mostly US and Chinese, says something about the potential conflict over data and networks, as revealed by the US and other countries' campaign of ostracism directed against China's Huawei, the world's largest provider of 5G technology.[10] The picture is also very complex. For instance, Huawei largely uses chips produced in the USA, and the Trump administration's ban on selling them led a few days later to Chinese President Xi Jinping's announcement of an investment of 1400 billion USD by 2025 to ensure the country's technological independence. The Trump administration, for its part, had blocked the acquisition by a Singaporean competitor of Qualcomm, one of the world's largest producers of semiconductors for 5G, and even considered taking a controlling stake in Nokia and Ericsson.

The emergence of nationalism, or perhaps even a digital sovereignism, that opposes the globalism of the Tech Giants is already among us, with Russia demanding that any data belonging to individuals within its jurisdiction be stored in servers physically located on national soil; the European Union, which does not allow personal data to be accessed by those who do not comply with certain safeguards (many websites in the US can no longer be visited by European citizens because they have not complied with the GDPR-General Data Protection Regulation); China, which does not allow its citizens to access WhatsApp, Gmail, Messenger, and some social media, or at least controls their content. I later discuss the proposals underway in the European Union, mainly at the initiative of Germany, to create a federated cloud infrastructure, a European super-cloud.

For cloud services, which I will talk about later, Amazon (which many only know for its role in logistics) has 48% of the market, Microsoft and Alibaba have 15.5 and 7.7%, respectively, with Google and IBM trailing behind, and all the rest very much fragmented. This market concentration also corresponds to a physical concentration, as servers are located in particular sites, which require extremely delicate security precautions. It is not clear whether and how there will be decentralisation. Incidentally, in a market such as China's, online payments are firmly in the hands of the duopoly Alipay (Alibaba) and Tenpay (Tencent), who also control the data generated by transactions.

In the meantime, data are bought and sold for a wide variety of purposes, the most visible of which are currently online advertising, estimated globally at 360 billion USD in 2020 with intermediaries earning more than 10% from transactions.[11] But this may only be a small profit compared to what can be squeezed out of personal data when they finally enter the biomedical, insurance, banking, and in general, the strategic and operational marketing of companies. It is not yet clear whether and how a market for corporate data, which for the time being are essentially fenced off by individual companies, could be created.

In terms of distribution, the implications of the concentration of data and the economic transactions resulting from their possession are alarming, as already mentioned in Chapter 2.

Missed opportunities

Data are not in themselves a public good. They may be excludable by, for instance, firewalls or encryption or other means, but what seems certain is that in principle their consumption does not create rivalry, in the sense that – like knowledge in general – their use by one subject does not detract from the possibility of another subject using them in turn. But in order to be used, raw data must be "clean", artificial intelligence algorithms must be trained, and secure storage and reliable extraction is not without cost. What is still unanswered is ultimately how ownership and access rights to data will be defined.

The movement in favour of open data contrasts with the proposal to create market institutions, which necessarily implies property rights, and instead asserts the apparently attractive idea of data as a public good. This approach somehow confuses knowledge, as a possible public good, with data, which, as I have just said, are actually not mutually exclusive, and above all – if left unmanaged – have no value. Paradoxically, the open data initiative is supported not only by scientists and some governments, but – with some caution – by some Tech Giants such as Microsoft and Alphabet, who evidently believe that if everyone puts their data in the cloud they have the best infrastructure and knowledge to make a profit, for instance by selling the cloud services themselves, or better still by selling value-added services, as Amazon's AWS, Microsoft Azure, Alibaba Cloud, and Google Cloud already do.

The response of governments to the tension between considering data as a commodity and considering it as a public good takes the form of privacy legislation, such as GDPR in the EU, which however does not concern corporate data and ultimately does not solve the underlying problem, namely the contradiction between the economic value that can be derived, on which the digital oligopoly of the Tech Giants is based, and the social value that is distributed downstream. Looking at this issue from a broader perspective, we have yet another example of the theme already encountered in the previous chapters: the agenda of the Tech Giants does not include maximising the social value of data. If this issue is not as well understood as the case of biomedical and planetary health knowledge, it is only because we have not yet realised all the potential that is being wasted by the disconnection between private and public interests in the digital economy.

The main question that arises is how to create infrastructures or institutions that enable cooperative forms of data use, in which ownership remains in the collective hands of those who created it. Some cities, such as Barcelona, have done this with projects that create municipal platforms for sharing citizens' personal data, somewhat (optimistically) seen as a local-scale answer to the Tech Giants.[12] More generally, some believe that Big Data storage centres (such as those of Amazon Web Services) are an inefficient answer to the flood of encoded information and that it should be processed as close as possible to where it is produced (edge computing).

But where is data actually generated? Today – not considering the RI – they are mainly generated through social media interactions, through email, through online bookings and purchases, through the use of credit cards and POS, through a simple visit to a website, and also in interactions with public administration and healthcare systems. In the future, they could be generated mainly by interconnected machines, the Internet of Things, which basically means that every single object with a logic card could generate signals that are transmitted, accumulated, analysed and processed remotely for all kinds of activities. An estimated 25 billion machines will thus be connected in 2025, essentially wirelessly. 5G technology could reportedly support one million connections per square kilometre.[13]

The mechanism that has presumably been established gravitates towards centralisation due to the phenomenon that, indeed, has been termed "data gravity": the attraction that data exerts on other data due to the obvious economies of scale, density and variety that result from the need for the information base to be as broad and diverse as possible. Take, for example, the potential offered by personal biomedical data. If we had data about an individual's complete genome, the diseases he or she has been diagnosed with, the drugs he or she takes, his or her continuous vital parameters and the time he or she spends on physical activity (e.g., with a wrist device such as a Fitbit), but also his or her shopping trolley at the supermarket and purchases in general, his or her physical and online movements, his or her social network, and his or her income declared to the tax authorities, we could derive a much more complete risk profiling than could be inferred from non-interfaced databases.

If this scenario appears disturbing in relation to the individual, it is sufficient to shift the unit of analysis to statistical aggregates of reference, assuming, of course, that the users supplying the data trust the operator of the integrated databases, which is the case today when a user accepts the small print conditions proposed by the operators of the various services with a click. If the databases are integrated, then so can the software for cleaning up the "noise" of storage, querying, and analysis. In this sense, artificial intelligence tends towards a natural monopoly, in the sense that the marginal cost of managing the bit is constantly decreasing.

However, this integration is by no means trivial, as anyone who has worked on large databases, such as ORBIS, knows. ORBIS hosts data on more than 380 million companies with detailed financial information on 40 million companies, including not only balance sheet data but also information on share ownership. Even slight variations in the company name, location, group membership, etc., make the merging of these data with data from other databases anything but trivial. For example, in the case of my research group, the reconstruction of ownership and data on telecommunication companies or CERN suppliers required laborious checks that could only be partly automated and, in many cases, they were carried out manually one by one, despite the fact that we used professionally managed, consolidated, relatively "clean" databases, not the raw data that can come from the traces left by visitors to a site, or radar readings from earth observation satellites, or from many other sources that require a lot of preliminary work to interpret.

These problems are well known within organisations of a certain size, such as large companies or public administration, where the integration of data between different departments often fails or proves to be much more laborious than expected. Only an ex-ante design of data management (often including the establishment of a chief data officer) that establishes data warehouses or data lakes with the corresponding integrated procedures from the outset can alleviate integration problems that can often be intractable or costly ex post. It is not a question of where the data are stored, whether in large centres accessible through cloud services or in decentralised but interconnected repositories. The issue is whether different sources of data are able to be analysed in a unified way with certain procedures. The data in many cases, however, are not static objects, but quasi-continuous streams in real time. Their combinations cannot be managed with "timeless" procedures, an issue that concerns a wide variety of applications, from the global supply chain of large manufacturing companies such as the automobile industry, to the monitoring of energy theft for electricity operators such as Enel, to the management of insurance contracts. This opens up a market for companies such as Oracle or IBM that offer to sell database management programmes built with a datamining and artificial intelligence approach to those who do not have the resources to build these programmes themselves (i.e., practically everyone, since the required professional skills on the labour market are scarce and demand at a high price). Start-ups are constantly entering the market proposing new AI programmes, but which and how many will reach the critical mass to compete with the oligopolists in the various segments cannot be predicted, although there will presumably be few due to the effect of a certain Darwinian selection, in this as in other fields, but also because – as in the case of the pharmaceutical sector – if a start-up comes up with commercially interesting ideas, it is likely to be taken over by one of the larger companies with offers that are too tempting to be refused.

In this perspective, the debate between Big Data centres and edge computing does not appear to define a clear-cut alternative, since integrated data storage and processing systems can be imagined without the data being physically concentrated: this does not detract from the fact that if there is a unitary organisation that manages the process of extraction, cleaning, processing, access, the natural monopoly applies to the organisation, not to a specific location. For example, it does not seem at all necessary that the data generated by the fleet of self-driving cars should flow into remote servers, but of course, if the local servers are connected and interfaced in an integrated manner it does not make much difference in terms of the economic mechanism that generates the decreasing marginal costs.

From a distributional point of view, apart from considerations of geographic and market concentration, the formation of a data processing proletariat seems likely, as I have already mentioned. As *The Economist* wrote:

> The question is rather how much such data workers will be paid. As things stand, their work may become systematically undervalued [...] big platforms are not just monopolies, but monopsonies, meaning that they have the power to hold down wages for data labour. Tellingly, none has ever really considered paying users for the data they generate [...] A data economy in which those who produce a large part of the main input are perennially underpaid is unlikely to be a healthy economy.[14]

The second of these two aspects, I believe, is the decisive one. Tens of millions of proletarians in data management and IT activities in general, people with their lives stuck to a screen (like call centre operators), are a social problem. But billions of human beings dispossessed of their data to generate the wealth of a few, in exchange for goods often of dubious value, are a matter of another order of magnitude. It is the return on a planetary scale to unacceptable capitalism without public rules, which deprives everyone of personal dignity, reducing us to free purveyors of knowledge about our lives in exchange for mere breadcrumbs.

In listing the benefits of the digital economy, however great they may seem to the individual and the individual company, the identification of opportunity costs is missing: what could be done, and what is not being done, with information science and technology to address the unresolved challenges of our time?

I will only give a few illustrative examples here. The concrete articulation of objectives and instruments can only come from the construction of public infrastructure that embraces the mission of a research, development, and service provision agenda in the collective interest. I will propose this in the next section, but let us immediately look at some issues to which the current configuration of the ICT market in the broad sense does not adequately respond.

The grand challenges I discussed in the previous two chapters are connected to new visions of human health and the health of the planet. A digital agenda with objectives related to these issues could, first of all, consider that today, for the first time in human history, we have the opportunity to comprehensively, systematically, and dynamically investigate the correlation between genetic heritage, the natural environment, and the socio-economic conditions of each of us.

As extraordinary as the advances in human medicine have been, an enormous wealth of knowledge about the interactions between our genes and our world goes to waste. The most important data are collected in a disorganised way, often as a result of research projects with economic or academic motives. Detailed information is in inaccessible, non-standardised archives, which can hardly be used for holistic studies of human health. If research is primarily aimed at drugs to treat certain diseases, it escapes our notice that many aspects of human health are not necessarily treatable effectively and efficiently with drugs in the first place. Combating behavioural, social, and environmental risk factors requires looking at the individual person as a whole. Despite the fact that excellent epidemiological research has established some of these correlations, and notwithstanding the ambitions of precision medicine, the database that is collected does not have the consistency and coherence required for an analysis in which a large number of variables are taken into account simultaneously. For example, the typical stratification of patients and control groups in clinical trials captures data such as age, gender, and certain clinical parameters, but is not systematically supplemented with data on the patients' genome, familiarity, ethnicity, socio-economic status, dietary habits, and exposure to environmental factors. To conduct this type of study requires repeated sampling, the size of which is beyond the industry's interest, but which would pave the way for research that is more clearly oriented towards health policies.

Indeed, the current approach is heavily conditioned by the fact that information, which is not systematic and not accessible to subsequent research in a useful way, is collected at specific moments in a person's life, for example, during illness, and not continuously before and after for public interest purposes. The paradox of the situation we live in is that these personal data are chaotically accumulating on the servers of the Tech Giants, based on criteria and with purposes that are inevitably those of profit-oriented organisations. This data is not collected in a way that is accessible to public health institutions, which, for example, during the Covid-19 pandemic had to invent tracking systems on a national basis with vastly differing outcomes. Yet the possibility of documenting our genetic identity at birth, of detecting mutations at predetermined intervals of time, of integrating these data in an equally systematic manner with other aspects of socio-healthcare relevance, is now technologically feasible at a sustainable cost, with very great potential benefits in the design of health policies, from prevention to treatment. The problems of ethics, cybersecurity, and encryption of this information in a system of integrated digital archives would be considerable, but not insurmountable, and no greater than those that already arise at present in a way that is scarcely homogeneous between jurisdictions. The game of Big Data and artificial intelligence is too important not to be played in the field of health with a clear and prominent public mission.

The other great challenge is to recognise that if we as individuals can get sick, the planet can also get sick. And because we inhabit it, we need to understand what data we need in order to dynamically monitor the health of the environment in which we live and to develop preventive and therapeutic measures for ourselves as individuals.

There is a long tradition of collecting data on the state of the atmosphere on just a few parameters for weather forecasting and a more recent systematic collection of data on air and water pollution, and more besides. But as with human health, much information is wasted. Individual research programmes typically lasting several years, but not permanent, collect and process certain data in certain contexts, but – as mentioned in the previous chapter – there is a lack of a coordinated international database infrastructure on the health of the planet and its determinants.

Despite the fact that an expensive fleet of earth observation satellites rotates over our heads generating a stream of valuable data, most of this data is not used because it appears to have no immediate commercial value. The same is true for ground-based pollution monitoring stations, for observations of the state of the seas and rivers, for monitoring vehicle traffic on the roads and real-time electricity production and consumption, for the environmental impact of animal husbandry and various other human activities. Data are collected, but they are poorly and little used in non-integrated archives. The paradox is that the scientific community of astronomers poses the problem of how to integrate data on the observation of the universe more than governments pose the problem of integrating data on our planet. As for human health, the information technologies that would enable this are at hand, but financial investors are not interested. The time horizon is too long for them.

A third element on which we are conspicuously squandering opportunities is universal access to information and to knowledge and the interconnection between people. The current system of telecommunications and the web economy actually operates under conditions of decreasing and often zero marginal costs. This fact, combined with the configuration of profit-oriented oligopolies, entails the need for companies to extract returns on data transmission and access in inefficient ways: with advertising, with subscription fees and price discrimination, and in many other ways, when the most efficient solution would be to offer digital communication free of charge as a basic public service, just as – at least in Europe – other services are offered at the expense of general taxation. The persistence even in the Union, certainly in Italy as we have seen with distance learning, of "digital divide" is unacceptable given the not insurmountable costs and the high benefit it would have in bridging the gaps, just as the public electricity service companies did in their time.

European Commission initiatives and a new proposal

If we discard the hypothesis of digital sovereignism, in which each government regulates users' access to the Internet in more or less drastic ways within its jurisdiction, supranational forms of regulation on a purely regulatory basis, such as the European Union's GDPR, the Digital Markets Act or the Digital Services Act,[15] appear to be inconclusive. Anti-trust actions are slow and uncertain.[16] One example is the investigations by the European Commission and the US Supreme Court into Apple's market power with the AppStore payment system, exclusively installed on every iPhone, from which 519 billion USD flowed in 2019 alone, with a substantial commission flow for Apple itself.[17] Perhaps some Tech Giants could opt, like Facebook, for self-regulating systems, either with committees and appeals procedures on the content, or with algorithms that give users some control over the data. The most effective strategy, however, would be the creation – at least at the European level – of a public infrastructure capable of competing with the Tech Giants and offering services that the latter are currently not interested in offering.

An embryonic symptom of this ambition is the Gaia-X project, initially proposed by Germany at the Dortmund Digital Summit (2019), but later joined by France and in which other countries and companies, research institutes, and organisations expressed interest. The initial ambitious idea seems to have been to create an Airbus Cloud in the manner of the consortium that effectively broke Boeing's market dominance in the aviation industry. The version currently on the table is that of a federation of clouds that agree with each other to adopt certain protocols, with specialised clubs such as GAIA-Health, GAIA-Mobility, and others according to a variable geometry. The model should be that of a cloud of clouds characterised by a single standard for sharing data, in a flexible form. The concept declared by Gaia-X in its founding documents is to build a user-friendly ecosystem by aligning the protocols of different network and interconnection providers, Cloud Solution Providers and High-Performance Computing centres, and by bringing specialised clouds into the system.

The areas of implementation identified so far by Gaia-X are as follows:

- implementation of reliable federated identities in terms of security and privacy right from the design phase of the system;
- data management services whose sovereignty is maintained, ensuring the identity of the source and recipient of the data, as well as the rights of access and use of the data;
- easy access to providers, nodes, and services through federated catalogues;
- integration of existing standards to ensure interoperability and portability across infrastructure, applications, and data;
- the creation of a framework for proper enforcement of rules with accreditation and certification services;
- the formation of a modular library of open-source software and standards to support a secure, trusted, interoperable infrastructure.

Forty use cases were presented in sectors such as Industry 4.0, Smart Living, Finance, Health, Public Sector, Mobility, and Agriculture illustrating the potential advantages. An example: in confirmation of what I said above about biomedical data relating to clinical trials, there is consensus that while AI methods could be extremely useful,

> a large part of the clinical data collected at present is not accessible for scientific studies and statistical analysis due to the different formats used for the unstructured nature of the data. This means that no useful insights for medicine can be gained from it.[18]

Gaia-X could implement reliable solutions for the use of healthcare data, in compliance with regulations, data protection, and cybersecurity. It could offer secure data storage capabilities and computational resources available to hospitals and small- to medium-sized enterprises in the sector with dedicated cloud services, accessible via standardised interfaces. It could also offer standardised anonymisation or pseudonymisation services so that different user groups could access the data in compliance with regulations, for example, to train AI models on this data. The most sensitive data could remain stored at a hospital, while other data could be shared for research network projects.

Currently (2023), Gaia-X seems to be a project still a work in progress, despite the adhesion in principle of over 350 companies and organisations with Italy in third place after Germany (with management entrusted to the Fraunhofer Institute for Software and Systems Technology and the participation of SAP, Siemens, Deutsche Telekom, etc.) and France. Among the Italian companies involved are Leonardo, Enel, Aruba, Retelit, and telecommunication companies such as TIM and Fastweb, as well as Poste Italiane, Banca Intesa, and various IT companies. The founding members of the Gaia-X Association are 11 German and 11 French organisations, which is perhaps an indication of a Berlin-Paris axis present in the initial design.

In Ursula von der Leyen's State of the Union Address (2020), the project was "sponsored" by the Commission with these words:

> On personalized data – business to consumer – Europe has been too slow and is now dependent on others. This cannot happen with industrial data [...] The amount of industrial data in the world will quadruple in the next five years – and so will the opportunities that come with it. We have to give our companies, SMEs, start-ups and researchers the opportunity to draw on their full potential [...] But the reality is that 80% of industrial data is still collected and never used. [...] We need common data spaces – for example, in the energy or healthcare sectors. This will support innovation ecosystems in which universities, companies and researchers can access and collaborate on data. And it is why we will build a European cloud as part of NextGenerationEU – based on GaiaX.[19]

This is an authoritative and courageous stance, especially in its recognition of the delay and the need to remedy it. The reference model, however, is not yet well defined and may not be up to the challenge of disengaging Europe from the dependency on "others" to which von der Leyen alludes. For instance, it is not clear whether, and with what role, the major players of global cloud services might participate. Let's look again at their market shares at the end of 2018: AWS 31.7% (25.4 billion USD); Microsoft Azure 16.8%; Google Cloud 8.5%; Alibaba Cloud 4%; IBM Cloud 3.8%; and others 35.2%, for a total market (estimated by the specialised market research company Canalys) of 80.4 billion, will also join the consortium.

Some experts are very critical of the space given to the speeches of some of their exponents at the virtual launch event of the project: the Pan European Gaia-X Summit, 18 November 2020, with 4000 participants. According to Fermigier and Franck (2020), with such a level of participation, the project could be captured and become a "Trojan horse" for the Tech Giants. They could access the grant funding provided by Next Generation EU. The authors also mention the failed previous attempts at building a French cloud:

> Gaia-X is a great opportunity to demonstrate what potentials a federated and collaborative system based on European values can unlock. By not attaching conditions for receiving public funding and by letting Hyperscalers influence the rules of openness and competition, it also poses a great risk of destroying the European ecosystem and hopes of sovereignty that the Gaia-X project was originally supposed to build and strengthen.[20]

The Hyperscalers alluded to here are the Tech Giants that offer "scalable" cloud and computing services, that is, expandable as an architecture, with virtually no limits on memory, computation, networking, and data storage.

The criticism should be taken seriously and the following proposal has a different approach to that of Gaia-X, at least in its current formulation.

Before presenting it, I think it is useful to briefly mention another European project with cloud ambitions, in this case relating to the scientific environment: EOSC-European Open Science Cloud. I quote here the presentation by Prof. Giorgio Rossi (European Science Cloud Virtual Event, University of Milan, 15 October 2020):

> the creation of data is growing exponentially (at the scale of Zettabytes – 10^{21} bytes) for research as well, so that researchers are already de facto prevented from accessing all digital knowledge relevant to their research field [...] What is needed is a robust Europe-wide environment for storing and analysing data with the necessary computing resources in order to offer equal opportunities to all European researchers (approx. 1.7 million and over 70 million professionals involved in science and technology-related activities) [...] [to] interconnect Research Infrastructures in order to overcome disciplinary silos by creating interoperable "data commons" necessary for the global challenges and "mission-oriented" research envisaged by Horizon Europe [...] [it is] necessary to create the competences for the management of FAIR data from the generation phase by the researcher (FAIR-by-design) to the production of data services for the user (identifiers, access, AI) by training new professional data-scientists and data-stewards alongside researchers of all disciplines [...] EOSC is conceived as a public good at the service of the whole research community. It will have to guarantee the quality of data and metadata, the care and long-term preservation of unrepeatable data collections (time series), the effective accessibility and availability of software and resources for data analysis.

To design EOSC, a Strategic Partnership is envisaged within the Horizon Europe Framework Programme, with funds made available by the European Commission and in-kind contributions from the participating states, including Italy, where ICDI-Italian Computing and Data Infrastructure has been set up, bringing together Italian research infrastructures, public research bodies, and universities. Gaia-X and EOSC are not the only European projects in fields related to the theme of this chapter. The picture is currently evolving but, to date, as I have already mentioned, around 8 billion euros of the EU budget has been earmarked for a Digital Europe Programme, which includes resources for projects of Community interest in areas such as supercomputing, artificial intelligence, cybersecurity, advanced vocational training, and the development of Digital Innovation Hubs. The Digital Europe Programme is considered complementary to other EU programmes, in particular, Horizon Europe for research and Connecting Europe Facility for fibre-optic projects in peripheral areas and other investments.

Despite these encouraging signs, Europe will find it difficult to catch up with the US and China in information technology and related areas without a real public infrastructure along the lines outlined in the previous chapters.[21]

Let me now turn to my own proposal. It would be necessary to design a European supranational entity that not only has coordination functions, but also has full managerial autonomy, budget, tangible, and intangible capital, and dedicated staff with the mission to create a public platform as an alternative to the Tech Giants. As with Biomed Europa and Green Europa, this would be a combination of research infrastructure and public enterprise, that is, a public infrastructure. The supranational agency managing this infrastructure would certainly have to resort to collaborations with third parties, as in the Gaia-X scheme, but with a clear distinction of roles. The secret of the success of CERN's "Geneva model" (but also of other RIs I have mentioned) lies in the fact that the experimental scientific collaborations with their broad and "federated" structure have a permanent point of reference in CERN's scientific, technological, and managerial infrastructure. This aspect can be seen very clearly in IT matters and is the basis for the invention of the WWW and the current grid, as well as many other features of data management activities. The system is designed to have the greatest flexibility in data access by thousands of researchers worldwide, connected via a vast network of nodes using standardised protocols, but it could not function without CERN's robust IT department, which has data centres with dedicated servers, computing resources, its own staff, and research projects focused on specific objectives.

The same can be said for the EMBL-European Bioinformatics Institute, which, while providing a service to hundreds of thousands of users in the most flexible way conceivable, is also solidly supported by its own physical server infrastructure, its own staff and the resources derived from being part of EMBL, a supranational body and not a federation of participating institutes.

On the other hand, the best-known US Tech Giants, although they are companies that have adopted organisational models in line with the "open" culture of Silicon Valley, have full control of the central and peripheral structures that are essential for their functioning, albeit with significant differences between them.

Only an accurate strategic plan would be able to define the details of a European public digital infrastructure, but it may be useful to indicate a few themes here:

a *Personal data.* Firstly, it is not yet clear to me that the personal data "game" (consumer to consumer and consumer to business) is completely lost for Europe. At the very least, alternatives should be explored. Take the case of Facebook, which was seen by many as the most unbeatable of technology platforms, with its billions of users and the daily petabytes of information it generates, but whose audience is segmented linguistically and normatively. Facebook actually manages a number of perhaps weakly interconnected pools (e.g., advertising investments in Italian are not connected to those in Russian or Arabic). Europe, also from a regulatory point of view, could be a sufficiently large pool to imagine that at least for certain categories of users an alternative platform could be offered that would give services and guarantees that Facebook does not give in terms of data protection, removal of hate content, retention of data ownership by the user, and many other undesirable and dangerous aspects from a democratic point of view.

b *The platforms.* Even Amazon, which emerged victorious and strengthened from the pandemic, might not be considered unbeatable if, at least for the European market space, one considers the logistics platforms offered by the postal systems, which as a whole have excellent operating standards compared to those in other parts of the world. Other examples can be given of hypothetical autonomous European platforms that could attract users in associations, schools, and professions. While these "civic" platforms should not be the priorities of the Digital Europe project, it would be worthwhile for the project to launch feasibility studies and proof-of-concept models, experimental prototypes, to imagine a freer future for the individual user, offering European citizens alternative platforms to those in the US (and China).

c *Professional data.* As far as so-called "industrial" data are concerned, which in reality include all kinds of data not generated by individuals, that is, data from public administrations, healthcare, universities, finance, and various public service sectors, the federative model of Gaia-X appears – as I have mentioned – to be inadequate in many respects, as well as being incompletely defined for the time being. The idea of a "cloud of clouds" could be a complement to an autonomous European cloud managed directly by the Digital Europa agency, with its own servers and staff, with specific know-how, without detracting from the possibility of specialised clouds such as EOSC. But it would clearly be an inefficient use of resources for each of these projects to set up its own IT infrastructure and then federate with others that will inevitably have designed their data centres, protocols, etc., in a different way. Nor should we underestimate the language and "tacit" knowledge aspect that is typical of organisations, solved at

CERN, EMBL, ESA, and elsewhere in the only possible way: with the use of English and with "house rules" that everyone must somehow abide by if they want to access the services offered as users, even if these users are thousands of kilometres away.

d *Investments*. One cannot then underestimate the investment in R&D specifically dedicated to such a project, which involves technological solutions for storing, retrieving, processing, analysing, and transmitting data, combining very high security with ease of access. If one does not want to buy ready-made solutions on the market offered by the Tech Giants but wants to develop a European IT sector that is competitive with that of the USA, Digital Europa needs to invest itself, and to a considerable extent. One only has to look at the R&D budgets of the key companies in the digital oligopoly to realise that a mishmash of research carried out by hospitals, power companies, banks, ministries, universities, etc., cannot create the library of code needed by a project with the ambitions set out by the president of the European Commission. Perhaps it might be useful to quote some figures on the R&D spending of some Tech Giants: according to Statista,[22] in 2020 Amazon claims to have spent 42.7 billion USD on R&D, Alphabet 27.6 billion USD, Microsoft 19.3 billion USD, Apple 18.8 billion USD, and Meta 18.5 billion USD. Only Big Pharma, automotive oligopolists (grappling with a radical change in technology), defence multinationals, and a few other sectors can claim these levels of R&D expenditure in the world. It is hard to see how one can challenge the Tech Giants without deploying adequate resources, and such resources cannot be dispersed in a myriad of projects of various orders of magnitude with a smaller R&D budget of those they intend to challenge.

e *The networks*. Then there are a series of technological adjustments to data transmission networks on which ITC companies, even those with public ownership, are lagging behind and which would require a more determined European policy than the current one: for example, in the Connecting Europe Facility allocations, the funds available for telecommunications are a modest fraction of those allocated to transport infrastructures, according to a now obsolete conception that assigns the priority of public investment to moving goods and people, leaving to the market the creation of infrastructures for the transportation of information.

f *The satellites*. While Europe lags behind the USA in other fields, this is not the case in industrial policy in the space sector, which has ESA as its point of reference. The fleet of satellites currently operated by ESA generates poorly utilised information in the downstream of certain fields, such as earth observation, which would greatly benefit from a functional integration in data processing in concert with Digital Europa. Moreover, innovative technological solutions could be envisaged to bring broadband Internet everywhere via satellite, a theme that some private US operators (initially including Google) are pursuing, in particular, with fleets of small, low-cost satellites in low orbits: see, for instance, the OneWeb project with 650 satellites and a plan to increase this to 48,000.[23] The project, supported mainly by US capital, risked bankruptcy and was saved for the time being by the British government (which has instead left the European radionavigation project Galileo) and an Indian fund. I mention this example to show how much the world of digital communication could change by embarking on new technological trajectories. Continuing with seemingly rather esoteric topics, the world's dependence on ICT technologies should imply adequate investment in how to predict or how to manage catastrophic risks to systems that might arise from rare but nonetheless possible events, such as extreme solar activity, a topic in which the private sector does not invest.

g *Computational capacity*. The scale of data to be handled in the near future, over the next five to ten years, is such that it is believed that new approaches to computing capabilities will be needed, regardless of how immense the progress from the UNIVAC era to modern computers has been. Today, we refer to at least three cutting-edge topics: exascale computing, large-scale integration of networked computers, and quantum computers. As far as the first topic is concerned, the aim is to design machines or systems capable of exceeding the threshold of 1018 FLOPS (floating point operations per second, a standardised measure of elementary instructions executed). These machines are expected to be indispensable for personalised medicine, meteorological models, simulations of the functioning of the human brain and other fields where the data to be computed in relation to the scenarios to be simulated go beyond current supercomputers (which have been operating at petascale for a decade or so). This may also require new chip production technologies, the global leader of which is in the Netherlands[24] and on which Intel, Samsung, and other leaders in the downstream semi-conductor market critically depend.[25] The second topic, which partly converges with the first, is the technological advancement required to move towards parallel or distributed computing systems that efficiently enable computer networks with large numbers of independent machines, physically located at great distances, to operate in an integrated and reliable manner. Finally, quantum computing promises to change (at least for certain types of operations) the very concept of binary code, from which the discussion in this chapter started, by adopting the property of quantum physics of allowing overlapping states (those in which Schrödinger's famous cat is neither alive – "state 1" – nor dead – "state 0", but a probabilistic mixture of the two states). Although classical computing, given enough time, could solve any problem posed to quantum computing, the problem is that the time needed for some problems could be extremely long,[26] whereas a future quantum computer could be much faster. It is significant that the first empirical demonstration, obviously on a purely illustrative scale of quantum supremacy (or perhaps more appropriately quantum advantage) seems to have been achieved by Google in collaboration with NASA and announced in an article in "Nature" in 2019,[27] according to which – to simplify a more complex topic – Google's quantum system would perform in 100 seconds a calculation that a classical supercomputer can perform in 10,000 years (a claim disputed by IBM in an interesting subsequent controversy). Although there is no shortage of European research projects in these cutting-edge fields (including at CERN), there does not seem to be the critical mass comparable to the work being done in the USA that could establish a truly unbridgeable gap in computer science and its applications on both sides of the Atlantic.

As with Biomed Europa and Green Europa, it is not a matter of imagining a closed and self-referential system, but rather being open to partnerships with already existing public and private organisations, primarily in the member states, building on adequate resources comparable with the annual research and development budgets of the major players in the field. The scale of a Digital Europa project should be that of a few billion euros per year in the hands of the new agency (much larger than amounts to be allocated for the digital economy in the Next Generation EU, and what's more in a rather dispersed manner). It is necessary to recruit the right people, the brightest minds in the world, to fund projects, to invest in equipment both in a campus that serves as a hub and in decentralised locations. As in the two previous examples, it seems possible to me that the initial and periodic public funding would to a large extent come directly back into the budget through a policy of fair pricing of certain types of services and through the management in the public interest of any intellectual property rights.

Appendix: Digital Markets Act and Digital Services Act

Overall the EU legislation is welcome but unable to structurally change the landscape. Very briefly:

a The Digital Services Act (DSA) aims at containing illegal content, disinformation, use of personal data for advertising. Its enforcement will start in 2025. Several national laws will need to be repealed or amended. Companies will be accountable for illegal content if they actually know such content is illegal; they will need to disclose to regulators their algorithms and implement transparent audit and risk management. There will be substantial fines for non-compliance. The EC will have specific enforcement powers.
b The Data Governance Act (DGA) has established a framework for the creation of common data spaces in the hope that data will be increasingly shared in sectors such as finance, health, and the environment.
c The Digital Markets Act (DMA) covers search engines; intermediation services (online stores); social networks; video sharing platforms, e-mail, and messaging; advertising operating systems; cloud services. DMA wants

to increase competition and targets market dominance and abuse of power against smaller competitors by major players: the "gatekeepers" (de facto the Tech Giants). Fines for non-compliance may reach 10% of turnover. Data collected from different services provided by the same player cannot be combined to extract information on platforms' users; advertisers and publishers will be more protected; self-preferencing, pre-installation, and bundling of own services will be limited; regulation related to bundling practices; interoperability, portability, and access to data for users will be enhanced.

d The General Data Protection Regulation (GDPR) since 2016 has created some rules about the use of personal data by the major digital players, granting certain rights to individuals and establishing certain obligations for companies.

e The future AI Act (2023) defining risk categories for artificial intelligence applications.

These are only some of the EU digital legislation in the last years aimed at increased competition and consumer protection in the digital markets. From a broader perspective, the electronic communication market in the past included other industries such as telecommunications. There are lessons to be learnt from earlier attempts to regulate such markets. In these industries, there is a combination of economies of scale on the supply side; direct and indirect network effects on the demand side (that further support monopolistic forces); economies of variety (meaning that different services provided have mutually reinforcing mechanisms); entry barriers related to past tangible and intangible assets owned by the incumbents, including brands, patents, and other intellectual property rights. Hence, such markets are too far from the competition paradigm to hope that regulators can obtain much more than some relatively limited, even if usually helpful, remedies. Consumers as individuals or small businesses are rarely effectively protected when a market is structurally an oligopoly or a monopoly, whatever the lawmakers and regulators, when they are not captured, try to do in terms of rules for access, prices, service quality, and other outcomes (Florio, 2013).

Appendix: the Fraunhofer model

A possible model of public infrastructure to draw inspiration from is the Fraunhofer-Gesellschaft model, founded in 1949, headquartered in Munich, one of Germany's great scientific associations that later evolved into a federal government structure for the promotion of applied research and technology (other associations such as Max Planck and Helmholtz are dedicated to basic research). I think it is useful to mention here a few key elements that show how what I call public infrastructure in this book can be structured, function, and achieve results.

I draw some figures from the 2018 Annual Report, which celebrates 70 years of the Society (and from subsequent updates). In 2018, Fraunhofer was a collection of 72 institutes and research units, some of which are part of virtual structures in different fields called Fraunhofer Clusters of Excellence. With a total annual budget of 2.6 billion euros, as much as 2.2 billion per year is generated by research contracts, both with the public sector and private companies (for 614 million euros, plus more than 100 million for other industrial revenues). Several thousand companies apply to the association each year, often for small contracts with a unit value of a few thousand euros for the solution of specific problems, in other cases for research contracts on the scale of several million euros.

A transfer from the federal government, and to a much lesser extent from the individual state governments, covers the basic activities while Fraunhofer gets the rest from the tender for research services. The association employs 26,600 scientists and technicians, including more than 7700 students and interns, most of them in engineering and natural sciences. In 2018, it spent 445 million euros on investments in infrastructure and equipment.

The governance is performed by an Executive Board, with management tasks undertaken together with the directors of the institutes, a Corporate Responsibility Board with supervisory tasks and integration of horizontal functions and missions, as well as the directors of the institutes. The institutes do not have their own legal status, but have a separation of accounts and budgets and develop their strategies with a large degree of autonomy within their market environment of research services and the relevant scientific and professional communities. In turn, the institutes are grouped into eight clusters, which indicate a broad thematic coverage (I report the operating budget and the number of institutes in brackets): ICT (250 million, 6 institutes), INNOVATION (a heterogeneous interdisciplinary cluster, 77 million, 5 institutes), Life Sciences (175 million, 7 institutes), Light and Surfaces (157 million, 16 institutes), Materials and Components (462 million, 16 institutes), Microelectronics (443 million, 11 institutes), Manufacturing (287 million, 11 institutes), and Defence (213 million, seven institutes working on technologies of military interest and fully funded by the German Ministry of Defence). In addition to these institutes, there are subsidiaries abroad with their own legal status and partnerships with companies and other research institutes. Key Strategic Initiatives have also been identified in the strategic plan up to 2022, which include, for example, inter-institute research on batteries, quantum technologies, and artificial intelligence. Two recent Clusters of Excellence are "Circular Economy of Plastics" and another on "Integrated Energy Systems". There are also 17 high-performance centres scattered across the territory that collaborate with local universities for transfer activities to support industry on a local scale. Several initiatives are in collaboration with the other three major German scientific associations: Max Planck, Helmholtz, and Leibnitz. Ninety per cent of the institute directors and 249 heads of departments also hold university positions, thus establishing strong links with the relevant academic communities, even though Fraunhofer is completely separate from the universities in terms of mission and structure.

The association has capital holdings in 90 companies, 66 of which are for technology transfer, as well as generating numerous spin-off companies (39 in 2018 alone) with the support of the Fraunhofer Venture department. The aim is to generate two spin-offs per thousand employees each year (in line with the international top performer in this field, the Massachusetts Institute of Technology). There are branches abroad with their own legal personality in the USA, Austria, Italy, the UK, Chile, Portugal, Sweden, and Singapore, to which 16 research centres belong, often in partnership with universities. There are also centres with other characteristics in Israel (on innovative drugs), Poland (components for the automotive industry), Japan, Australia, and elsewhere.

An indicator of the success of Fraunhofer's activities, in addition to its ability to attract national and international funding also from companies, is the filing of patents. For the past ten years, the association has been ranked among the best in Germany and within the European Patent Office. In 2018 alone, inventors employed by the association made public reports on 734 inventions, 612 of which involved the filing of patent applications: almost three patents for every working day. In Germany, a total of 3272 patents are registered with Fraunhofer, and the portfolio of patent families in different countries comprises 6881. There are currently 2515 licensing agreements, 384 of which were finalised in 2018, with 109 million euros in revenue. The annual reports present some of the major recent innovations in various fields. The most recent is the 2021 report: more than 30,000 employees, 76 institutes, a budget of 2.9 billion euros, of which 2.5 billion euros from research contracts, and 521 new patents filed. It is a good example of an innovative public infrastructure that could inspire a European project.

Notes

1 Albeit with some ambiguity because base 2 is sometimes substituted for base 10, so that a gigabyte (GB) is defined as 10^9 bytes, corresponding to approximately 2^{30} bytes or a gibibyte (GiB).

2 COST, 2010.

3 https://kinsta.com/blog/facebook-statistics/

4 IDC, a specialised research company.

5 https://www.idc.com/

6 The Economist, 25 January 2020a, p.26. An example of these projects is Multics (Multiplexed Information and Computing Service) – less known to the general public than the Internet – that in 1969 brought together MIT, Bell Laboratories, and General Electric, one system which made the history of computers by allowing multiprogramming activities and multitasking through time optimisation of resources of calculation.

7 Weinberger, 2017.

8 A new agency of the US Department of Defence, the Joint Artificial Intelligence Center, has been created to use AI technologies applied to the military (e.g. for drone target recognition), at the proposal of the Defence Innovation Board, a body that coordinates various programmes of the Pentagon. It is revealing that the chairman of the DIB is a former board member of Alphabet.

9 It collapsed to 271 billion at the time I am writing (October 27, 2022).

10 Huawei controls about 30% of the 5G equipment market, while Samsung has about 23%, Scandinavian Nokia and Ericsson hold 15 and 12% respectively, although alternative technologies such as OpenRAN may exist in the future. Since July 2020, the US government has taken various measures against Huawei, invoking reasons of national security.

11 https://www.imarcgroup.com/internet-advertising-market

12 Koryan and Narayan (2021) provide a synthesis of lively recent discussion among supporters of different models for socialising data value, aiming at counteracting asymmetries of power in the digital economy: between Tech Giants and consumers, small business, nation states, less developed regions. In general regulations such as the EU GDPR are seen as "individualist" approaches that privileges privacy and data security and ineffective in terms of fairness. These alternative model are in fact at different levels of maturity, as some of them are just initial ideas. They include: A) Various forms of "data stewardship" such as sharing pools among partners. The more important ones involve some large companies, and are regulated by private law. While "horizontally" these arrangements may work, their bargaining power "vertically" with the Tech Giants, are limited on non existent. Data co-operatives tend to be a variant with a democratic governance within the group, but probably of limited scope without mandatory mechanisms. Public data trusts often involves municipalities or other public entities and their citizens/users. Their financial and technical sustainability is not yet proven. B) Solidarity based data governance, particularly in fields as health care where patients may mutually benefit of sharing information, which is currently mostly appropriated by commercial data users. C) Semi-commons, based on the principle that users have non-exclusive access to the data they have provided, or to a layer of certain types of data, but are not individually their owners. D) Data re-using mechanisms, meaning that other actors can access and use data collected by somebody else in the first place, and for different purposes, under certain conditions. E) Democratic data governance, which does not assume that there is individual ownership of data, but a collective entitlement by a "population" of providers-users that enter in a relation. F) Peer-to-Peer production, developing to a larger scale examples of voluntary cooperation such as Wikipedia. While it interesting to look at these ideas and initial experiences, it seems obvious that without a strong public initiative they would take too much time to offer viable alternatives to the Tech Giants. In any case, they could be a complement to a public infrastructure such as the one I propose in this chapter.

13 https://www.ericsson.com/en/internet-of-things

14 The Economist, 20 February 2020b.

15 https://digital-strategy.ec.europa.eu/en/policies/digital-services-act-package

16 A critical discussion of EU legislation on the digital economy goes beyond the scope of this book. See Appendix: Digital Markets Act and Digital Services Act.

17 https://ec.europa.eu/commission/presscorner/detail/en/ip_20_1073, https://techcrunch.com/2019/05/13/supreme-court-rules-against-apple-allowing-an-app-store-antitrust-case-to-proceed/?guce_referrer=aHR0cHM6Ly93d3cuZ29vZ2xlLmNvbS8&guce_referrer_sig=AQAAAN19SCItI_ge5QvuM14kxdRdgi5LPvHKKhIth9s_JDFwWjgT69VLCrwbR3P-AwtPekWn7oxfvJG5U0SCcleaIEB8QW7fRhb6FwX-8y0HgDqRy22eMqFvCIn4onnm7OP2zJROxoRPhAmj7En3NV4Y0TnRnfo79PLZUVntStDMvkGt&guccounter=2

18 https://www.data-infrastructure.eu/GAIAX/Navigation/EN/Home/home.html

19 European Commission, *State of the Union Address by President von der Leyen at the European Parliament Plenary*: https://ec.europa.eu/commission/presscorner/detail/en/SPEECH_20_1655

20 Fermigier, Franck, 2020.
21 The global dependence on China in terms of revenue is around 30–35% for electronic components, computer hardware, software, and Internet services, household appliances, retail internet sales, semiconductors, and at least 20% for electronic equipment in general and telecommunications in particular.
22 https://www.statista.com/statistics/265645/ranking-of-the-20-companies-with-the-highest-spending-on-research-and-development/
23 https://en.wikipedia.org/wiki/OneWeb_satellite_constellation
24 ASML, whose machines are able to design circuits using ultraviolet radiation at the nanometre scale.
25 Little known to the public, this company has a higher market value than Volkswagen, Siemens, or Airbus, which speaks volumes about the strategic role of these cutting-edge technologies for the future.
26 Arute et al., 2019.
27 Arute et al., 2019.

Conclusion

What can be done?

> Just as the electricity of a whole atmosphere is concentrated in the tip of the lightning rod, an immeasurable number of events then come together in the narrowest span of time. What otherwise leisurely occurs sequentially and simultaneously is condensed into a single moment that determines and decides everything.
>
> **Stefan Zweig, *Decisive Moments in History*, 1943**

A lot of electricity has accumulated in the atmosphere over the last decade. A decisive moment was the announcement of the bankruptcy of Lehman Brothers. One of the world's largest investment banks ('triple A', the highest reliability in agency ratings) suddenly collapsed (15th September 2008). A chain of catastrophic events in the financial markets was triggered. The Great Recession that followed was the trauma that called into question the narrative of self-regulation of the financial markets and brought the state back into play as the economy's lifeline. The Great Recession had political consequences. The sense of social alarm contributed to the election of Obama to the US presidency, with a moderately progressive agenda on employment support, health insurance coverage, and environmental policy: an agenda that was nevertheless inadequate to create a broad and lasting social and electoral coalition.

Indeed, an opposite reaction was triggered. In the country of opportunity, which was increasingly becoming one of great inequalities and fractures, there was another decisive moment. On 8th November 2016, an eccentric billionaire with a protectionist and nationalist agenda, mainly anti-Chinese, but also anti-European, would succeed in creating an unprecedented coalition. Voters, who were mainly white and unsure of their future, concentrated in a few key states with a declining industrial tradition, especially in the peripheral areas, surprisingly voted together with voters in the historical conservative strongholds. Thanks in part to the aggressive use of old and new media, Donald Trump showed how fragile the institutions of democracy are when its social foundations are shaken by the perception of injustice. Three years after his election, that President announced the withdrawal of the

DOI: 10.4324/9781003381532-7

United States from the Paris Agreement on climate change, an unprecedented rupture in multilateral international relations, but also a planetary signal of the splits we have to reckon with and that closely link economics and finance, social inequality, public policy, and the great challenges of this century.

A few weeks after the US withdrawing from the Paris Agreement, on 31 December 2019, the Wuhan Health Commission officially notified the World Health Organization of an outbreak of interstitial pneumonia of unknown origin. Trump's USA then promptly withdrew from the WHO, accusing it of connivance with China. After a year of a chaotically managed pandemic, on 6 January 2021, followers of Trump, having been defeated in the election after his first term but unwilling to surrender, stormed Capitol Hill. They had been summoned via social media, incited by the White House itself, in the most serious crisis of American democracy in over a century. Twitter permanently closed the US president's profile with its 89 million followers.

In these events, only apparently unrelated, the main ingredients of our time recur: economic instability, social insecurity, climate change, planetary health threats, geopolitical imbalances, the power of the Tech Giants, and the fragility of democracy. Events flow in parallel, as Zweig said, but the crises are convergent.

There are cracks in the previous neoliberal consensus: the glorification of the oligopoly and the acceptance as inescapable of social inequality. That consensus kept critics on the sidelines, with ill-concealed annoyance. For many years, I tried to show – with the analytical tools of the applied economist – that policies of generalised privatisation of public services, on the British model of Margaret Thatcher, undermined essential means of social cohesion. Trust in the abstraction of market efficiency and the miraculous virtues of its regulation by bureaucratic agencies was excessive and suspect. Those "reforms" undermined universal health care, environmental policies, and publicly owned enterprises in key sectors, such as energy, telecommunications, railways, and others, and simultaneously weakened the credibility of public institutions among citizens. If the state is not acknowledged as providing the services that hold society together, while inequality increases and opportunities for most people worsen, then taxes, open borders and democracy begin to appear the enemy of "the people", particularly the impoverished "middle classes". I was not certainly alone to criticise the neoliberal ideology and policy embodied in the "Washington Consensus", but mainstream economics and policymaking provided a powerful narrative. The emergence of the Great Recession and the disruption of the US democracy with the Trump presidency revealed the flaws of that narrative.[1]

The pandemic caught the West at the height of a wave of neo-nationalist movements, with the classic mixture of racism, xenophobia, tax revolt, mockery of science, and the emergence of "strong men". Even now, as I write, tens of millions of US and EU citizens are convinced that the pandemic is a conspiracy, vaccines are a scam, and politicians spread terror for their own hidden ends. Trump lost the election, but for the majority of his voters climate change is fake news, social media is a conspiracy, facemasks constitute violence, and judges are traitors. Trump overwhelmingly lost in the vote, defeated everywhere in the cities, but he holds the oldest political party in the West to hostage. In Europe, after the nationalist drama of Brexit, greeted with joy by Trump himself and by the enemies of the European project, after the authoritarian drifts in Poland, Hungary, and elsewhere, after the explosion of the far-right vote in countries like France, Italy, and others, it is time to stop and think about the need to change policies. Perhaps the moderate ruling classes of liberal-democratic persuasion (as well as those of the fading social-democratic tradition) are beginning to realise that the mixture of budgetary austerity, globalisation without curbs on social and fiscal dumping, privatisation, and liberalisation of public services, has endangered the survival of economic and political institutions as we have known them since the Second World War. As in the 1920s, anything can happen. The outcome of the play is uncertain.

Next Generation EU, the set of extraordinary measures to cope with the health, economic, and climate crisis at the same time, measures financed with joint debt by the EU member states, is perhaps a sign of some rethinking on the part of the establishment. It is in this context that the European Commission has announced initiatives that were unthinkable a few years ago: among them, a European medicines strategy, a policy of data governance and the creation of public digital platforms, as well as an ambitious goal of decarbonising the economy. The Biden administration in the US has adopted a more progressive agenda than Obama's (not to mention Clinton's). Among its first acts: bringing the US back into the Paris Climate Agreement and into the World Health Organization, launching extraordinarily expansive economic measures, taking the vaccination campaign vigorously into its own hands, reassessing the role of science, reopening a public debate on discrimination.

An energy crisis in now shaking again the neoliberal paradigm. Everybody now understands that energy markets alone are unable to deal with huge price spikes, beyond the Russian invasion of Ukraine. Without radically innovative policies, the world will remain dominated by uncontrollable oligopolistic combinations, with the corollary of dangerous social imbalances, insufficient curbs on global threats from the coming economic, health, and environmental crises, and risks to democratic institutions. The global oligopoly cannot ensure good governance, a good society, and inclusive and orderly economic growth. We need to turn the page from apologetic narratives, to which too many politicians and economists have lent themselves, and we need to do so by opening a debate on possible alternatives. A window of opportunity has opened.

The three proposals I have offered for discussion here are a contribution to an agenda that is largely still to be written. They are only a fragment of the new policies that would be needed to tackle the ills of our planet: social inequality, climate change, health and demographic crises, and a knowledge economy that is taking on unacceptable forms of autocratic power. No policy proposal is risk-free exempt. Can we be sure that knowledge-intensive public enterprises, if implemented, are then not captured by the oligopolies that they aim at containing? The contribution of this book is to frame the proposals in terms of ownership, governance, funding, legal arrangements, organisation, and internalisation of public mission, learning from the experience of research infrastructures. This goes beyond the concept of mission-oriented policies. A global perspective would be in principle appropriate, the focus of the proposals on the European Union, with its institutions, albeit far from perfect, is meant to offer a concrete legal and political environment to the concept.

An economist can only make proposals and hope that they are taken into consideration for what they are. In summary. Three new European agencies with well-defined missions: biomedical research and the development of innovations for human health in which industry is not interested or would only be interested if subsidised by states even more than now; the development of winning technologies for the energy transition at the scale of commercial demonstration with potential global impact; European public data governance platforms, alternatives to the US Governments and Chinese ones, based on principles other than the privatisation of knowledge. All this can be done at a lower cost than the largely fossilised EU agricultural policy.

These could represent three cards to be played in the face of the challenges of the next 30 years, financed by Next Generation EU and complementary mechanisms. They could also together be a step forward in the political construction of Europe.

Governments need to find new democratic legitimacy, which does not come automatically with elections. In the case of the EU, with a common budget of negligible size compared to that of China and the USA, the risk is that the perception of citizens is that the EU institutions are irrelevant. Apart from a currency, which is not shared by all member states, the Union is otherwise often seen as essentially a patchwork of rules and subsidies (for agriculture, regional spending, student mobility, and a few other programmes). Too little to build a sense of citizenship and belonging. I am convinced that organisations like the European Space Agency or CERN do more for European identity than we think. New ones need to be created, capable of enthusiasm with plans that citizens can feel are important, necessary, and truly shared. The research infrastructure model points a way forward for the European Union itself. A step forward would be taken if citizens could also identify with European public projects in pharmaceutical research, green technologies, and digital services. While such projects would not be sufficient on their own, they would go a long way in the right direction.

Note

1 Williamson J. (1990), in a famous paper provides a manifesto for neoliberalism, initially addressed mainly to Latin America.

Bibliography

Abrignani, S. (2020, november 24). La necessità di realizzare un vaccino per tutti i coronavirus, in «Corriere della Sera». https://www.corriere.it/salute/malattie_infettive/20_novembre_24/necessita-realizzare-vaccino-tutti-coronavirus-0170b80a-2e47-11eb-9814-5d0b7c9bd2b5.shtml

Angelis, A., Alonso, C.S., Kyriopoulos, I., & Mossialos, E. (2022). Funding sources of therapeutic and vaccine clinical trials for COVID-19 vs non–COVID-19 indications, 2020–2021. *JAMA Network Open*, *5*(8), e2226892.

Archibugi, D., & Filippetti, A. (Eds.). (2015). *The handbook of global science, technology, and innovation*. John Wiley & Sons.

Arute, F., Arya, K., Babbush, R., et al. (2019). Quantum supremacy using a programmable superconducting processor. *Nature*, *574*(7779), 505–510.

Arrow, K.J. (1996). The economics of information: An exposition. *Empirica*, *23*(2), 119–128.

Atkinson, A.B., 2015. *Inequality. What can be done?* Harvard University Press.

Autio, E., Hameri, A.P., & Vuola, O. (2004). A framework of industrial knowledge spillovers in big-science centers. *Research Policy*, *33*(1), 107–126.

Autor, D., Dorn, D., Katz, L.F., Patterson, C., & Van Reenen, J. (2020). The fall of the labor share and the rise of superstar firms. *The Quarterly Journal of Economics*, *135*(2), 645–709.

Bastianin, A., Del Bo, C. F., Florio, M., & Giffoni, F. (2022). Projecting the socio-economic impact of a big science center: the world's largest particle accelerator at CERN. *Applied Economics*, 1–22.

Battistoni, G., Genco, M., Marsilio, M., Pancotti, C., Rossi, S., & Vignetti, S. (2016). Cost–benefit analysis of applied research infrastructure: Evidence from health care. *Technological Forecasting and Social Change*, *112*, 79–91.

Beagrie, H., & Houghton, J. (2021). *Data-driven discovery: The value and impact of EMBL-EBI managed data resources*, Report EMBL-EBI, https://www.embl.org/documents/wp-content/uploads/2021/10/EMBL-EBI-impact-report-summary-2021.pdf.

Berners-Lee, T. (1999). *Weaving the web: The original design and ultimate destiny of the world wide web by its inventor*. Harper.

Bernier, L., Florio, M., & Bance, P. (Eds.). (2020). *The Routledge handbook of state-owned enterprises*. Routledge.

Birch, K., & Muniesa, F. (Eds.). (2020). *Assetization: Turning things into assets in technoscientific capitalism*. MIT Press.

Bognetti, G. (2020). History of western state-owned enterprises: From the Industrial Revolution to the age of globalization. In L. Bernier, M. Florio, & P. Bance (Eds.), *The Routledge handbook of state-owned enterprises* (pp. 25–44). Routledge.

Borghi, E., Del Bo, C., & Florio, M. (2016). Institutions and firms' productivity: Evidence from electricity distribution in the EU. *Oxford Bulletin of Economics and Statistics*, *78*(2), 170–196.

Bouillon, R., Slordahl, S., Nogueira, M.M., et al. (2015). Public investment in biomedical research in Europe. *The Lancet*, *386*, 1311–1418.

Brown, D. (2019). Medicine for all. The case for a public option in the pharmaceutical industry. *Democracy Collaborative*, 31.

Brown, D., Chow, H., Hanna, T., & McDonald, D. (2019). *Democratic public ownership in the UK pharmaceutical sector*. Working paper The Democracy Collaborative, Global Justice Now, and Just Treatment.

Camporesi, T., Catalano, G., Florio, M., & Giffoni, F. (2017). Experiential learning in high energy physics: A survey of students at the LHC. *European Journal of Physics*, *38*(2), 025703.

Carrazza, S., Ferrara, A., & Salini, S. (2016). Research infrastructures in the LHC era: A scientometric approach. *Technological Forecasting and Social Change*, *112*, 121–133.

Castelnovo, P., Del Bo, C.F., & Florio, M. (2018). Quality of institutions and productivity of State-Invested Enterprises: International evidence from major telecom companies. *European Journal of Political Economy*, *58*, 102–117.

Castro-Hermosa, S., Top, M., Dagar, J., Fahlteich, J., & Brown, T.M. (2019). Quantifying performance of permeation barrier-encapsulation systems for flexible and glass-based electronics and their application to perovskite solar cells. *Advanced Electronic Materials*, *5*(10), 1800978.

Catalano, G., López, G.G., Sánchez, A., & Vignetti, S. (2021). From scientific experiments to innovation: Impact pathways of a Synchrotron Light Facility. *Annals of Public and Cooperative Economics*, *92*(3), 447–472.

Chakravarthy, R., Cotter, K., DiMasi, J., Milne, C.P., & Wendel, N. (2015). Public- and private-sector contributions to the research and development of the most transformational drugs in the past 25 years: From theory to therapy. *Therapeutic Innovation & Regulatory Science*, *50*(6), 759–768.

Cleary, E.G., Beierlein, J.M., Khanuja, N.S., McNamee, L.M., & Ledley, F.D. (2018). Contribution of NIH funding to new drug approvals 2010–2016. *Proceedings of the National Academy of Sciences*, *115*(10), 2329–2334.

Coll, S. (2012). *Private empire: ExxonMobil and American power*. Penguin.

COST European Cooperation in Science and Technology. (2010). *Benefits of Research Infrastructures beyond Science. The Example of the Square Kilometre Array (SKA)*, Final report, COST Office: Brussels.

Credit Suisse. (2021). *Global wealth report 2021*. Credit Suisse Research Institute.

de Solla Price, D.J. (1963). *Little science, big science*, Columbia University Press Edition.

Dong, E., Du, H., & Gardner, L. (2020). An interactive web-based dashboard to track COVID-19 in real time. *The Lancet Infectious Diseases*, *20*(5), 533–534.

Dredge, C., & Scholtes, S. (2021). The health care utility model: A novel approach to doing business. *NEJM Catalyst Innovations in Care Delivery*, 2(4).

Edquist, C., Vonortas, N.S., Zabala-Iturriagagoitia, J.M., & Edler, J. (2015). *Public procurement for innovation*. Edward Elgar Publishing.

Edquist, C., & Zabala-Iturriagagoitia, J.M. (2012). Public procurement for innovation as mission-oriented innovation policy. *Research Policy*, *41*(10), 1757–1769.

EFPIA. (2020). *The Pharmaceutical Industry in Figures*, Annual Statistics Report.

European Commission. (2014). *Guide to cost-benefit analysis of investment projects: Economic appraisal tool for cohesion policy 2014–2020*, Directorate-General for Regional and Urban Policy.

Fan, V.Y., Jamison, D.T., & Summers, L.H. (2018). Pandemic risk: How large are the expected losses?. *Bulletin of the World Health Organization*, *96*(2), 129.

Fermigier, S., & Franck, S. (2020). Gaia-X: A trojan horse for Big Tech in Europe. *Euractiv*,https://www.euractiv.com/section/digital/opinion/gaia-x-a-trojan-horse-for-big-tech-in-europe/

Ferrajoli, L. (2020, March 21). The case for a planetary constitution. *Il Manifesto Global Edition*. https://global.ilmanifesto.it/the-case-for-a-planetary-constitution/

Ferrara, A., & Salini, S. (2012). Ten challenges in modeling bibliographic data for bibliometric analysis. *Scientometrics*, *93*(3), 765–785.

Fire, M., & Guestrin, C. (2019). Over-optimization of academic publishing metrics: Observing Goodhart's Law in action. *GigaScience*, *8*(6), giz053.

Florio, M. (2004). *The great divestiture: Evaluating the welfare impact of the British privatizations, 1979–1997*. MIT Press.

Florio, M. (2013). *Network industries and social welfare: The experiment that reshuffled European utilities*. Oxford University Press.

Florio, M. (2019). *Investing in science: Social cost-benefit analysis of research infrastructures*. MIT Press.

Florio, M., Castelnovo, P., Lupi, V., Morretta, V., Vurchio, D., Zirulia, L., Di Ciaccio, S., & Piermaria, M. (2022). *The socio-economic impact of public policies in the space sector in Italy*, Working Paper CIRIEC No. 2022/01.

Florio, M., Forte, S., & Sirtori, E. (2016). Forecasting the socio-economic impact of the Large Hadron Collider: A cost–benefit analysis to 2025 and beyond. *Technological Forecasting and Social Change*, *112*, 38–53.

Florio, M., & Gamba, S. (2021). Biomed Europa: After the coronavirus, a public infrastructure to overcome the pharmaceutical oligopoly. *Annals of Public and Cooperative Economics*, *92*(3), 387–409.

Florio, M, Gamba, S., & Pancotti C., (2023). *Mapping of long-term public and private investments in the development of Covid-19 vaccines*, publication for the special committee on COVID-19 pandemic: lessons learned and recommendations for the future (COVI), Policy Department for Economic, Scientific and Quality of Life Policies, European Parliament, Luxembourg. https://www.europarl.europa.eu/RegData/etudes/STUD/2023/740072/IPOL_STU(2023)740072_EN.pdf

Florio, M., & Giffoni, F. (2019). L'impatto sociale della produzione di scienza su larga scala: Come governarlo?. *L'industria*, *40*(4), 661–692.

Florio, M., Giffoni, F., Giunta, A., & Sirtori, E. (2018). Big science, learning, and innovation: Evidence from CERN procurement. *Industrial and Corporate Change*, *27*(5), 915–936.

Florio, M., Pancotti, C., & Prochazka, D.A. (2021). *European pharmaceutical research and development: Could public infrastructureovercome market failures?*, STOA - European Parliament, Brussels. https://www.europarl.europa.eu/RegData/etudes/STUD/2021/697197/EPRS_STU(2021)697197_EN.pdf

Fraunhofer-Gesellschaf. (2021). Annual Report 2021. *Knowledge and prosperity: Impact and innovation driven by pioneering research*, https://www.fraunhofer.de/s/ePaper/Annual-Report/2021/index.html#0.

Gagnon, M.A., & Lexchin, J. (2008). The cost of pushing pills: A new estimate of pharmaceutical promotion expenditures in the United States. *Plos Medicine*, *5*(1), e1.

Galison, P., Hevly, B., & Weinberg, A.M. (1992). Big science: The growth of large-scale research. *Physics Today*, *45*(11), 89.

Geisz, J.F., France, R.M., Schulte, K.L. et al. (2020). Six-junction III–V solar cells with 47.1% conversion efficiency under 143 Suns concentration. *Nature Energy*, *5*(4), 326–335.

Georghiou, L., Guellec, D., Ostry, J., Revoltella, D., Soete, L., & Veugelers, L. (2017). *The economic rationale for public R&I finding and its impact*, European Commission, Directorate-General for Research and Innovation.

Gibbons, M. (1999). Science's new social contract with society. *Nature*, *402*(6761), C81–C84.

Giffoni, F., & Florio, M. (2023). Public support of science: A contingent valuation study of citizens' attitudes about CERN with and without information about implicit taxes. *Research Policy*, *52*(1), 104627.

Global Preparedness Monitoring Board GPMB. (2019). *A world at risk, annual report on global preparedness for health emergencies*. https://www.gpmb.org/docs/librariesprovider17/default-document-library/annual-reports/gpmb-2019-annualreport-en.pdf?sfvrsn=bd1b8933_36

Gosling, F.G. (1999). *The Manhattan Project: Making the atomic bomb*. Diane Publishing.

Hackett, E.J., Lynch, M., & Wajcman, J. (Eds.). (2007). *The handbook of science and technology studies*. MIT Press.

Hamann, M., Berry, K., Chaigneau, T., et al. (2018). Inequality and the biosphere. *Annual Review of Environment and Resources*, *43*, 61–83.

Hess, C., & Ostrom, E. (2007). Introduction: An overview of the knowledge commons. In C. Hess, & E. Ostrom (Eds.), *Understanding knowledge as a commons: From theory to practice* (pp. 3–26). MIT Press.

Higher Education Strategy Associates (HESA). (2022). *World Higher Education: Institutions, Students and Funding*, HESA Main Report.

Hughes, J.A. (2003). *The Manhattan Project: Big science and the atom bomb*. Columbia University Press.

International Energy Agency (IEA). (2021). *World energy outlook 2021*. https://iea.blob.core.windows.net/assets/4ed140c1-c3f3-4fd9-acae-789a4e14a23c/WorldEnergyOutlook2021.pdf

Irvine, J., & Martin, B.R. (1984). CERN: Past performance and future prospects: II. The scientific performance of the CERN accelerators. *Research Policy*, *13*(5), 247–284.

Jasny, B.R., & Kennedy, D. (2001). The human genome. *Science*, *291*(5507), 1153–1153.

Jonas, O.B. (2013). *Pandemic risk*. World Bank.

Kornai, J. (1992). *The socialist system: The political economy of communism*. Princeton University Press.

Koryan, A., & Narayan, V. (2021). *Socializing data value: Reflections on the state of play*, IT for Change/Friedrich-Ebert-Stiftung.

Lafleur, C. (2010). Costs of US piloted programs. *The Space Review*. https://www.thespacereview.com/article/1579/1

Lander, E. et al. (International Human Genome Sequencing Consortium, Whitehead Institute for Biomedical Research, Center for Genome Re- search) (2001). Initial sequencing and analysis of the human genome. *Nature*, *409*(6822), 860–921.

Lazonick, W., Hopkins, M., Jacobson, K., Sakinç, M.E., & Tulum, Ö. (2017). US pharma's business model: Why it is broken, and how it can be fixed. In D. Tyfield, R. Lave, S. Randalls, & C. Thorpe (Eds.), *The Routledge handbook of the political economy of science* (pp. 83–100). Routledge.

Lazzarini, S.G., Mesquita, L.F., Monteiro, F., & Musacchio, A. (2021). Leviathan as an inventor: An extended agency model of state-owned versus private firm invention in emerging and developed economies. *Journal of International Business Studies*, *52*(4), 560–594.

Lexchin, J. (2018). Pharmaceutical company spending on research and development and promotion in Canada, 2013–2016: A cohort analysis. *Journal of Pharmaceutical Policy and Practice*, *11*(1), 1–6.

Li, D. (2017). Expertise versus bias in evaluation: Evidence from the NIH. *American Economic Journal: Applied Economics*, *9*(2), 60–92.

Lundvall, B.A. (1985). Product innovation and user-producer interaction. *The Learning Economy and the Economics of Hope*, *19*, 19–60.

Mairate, A. (2023). *The macroeconomic implications of the green transition.* A New Era for Europe Volume II – Selected Issues Edited by István P. Székely and Marco Ratto.

Malone, T.W., & Bernstein, M.S. (Eds.). (2022). *Handbook of collective intelligence.* MIT press.

Martin, B. (1996). The use of multiple indicators in the assessment of basic research. *Scientometrics*, *36*(3), 343–362.

Martin, B.R., & Irvine, J. (1983). Assessing basic research: Some partial indicators of scientific progress in radio astronomy. *Research Policy*, *12*(2), 61–90.

Martin, C.S., Repo, S., Arenas Márquez, J., et al. (2021). Demonstrating public value to funders and other stakeholders-the journey of ELIXIR, a virtual and distributed research infrastructure for life science data. *Annals of Public and Cooperative Economics*, *92*(3), 497–510.

Mazzucato, M. (2013). *The entrepreneurial state: Debunking public vs. private sector myths*. Anthem Press, London.

Mazzucato, M. (2018a). *The value of everything: Making and taking in the global economy*. Hachette UK.

Mazzucato, M. (2018b). *Mission-oriented research & innovation in the European: A problem-solving approach to fuel innovation-led growth*. European Commission, Directorate-General for Research and Innovation.

Mazzucato, M. (2018c). Mission-oriented innovation policies: Challenges and opportunities. *Industrial and Corporate Change*, *27*(5), 803–815.

Mazzucato, M., Li, H.L., & Darzi, A. (2020). Is it time to nationalise the pharmaceutical industry?. *British Medical Journal*, *368*, m769.

Millward, R. (2013). *The state and business in the major powers: An economic history 1815–1939*. Routledge.

Nordberg, M., Campbell, A., & Verbeke, A. (2003). Using customer relationships to acquire technological innovation: A value-chain analysis of supplier contracts with scientific research institutions. *Journal of Business Research*, *56*(9), 711–719.

OECD. (2017). *New health technologies: Managing access.* OECD Publishing.

OECD. (2018). *Pharmaceutical innovation and access to medicines, value and sustainability*. OECD Publishing.

OECD. (2019). *Antimicrobial resistance. Tackling the burden in the European Union.* OECD Publishing.

OECD. (2022). *OECD Economic Outlook, Volume 2022 Issue 2*, OECD Publishing. https://doi.org/10.1787/f6da2159-en.

Pagano, U. (2014). The crisis of intellectual monopoly capitalism. *Cambridge Journal of Economics*, *38*(6), 1409–1429.

Pinski, G., & Narin, F. (1976). Citation influence for journal aggregates of scientific publications: Theory, with application to the literature of physics. *Information Processing & Management*, *12*(5), 297–312.

Rea, P.A., Pauly, M.V., & Burns, L.R. (2018). *Managing discovery in the life sciences: Harnessing creativity to drive biomedical innovation*. Cambridge University Press.

Rikap, C. (2022). Becoming an intellectual monopoly by relying on the national innovation system: The State Grid Corporation of China's experience. *Research Policy*, *51*(4), 104472.

Romer, P.M. (1990). Endogenous technological change. *Journal of Political Economy*, *98*(5, Part 2), S71–S102.

Sachs, J.D., Karim, S.S.A., Aknin, L., Allen, J., Brosbøl, K., Colombo, F., et al. (2022). The Lancet Commission on lessons for the future from the COVID-19 pandemic. *The Lancet*, *400*(10359), 1224–1280.

Samset, B.H., Fuglestvedt, J.S., & Lund, M.T. (2020). Delayed emergence of a global temperature response after emission mitigation. *Nature Communications*, *11*(1), 1–10.

Scannell, J.W., Blanckley, A., Boldon, H., & Warrington, B. (2012). Diagnosing the decline in pharmaceutical R&D efficiency. *Nature Reviews Drug Discovery*, *11*(3), 191–200.

Schumpeter, J.A. (1942). *Capitalism, socialism and democracy*. Harper & Brothers

Scott, D.M., & Jurek, R. (2014). *Marketing the moon: The selling of the Apollo lunar program*. MIT Press.

Shannon, C.E. (1948). A mathematical theory of communication. *The Bell System Technical Journal*, 27(3), 379–423.

Simon, H.A. (1991). Organizations and markets. *Journal of Economic Perspectives*, *5*(2), 25–44.

Smil, V. (2021). *Grand transitions: How the modern world was made*. Oxford University Press.

Sorenson, O. (2018). Innovation policy in a networked world. *Innovation Policy and the Economy*, *18*(1), 53–77.

Sraffa, P. (1960). *Production of commodities by means of commodities*. Cambridge University Press.

SSR Health. (2016). *Biopharmaceutical R&D Productivity*, Report, http://www.ssrhealth.com/

Stern, N. (2007). *The economics of climate change: The Stern review*. Cambridge University press.

Stern, N., & Stiglitz, J.E. (2017). *Report of the high-level commission on carbon prices*. World Bank.

Stiglitz, J.E. (1999). Knowledge as a Global Public Good. In I. Kaul, I. Grunberg, & M.A. Stern (Eds.), *Global public goods: International cooperation in the 21st century*, (vol. 308, pp. 308–325).

Taghreed, A., Ambinintsoa, H.R., & Soumya, S. (2019). Biomedical research; what gets funded where?. *Bulletin of the World Health Organization*, *97*(8), 516.

Testoni, F.E., García Carrillo, M., Gagnon, M.A., Rikap, C., & Blaustein, M. (2021). Whose shoulders is health research standing on? Determining the key actors and contents of the prevailing biomedical research agenda. *PloS One*, *16*(4), e0249661.

The Economist. (2020a, January, 25). *How to invent the future. Recreating ARPA, the most successful research agency in history*, p. 26.

The Economist. (2020b, February 20). *Who will benefit most from the data economy? It is already unequal and that inequality could get worse*. https://www.economist.com/special-report/2020/02/20/who-will-benefit-most-from-the-data-economy.

The Economist. (2020c, February 22). The great Bezos giveaway. *Climate Philantrophy*, 10.

The Fraunhofer-Gesellschaft. (2019). Annual report 2019, *Our Future Mission: Research for Sustainable Value Creation*, https://www.fraunhofer.de/content/dam/zv/en/Publications/Annual-Report/2019/Fraunhofer-Annual-Report-2019.pdf

U.S. Government Accountability Office. (2017). *Drug industry: Profits, research and development spending, and merger and acquisition deals*. https://www.gao.gov/assets/gao-18-40.pdf

UNESCO. (2015). *UNESCO Science Report: Towards 2030*. UNESCO Publishing.

UNESCO. (2021). *UNESCO Science Report: The race against time for smarter development*. UNESCO Publishing. https://unesdoc.unesco.org/ark:/48223/pf0000377433

Watson, P. (2010). *The German genius: Europe's third renaissance, the second scientific revolution and the twentieth century*. Simon and Schuster.

Weinberg, A.M. (1961). Impact of large-scale science on the United States: Big science is here to stay, but we have yet to make the hard financial and educational choices it imposes. *Science*, *134*(3473), 161–164.

Weinberger, S. (2017). *The imagineers of war: The untold history of DARPA*. The Pentagon.

Williamson, J. (1990). What Washington means by policy reform. *Latin American Adjustment: How Much Has Happened*, *1*, 90–120.

Williamson, O.E. (2008). Outsourcing: Transaction cost economics and supply chain management. *Journal of Supply Chain Management*, *44*(2), 5–16.

World Health Organization. (2016). *Evaluation of the impact of WHO publications*. Corporate evaluation commissioned by the WHO Evaluation Office. https://www.who.int/docs/default-source/documents/evaluation/report-evaluation-impact-who-publications.pdf?sfvrsn=577627c5_2

Wouters, O.J., McKee, M., & Luyten, J. (2020). Estimated research and development investment needed to bring a new medicine to market, 2009–2018. *Jama*, *323*(9), 844–853.

Index

Pages in **bold** refer to tables and pages followed by "n" refer to notes.